Mysticism and the Spiritual Quest

A Crosscultural Anthology

Phyllis Zagano

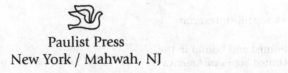

Paulist Press
New York / Mahwah, NJ

Cover image by Connie Wellnitz / Digital Vision
Cover design by Sharyn Banks
Book design by Lynn Else

Library of Congress Cataloging-in-Publication Data

Mysticism and the spiritual quest : a crosscultural anthology / Phyllis Zagano.
    pages cm
  Includes bibliographical references.
  ISBN 978-0-8091-4626-0 (alk. paper) — ISBN 978-1-58768-371-8
  1. Religions. 2. Mysticism. 3. Spirituality. I. Zagano, Phyllis, editor of compilation.
  BL80.3.M97 2013
  204`.22—dc23

2013030686

ISBN: 978-0-8091-4626-0 (paperback)
ISBN: 978-1-58768-371-8 (e-book)

Published by Paulist Press
997 Macarthur Boulevard
Mahwah, New Jersey 07430

www.paulistpress.com

Printed and bound in the
United States of America

To the memory of Lawrence E. Boadt, CSP

Contents

Contents

Contents

Contents

Editor's Acknowledgments

The concept for the present anthology grew from conversations with the late Father Larry Boadt, CSP, former publisher of Paulist Press, who graciously supported the project and to whom this book is dedicated. It was his idea to draw from the many original texts already within the various Paulist Press collections and join the selections in one anthology to form a genuine crosscultural anthology for use in both secular and denominational institutions.

The experts who prepared the individual introductions, Joshua Schapiro, PhD (Buddhism), Jeffery D. Long, PhD (Hinduism and Chinese religions), Hussein Rashid, PhD (Islam), and Ori Z. Soltes, PhD (Judaism) also provided consultation on selections of individual texts and translations.

Obviously, no work like this is ever completed without the able assistance of many others. I am indebted to the able librarians of Hofstra University, particularly David E. Woolwine, PhD, and to the Hofstra interlibrary loan staff. Monica M. Yatsyla, Manager of Instructional Design Services at Hofstra University, devised the coding system used throughout the project to manage the many separate files and also oversaw creation of electronic documents from the many sources used here. Student assistants in the Religion Department—Lauren Carlucci, Amanda Eliot, Rebecca Gianarkis, Henry Fuller, Amanda Ortega, Kaylee Platt, and Thomas Wright—provided all manner of research, technical, and secretarial assistance during the many years this work was in preparation. My professional assistants, Eileen M. Myles and Carmela Leonforte-Plimack, PhD, each cheerfully helped with this project from time to time, as did Joanne S. Herlihy, Senior Executive Secretary of the Department of Religion.

Following Larry Boadt's untimely death, the project was cheered on by many at Paulist Press, especially Bob Byrns, Sales Manager; Donna Crilly, Managing Editor; and Nancy de Flon, PhD, academic editor, who guided the work to completion. To these and the many others at Paulist who had a hand in the anthology—from proofreading to design to typesetting to production—I owe deep thanks and happy gratitude that the work is now complete.

Introduction

The terms *mysticism* and *spirituality* have gained new currency both in academic and general discourse, perhaps indicating a new turn to the subject in thought and conversation. Certainly, self-study and introspection are popular topics, as racks of self-help books in libraries and bookstores demonstrate. The paradoxical danger of all the popularity of the study of spirituality, however, is solipsism: the individual could eventually become involved only with the self, to the detriment of involvement with society. Inarguably, the proper reception of mysticism and spirituality as fields of interest will drive the individual out of the self, in fact, away from the self-interest that first engaged the inquirer.

Even so, the academic study of religion is not directed at personal spiritual growth. While the topics engaged in the study of mysticism and the spiritual quest are, in fact, the building blocks of religious spiritualities, there is no need for the objective mind to accede to any (or all) of the religious beliefs represented here to agree that understanding the various ways of being in the world each represents is an important task to undertake. In fact, the study of comparative mystic traditions and spiritualities can inform the understanding of international politics, comparative legal systems, and the cultural expressions of art, music, and literature.

The present anthology of writings is proposed for undergraduate and graduate spirituality courses, those perhaps entitled "Mysticism and the Spiritual Quest: East and West" or "Spirituality: East and West." Such courses often fill the undergraduate requirement for either a "crosscultural" course or a course in the study of world religions. Students at the graduate level, with few exceptions, are already focused on one or another tradition, and the anthology would well meet the need for a general crosscultural spiritualities course, recognizing that this is neither a text in comparative religions nor in comparative theologies, but rather one that demonstrates the means by which various religious come to an understanding of the spiritual quest and of mysticism within their respective traditions.

That mysticism is traditionally defined as the yearning for direct connection to a transcendent reality and is typically referred to as the esoteric dimension of the religious search forms the basis for the selection of the texts in this anthology. Though evident as a global phenomenon, mystical traditions most notably have developed and continue to develop in the monotheistic faiths of Judaism, Christianity, and Islam, as well as in the many religious traditions of India, China, Japan, and the world of Islam. The texts here presented form a representative selection of the spiritualities of these faiths.

The selections that follow, arranged roughly in chronological order according to the creation of their earliest texts, demonstrate the various facets of the mystic quest and the understandings of spirituality. If spirituality is to be understood as the ways in which humans relate to self and to others and specifically to whatever overarching principal or principle governs human existence, then the many languages of mysticism and the spiritual quest must be understood within their cultural contexts. Hence, rather than a general introduction to each of the six sections: Hinduism, Chinese Traditions, Buddhism, Judaism, Christianity, and Islam, specific introductions to each selected text situate it in the history of its tradition and of the world. Each introduction explains who is credited with creating the passage and how that person—or at least how that passage—fits in the given tradition. Biographical details connect the writer or scribe to his or her individual culture and to the world at large. Each introduction also considers the selection objectively, explaining how it is demonstrative of the writer's individual work, of the writer's tradition, and how it speaks to the general questions of mysticism and the spiritual quest, often pointing to how the writer and the selection relate to other writers and selections in the book.

The introductions have been written by experts in the study of Hinduism, Chinese traditions, Buddhism, Judaism, Christianity, and Islam.

Hinduism is represented by selections from the *Upanishads* (*Katha Upanishad, Mundaka Upanishad, Chandogya Upanishad*), the *Yoga Sutras* (Yoga Aphorisms, *Eight Limbs of Yoga*), and the *Bhagavad Gita* (Way of Selfless Action, Way of Loving Faith), and the *Brahma Sutras*.

Chinese traditions are represented by selections from the *Tao Te Ching* of Lao Tzu, and the writings of Chuang Tzu.

Buddhism is represented by selections from *The Dhammapada, The Heart Sūtra, The Lotus Sūtra*, Perfection of Wisdom as the Middle Way, the *Saundarananda, The Tibetan Book of the Dead*, and the *Letter to Lord Nakamura*.

Judaism is represented by selections from the *Song of Songs*, Philo of Alexandria, The Early Kabbalah, *Zohar*, and Abraham Isaac Kook.

Christianity is represented by selections from the Gospel of John, the First Letter of St. Paul to the Corinthians, Augustine of Hippo, Bernard of Clairvaux, Francis of Assisi and Clare of Assisi, Anchorite spirituality, Julian of Norwich, Walter Hilton, and John of the Cross.

Islam is represented by selections from the Qur'an, Rabia, Junayd, Hallaj, Al- Ghazāli, 'Attār, Ibn Arabī, and Rumi.

A complete bibliography of sources and secondary materials completes the anthology.

I have used many original works, anthologies, and textbooks during my many years of teaching courses in mysticism and spirituality at the undergraduate and graduate levels in both secular and denominational colleges and universities. Course books, however, have not appeared to mirror the growing interest in comparative spiritualities.

Following wide consultation and a significant amount of

research, especially into the few current and out-of-print titles that approach the topics of mysticism and the spiritual quest from a crosscultural perspective, and with consultation with both students and other faculty who have taught courses with these foci, I decided on the selections that follow. While one or another work may be missing from the instructor's list of favorites, the book is designed to provide wide latitude for instructors and students alike while remaining focused on the presentation of original texts.

That the world is in dire need of more and greater mutual understanding between and among its people is a fact that each of the world's religions recognizes and addresses. May the study of these texts enhance and encourage such mutual understanding.

June 29, 2013
Hempstead, New York

ONE

HINDUISM

HINDUISM

The *Upanishads*

INTRODUCTION

The *Upanishads* are a collection of inspired writings that make up the final portion of the Hindu scriptures known as the *Vedas* (or "Wisdom"). They mainly take the form of dialogues between teachers and students. In their current form, they were composed between about the middle of the first millennium BCE and the early centuries of the Common Era (thus roughly between 500 BCE and 200 CE). These dates refer to the forms that these texts have finally taken; however, the entire process of their composition and oral transmission actually spanned many centuries. Therefore, even if we locate the *Chandogya Upanishad* between roughly 500 and 400 BCE, and the *Katha* and *Mundaka Upanishads* between roughly 400 and 300 BCE, all of these texts contain teachings that may date back to an era considerably earlier than 500 BCE.

The Sanskrit word *upanishad* has the meaning "secret teaching," or esoteric doctrine. It carries the connotation of words whispered from teacher to student, requiring the student to "sit close" to the teacher (the literal meaning of *upanishad* being "sitting close by" or "sitting next to"). The teachings of the *Upanishads* were passed on orally, from teacher to student, for many centuries, and many *Upanishads* contain lengthy lists of lineages that trace their teachings back to sages of ancient times. The texts themselves are anonymous; because they contain the collected wisdom of lineages of many teachers, they cannot be ascribed to a single author.

Because the *Upanishads* were the final part of the Vedic literature to be compiled, and also because their teaching is seen as the final, most profound level of meaning of the Vedic tradition, the philosophy that they teach is also known as *Vedanta*, or "the end of the *Veda.*" Vedanta is the central philosophy of Hinduism and forms the conceptual basis of much of Hindu thought and practice.

The basic concepts of Vedanta that form the centerpiece of most of the teaching given in the *Upanishads* are *Brahman*—the Infinite, transcendent reality from which all of existence has emerged, the Ground of Being—and *Atman*, a term that is translated in these selections as "the Self."[1] This is not the individual self or soul—though that concept is also affirmed in these texts—but a universal Self that dwells in the hearts of all beings, residing in the body along with the individual soul like two birds sitting on a single tree branch (an image found recurrently in the *Upanishads*, including in the selections given here).

The "secret teaching" at the heart of the *Upanishads*, and of Vedanta philosophy, is that Brahman and the Self are one—that the transcendent reality that is the basis of all existence is also the soul of all beings, the indwelling consciousness that resides in us all. Mysticism and the spiritual quest are intimately tied to the teaching of the *Upanishads*. If mysticism is defined as "the yearning for direct connection to a transcendent reality," and if realizing the direct connection—indeed the *identity*—of the Self and Brahman is the goal of Vedanta, then Vedanta is a deeply, inherently—perhaps even paradigmatically—mystical tradition.

The specific spiritual quest that Vedantic mysticism fulfills is the quest for a state of freedom from the cycle of death and rebirth and the inevitable suffering that life within this cycle involves. The realization of Brahman as one's true identity, according to the *Upanishads*, frees one from bondage to this cycle, a bondage predicated upon ignorantly misidentifying oneself with the limited individual soul rather than with the Infinite that is free from *desire*—the force that drives one again and again into embodied existence.

Jeffery D. Long

---

1 *Brahmin* is a Hindu term for a scholar class and refers to an individual. *Brahman* refers to the Supreme Self. *Brahma* refers to the creative aspect of the universal consciousness.

THE *KATHA UPANISHAD*

The *Katha Upanishad* is an anonymous work most probably composed between 400 and 300 BCE. The text consists chiefly of a dialogue between a boy named Nachiketa and Yama, the god of death. Nachiketa seeks to learn the secret of immortality and what occurs after the death of the physical body. Yama, or Death, reveals to him the doctrine of death, rebirth, and freedom from rebirth—a freedom the attainment of which is intimately tied to mysticism and the spiritual quest.

The *Upanishads*, as a group, form something like an appendix to the more ancient Vedic texts and claim to reveal the true, inner meaning of the earlier writings and of the rituals described by those earlier writings. The reference in this selection to "the fire sacrifice that leads to heaven," and Yama, or Death, naming this sacrifice after Nachiketa is an example of the rootedness of the mystical reflections of the *Upanishads* in the ritual performance of the ancient Vedic religion. The earlier Vedic texts to which the *Katha Upanishad* is appended are those that explain how this fire ritual is to be performed (a set of texts called the *Yajur Veda*), and the *Katha Upanishad* can be seen as exploring the deeper meaning of this ritual (as well as, of course, the origin of its name).

It is important to note that the "heaven" to which this ritual leads is a temporary abode. One eventually dies in this heaven and is reborn back in this world. Even gods like Death are mortal, albeit extremely long-lived, in the Hindu tradition. The only true immortality, according to this tradition, is freedom from the cycle of repeated death and rebirth—which is the main focus of the dialogue between Nachiketa and Death.

Like most of the *Upanishads*, the *Katha Upanishad* takes the form of a dialogue between a teacher and a student. In this case, Nachiketa is the student and Death himself is the teacher. Who better to instruct one in the mysteries of death and the afterlife than Death? One of the basic teachings of Vedantic philosophy, and thus of Hinduism, is that death is typically followed by rebirth: that, after the death of the physical body, the soul continues to exist and is reborn, taking on another physical body in which it continues its journey. This journey ends only when one attains freedom from the rebirth process. This freedom—freedom from the suffering inevitably involved in coming back again and again into a world of death, disease, and limitation—is the ultimate goal of Vedantic practice.

This freedom is intimately tied to mysticism and the spiritual quest. For if mysticism is defined as "the yearning for direct connection to a transcendent reality," then mysticism can be said to be a necessary condition for freedom from rebirth—which, according to this text, occurs only when one realizes the direct connection between, and indeed the *identity* of, the Self and Brahman, the Infinite.

According to Death, Nachiketa shows wisdom in asking not for wealth or physical pleasure but for the knowledge that leads to liberation from rebirth; for one who pursues temporary goods receives only such goods and "falls again and again, birth after birth," into the jaws of Death. But one who realizes the Self "is freed alike from pleasure and pain" and finds the "dwelling place of all felicity."

But what is the Self? And how is the Self to be realized? Death speaks about the Self primarily in terms of what it is *not*. It is not born. It does not die. It is "separate from the body, the senses, and the mind." It is not destroyed when the body is destroyed. It inhabits all form, but is itself formless. It is "subtle, deep-hidden in the lotus of the heart." Knowing the Self in its true nature, one "transcends all grief."

Realizing the Self is not a matter of mere intellectual knowledge. The Self "is not known through the study of scriptures, nor through subtlety of the intellect, nor through much learning." It is known, rather, through mysticism—again, through the yearning for direct connection to a transcendent reality. The Self is known by the one who longs for it. "Verily unto him does the Self reveal his true being."

As part of the Vedic canon, the *Katha Upanishad*, like all of the *Upanishads*, is a highly authoritative scriptural text for Hindus. Its teaching is echoed in other selections from the *Upanishads* and the later Hindu texts cited in this volume. The *Bhagavad Gita*, in particular, picks up this text's theme of the immortality of the Self, even utilizing the same words—"If the slayer think that he slays, if the slain think that he is slain, neither of them knows the truth. The Self slays not, nor is he slain"—and the image of the body as a chariot in which the Self rides.

Jeffery D. Long

Om...
May Brahman protect us,
May he guide us,
May he give us strength and right understanding.
May love and harmony be with us all.
OM...Peace—peace—peace.

On a certain occasion Vajasrabasa, hoping for divine favor, performed a rite which required that he should give away all his possessions. He was careful, however, to sacrifice only his cattle, and of these only such as were useless—the old, the barren the blind, and the lame. Observing this niggardliness, Nachiketa, his young son, whose heart had received the truth taught in the scriptures, thought to himself: "Surely a worshiper who dares bring such worthless gifts is doomed to utter darkness!" Thus reflecting, he came to his father, and cried:

"Father, I too belong to thee: to whom givest thou me?"

His father did not answer; but when Nachiketa asked the question again and yet again, he replied impatiently: "Thee I give to Death!"

Then Nachiketa thought to himself: "Of my father's many sons and disciples I am indeed the best, or at least of the middle rank, not the worst; but of what good am I to the King of Death?" Yet, being determined to keep his father's word, he said:

"Father, do not repent thy vow! Consider how it has been with those that have gone before, and how it will be with those that now live. Like corn, a man ripens and falls to the ground; like elm, he springs up again in his season."

Having thus spoken, the boy journeyed to the house of Death.

But the god was not at home, and for three nights Nachiketa waited. When at length the King of Death returned, he was met by his servants, who said to him: "A Brahmin, like to flame of fire, entered thy house as guest, and thou wast not of there. Therefore must a peace offering be made to him. With accustomed rites, O King, thou must receive thy guest, for if a householder show not due hospitality to a Brahmin, he will lose what he most desires—the merits of his good deeds, his righteousness, his sons, and his cattle."

Then the King of Death approached Nachiketa and welcomed him with courteous words.

"O Brahmin," he said, "I salute thee. Thou art indeed a guest worthy of all reverence. Let, I pray thee, no harm befall me! Three nights hast thou passed in my house and hast not received my hospitality; ask of me, therefore, three boons—one for each night."

"O Death," replied Nachiketa, "so let it be. And as the first of these boons I ask that my father be not anxious about me, that his anger be appeased, and that when thou sendest me back to him, he recognize me and welcome me."

"By my will," declared Death, "thy father shall recognize thee and love thee as heretofore; and seeing thee again alive, he shall be tranquil of mind, and he shall sleep in peace."

Then said Nachiketa: "In heaven there is no fear at all. Thou, O Death, art not there, nor in that place does the thought of growing old is make one tremble. There, free from hunger and from thirst and far from the reach of sorrow, all rejoice and are glad. Thou knowest, O King, the fire sacrifice that leads to heaven. Teach me that sacrifice, for I am full of faith. This is my second wish."

Whereupon, consenting, Death taught the boy the fire sacrifice, and all the rites and ceremonies attending it. Nachiketa repeated all that he had learned, and Death, well pleased with him, said: "I grant thee an extra boon. Henceforth shall this sacrifice be called the Nachiketa Sacrifice, after thy name. Choose now thy third boon."

And then Nachiketa considered within himself, and said:

"When a man dies, there is this doubt: Some say, he is; others say, he is not. Taught by thee, I would know the truth. This is my third wish."

"Nay," replied Death, "even the gods were once puzzled by this mystery. Subtle indeed is the truth regarding it not easy to understand. Choose thou some other boon, O Nachiketa." But Nachiketa would not be denied.

"Thou sayest, O Death, that even the gods were once puzzled by this mystery, and that it is not easy to understand. Surely there is no teacher better able to explain it than thou—and there is no other boon equal to this."

To which, trying Nachiketa again, the god replied:

"Ask for sons and grandsons who shall live a hundred years. Ask for cattle, elephants, horses, gold. Choose for thyself a mighty kingdom. Or if thou canst imagine aught better, ask for that—not for sweet pleasures only but for the power, beyond all thought, to taste their sweetness. Yea, verily, the supreme enjoyer will I make thee of every good thing. Celestial maidens, beautiful to behold, such indeed as were not mean for mortals—even these, together with their bright chariots and their musical instruments, will I give unto thee to serve thee. But for the secret of death, O Nachiketa do not ask!"

But Nachiketa stood fast, and said: "These things endure only till the morrow, O Destroyer of Life, and the pleasures they give wear out the senses. Keep thou therefore horses and chariots, keep dance and song, for thyself! How shall he desire wealth, O Death, who once has seen thy face? Nay, only the boon that I have chosen—that only do I ask. Having found out the society of the imperishable and the immortal, as in knowing thee I have done, how shall I, subject to decay and death, and knowing well the vanity of the flesh—how shall I wish for long life?

"Tell me, O King, the supreme secret regarding which men doubt. No other boon I ask."

Whereupon the King of Death, well pleased at heart, began to teach Nachiketa the secret of immortality.

KING OF DEATH:

The good is one thing; the pleasant is another. These two, differing in their ends, both prompt to action. Blessed are they that choose the good; they that choose the pleasant miss the goal.

Both the good and the pleasant present themselves to men. The wise, having examined both, distinguish the one from the other. The wise prefer the good to the pleasant; the foolish, driven by fleshly desires, prefer the pleasant to the good.

Thou, O Nachiketa, having looked upon fleshly desires, delightful to the senses, hast renounced them all. Thou hast turned from the miry way herein many a man wallows.

Far from each other, and leading to different ends, are ignorance and knowledge. Thee, O Nachiketa, I regard as one who aspires after knowledge, for a multitude of pleasant objects were unable to tempt thee.

Living in the abyss of ignorance yet wise in their own conceit, deluded fools go round and round, the blind led by the blind.

To the thoughtless youth, deceived by the vanity of earthly possessions, the path that leads to the eternal abode is not revealed. *This world alone is real; there is no hereafter*—thinking thus, he falls again and again, birth after birth, into my jaws.

To many it is not given to hear of the Self. Many, though they hear of it, did not understand it. Wonderful is he who speaks of it. Intelligent is he who learns of it. Blessed is he who, taught by a good teacher, is able to understand it.

The truth of the Self cannot be fully understood when taught by an ignorant man, for opinions regarding it, not founded in knowledge, vary one from another. Subtler than the subtlest is this Self, and beyond all logic. Taught by a teacher who knows the Self and Brahman as one, a man leaves vain theory behind and attains to truth.

The awakening which thou hast known does not come through the intellect, but rather, in fullest measure, from the lips of the wise. Beloved Nachiketa, blessed, blessed art thou, because thou seekest the Eternal. Would that I had more pupils like thee!

Well I know that earthly treasure lasts but till the morrow. For did not I myself, wishing to be King of Death, make sacrifice with fire? But the sacrifice was a fleeting thing, performed with

11

fleeting objects, and small is my reward, seeing that only for a moment will my reign endure.

The goal of worldly desire, the glittering objects for which all men long, the celestial pleasures they hope to gain by religious rites, the most sought-after of miraculous powers—all these were within thy grasp. But all these, with firm resolve, thou hast renounced.

The ancient, effulgent being, the indwelling Spirit, subtle, deep-hidden in the lotus of the heart, is hard to know. But the wise man, following the path of meditation, knows him, and is freed alike from pleasure and from pain.

The man who has learned that the Self is separate from the body, the senses, and the mind, and has fully known him, the soul of truth, the subtle principle—such a man verily attains to him, and is exceeding glad, because he has found the source and dwelling place of all felicity. Truly do I believe, O Nachiketa, that for thee the gates of joy stand open.

NACHIKETA:

Teach me, O King, I beseech thee, whatsoever thou knowest to be beyond right and wrong, beyond cause and effect, beyond past, present, and future.

KING OF DEATH:

Of that goal which all the Vedas declare, which is implicit in all penances, and in pursuit of which men lead lives of continence and service, of that will I briefly speak.

It is—OM.

This syllable is Brahman. This syllable is indeed supreme. He who knows it obtains his desire.

It is the strongest support. It is the highest symbol. He who knows it is reverenced as a knower of Brahman.

The Self, whose symbol is OM, is the omniscient Lord. He is not born. He does not die. He is neither cause nor effect. This

Ancient One is unborn, imperishable, eternal: though the body be destroyed, he is not killed.

If the slayer think that he slays, if the slain think that he is slain, neither of them knows the truth. The Self slays not, nor is he slain.

Smaller than the smallest, greater than the greatest, this Self forever dwells within the hearts of all. When a man is free from desire, his mind and senses purified, he beholds the glory of the Self and is without sorrow.

Though seated, he travels far; though at rest, he moves all things. Who but the purest of the pure can realize this Effulgent Being, who is joy and who is beyond joy?

Formless is he, though inhabiting form. In the midst of the fleeting he abides forever. All-pervading and supreme is the Self. The wise man, knowing him in his true nature, transcends all grief.

The Self is not known through study of the scriptures, nor through subtlety of the intellect, nor through much learning; but by him who longs for him is he known. Verily unto him does the Self reveal his true being.

By learning, a man cannot know him; if he desist not from evil, if he control not his senses, if he quiet not his mind, and practice not meditation.

To him Brahmins and Kshatriyas are but food, and death itself a condiment.

Both the individual self and the Universal Self have entered the cave of the heart, the abode of the Most High, but the knowers of Brahman and the householders who perform the fire sacrifices see a difference between them as between sunshine and shadow.

May we perform the Nachiketa Sacrifice, which bridges the world of suffering. May we know the imperishable Brahman, who is fearless, and who is the end and refuge of those who seek liberation.

Know that the Self is the rider, and the body the chariot; that the intellect is the charioteer, and the mind the reins.

The senses, say the wise, are the horses; the roads they travel

13

are the mazes of desire. The wise call the Self the enjoyer when he is united with the body, the senses, and the mind.

When a man lacks discrimination and his mind is uncontrolled, his senses are unmanageable, like the restive horses of a charioteer. But when a man has discrimination and his mind is controlled, his senses, like the well-broken horses of a charioteer, lightly obey the rein.

He who lacks discrimination, whose mind is unsteady and whose heart is impure, never reaches the goal, but is born again and again. But he who has discrimination, whose mind is steady and whose heart is pure, reaches the goal, and having reached it is born no more.

The man who has a sound understanding for charioteer, a controlled mind for reins—he it is that reaches the end of the journey, the supreme abode of Vishnu, the all-pervading.

The senses derive from physical objects, physical objects from mind, mind from intellect, intellect from ego, ego from the unmanifested seed, and the unmanifested seed from Brahman—the Uncaused Cause.

Brahman is the end of the journey. Brahman is the supreme goal. This Brahman, this Self, deep-hidden in all beings, is not revealed to all; but to the seers, pure in heart, concentrated in mind—to them is he revealed.

The senses of the wise man obey his mind, his mind obeys his intellect, his intellect obeys his ego, and his ego obeys the Self.

Arise! Awake! Approach the feet of the master and know THAT. Like the sharp edge of a razor, the sages say, is the path. Narrow it is, and difficult to tread!

Soundless, formless, intangible, undying, tasteless, odorless, without beginning, without end, eternal, immutable, beyond nature, is the Self. Knowing him as such, one is freed from death.

THE *MUNDAKA UPANISHAD*

The *Mundaka Upanishad* is an anonymous work probably composed between 400 and 300 BCE. This text places a special emphasis upon the value of the renunciation of worldly aims and the transitory nature of the fruits of Vedic ritual and recommends that the spiritual aspirant leave such aims and activities behind to seek an enlightened teacher, or *guru*.

The *Upanishads*, as a group, form something like an appendix to the more ancient Vedic texts and claim to reveal the true, inner meaning of the earlier writings and of the rituals described by those earlier writings. The *Mundaka Upanishad* is particularly striking in its teaching that the ancient Vedic rituals, intended to bring about specific this-worldly goals such as long life and prosperity, are ultimately a trap—a source of suffering and further bondage to the cycle of death and rebirth. One who is wise sees the rituals as pointing beyond themselves and their immediate ends toward the transcendent reality that infuses them with power in the first place: Brahman.

Like most of the *Upanishads*, the teaching of the *Mundaka Upanishad* is aimed at those who aspire not to a continuation of the life of this world and the fleeting pleasures of the senses, but to true immortality, which in the Hindu traditions means freedom from the cycle of rebirth.

This freedom is intimately tied to mysticism and the spiritual quest. If mysticism is defined as "the yearning for direct connection to a transcendent reality," then mysticism can be said to be a necessary condition for freedom from rebirth—which, according to this text, occurs only when one realizes the direct connection, and indeed the *identity*, of the Self and Brahman, the Infinite.

The text begins with the sacred syllable OM. This syllable is untranslatable. It is believed to contain within itself the essence of all of existence—to be Brahman in the form of sound. Meditating

15

silently upon this syllable or chanting it aloud is a central practice of the Vedantic tradition.

The text moves swiftly to a condemnation of formal, ritualistic religious practice that is aimed at finite goals. It is not that such ritual practice is ineffective—it does yield the fruit at which it is aimed. But this fruit is transient and not the source of the highest felicity. The "heaven" to which such works lead is a temporary abode, in which one may reside for a limited period, depending upon the works, or *karma*, that one has performed. But works are always finite in their results. One eventually dies in this heaven—even the gods are mortal, albeit long-lived, in the Hindu tradition—and is reborn in this world, or, as the text says, "flung back to earth." Persons who pursue such goals are contrasted with "wise, self-controlled, and tranquil souls, who are contented in spirit, and who practice austerity and meditation in solitude and silence, are freed from all impurity, and attain by the path of liberation to the immortal, the truly existing, the changeless Self."

The mystic, one who yearns for direct connection to a transcendent reality, needs to seek out a teacher who has already established such a connection. "To a disciple who approaches reverently, who is tranquil and self-controlled, the wise teacher gives that knowledge...by which is known the truly existing, the changeless Self." In its emphasis on the importance of a living, enlightened teacher, the *Mundaka Upanishad* is at one with most Hindu traditions, which emphasize such direct teaching over the study of scripture or intellectual knowledge.

The Self is described in the *Mundaka Upanishad* as "self-luminous." It is not so much a conscious entity as it is consciousness itself—the light by which all other objects are illuminated. It has no specific form of its own. It "dwells within all and without all," being all-pervasive. It is an inner reality, but also a cosmic reality, from which all beings arise. The Self is "both personal and impersonal." It can be approached as a personal deity or realized as the abstract principle of all existence. The individual self and cosmic Self, or Brahman, both dwell within the body, like two birds in a tree. The first bird eats "the sweet and bitter fruits of the tree" and grieves until it realizes its ultimate identity with the second: the divine.

As part of the Vedic canon, the *Mundaka Upanishad*, like all the *Upanishads*, is a highly authoritative scriptural text for Hindus. Its teaching is echoed in other selections from the *Upanishads* and in later Hindu texts cited in this volume.

Jeffery D. Long

OM...

With our ears may we hear what is good.

With our eyes may we behold thy righteousness. Tranquil in body, may we who worship thee find rest. OM...Peace—peace—peace.

Finite and transient are the fruits of sacrificial rites. The deluded, who regard them as the highest good, remain subject to birth and death.

Living in the abyss of ignorance, yet wise in their own conceit, the deluded go round and round, like the blind led by the blind.

Living in the abyss of ignorance, the deluded think themselves blest. Attached to works, they know not God. Works lead them only to heaven, whence, to their sorrow, their rewards quickly exhausted, they are flung back to earth.

Considering religion to be observance of rituals and performance of acts of charity, the deluded remain ignorant of the highest good. Having enjoyed in heaven the reward of their good works, they enter again into the world of mortals.

But wise, self-controlled, and tranquil souls, who are contented in spirit, and who practice austerity and meditation in solitude and silence, are freed from all impurity, and attain by the path of liberation to the immortal, the truly existing, the changeless Self.

Let a man devoted to spiritual life examine carefully the ephemeral nature of such enjoyment, whether here or hereafter, as may be won by good works, and so realize that it is not by works that one gains the Eternal. Let him give no thought to transient things, but, absorbed in meditation, let him renounce the world. If he would know the Eternal, let him humbly approach a Guru devoted to Brahman and well-versed in the scriptures.

To a disciple who approaches reverently, who is tranquil and self-controlled, the wise teacher gives that knowledge, faithfully

18

and without stint, by which is known the truly existing, the changeless Self.

The Imperishable is the Real. As sparks innumerable fly upward from a blazing fire, so from the depths of the Imperishable arise all things. To the depths of the Imperishable they in turn descend.

Self-luminous is that Being, and formless. He dwells within all and without all. He is unborn, pure, greater than the greatest, without breath, without mind.

From him are born breath, mind, the organs of sense, ether, air, fire, water, and the earth, and he binds all these together.

Heaven is his head, the sun and moon his eyes, the four quarters his ears, the revealed scriptures his voice, the air his breath, the universe his heart. From his feet came the earth. He is the innermost Self of all.

From him arises the sun-illumined sky, from the sky the rain, from the rain food, and from food the seed in man which he gives to woman.

Thus do all creatures descend from him.

From him are born hymns, devotional chants, scriptures, rites, sacrifices, oblations, divisions of time, the doer and the deed, and all the worlds lighted by the sun and purified by the moon.

From him are born gods of diverse descent. From him are born angels, men, beasts, birds; from him vitality, and food to sustain it; from him austerity and meditation, faith, truth, continence, and law.

From him spring the organs of sense, their activities, and their objects, together with their awareness of these objects. All these things, parts of man's nature, spring from him.

In him the seas and the mountains have their source; from him spring the rivers, and from him the herbs and other life-sustaining elements, by the aid of which the subtle body of man subsists in the physical body.

Thus Brahman is all in all. He is action, knowledge, goodness supreme. To know him, hidden in the lotus of the heart, is to untie the knot of ignorance.

Self-luminous is Brahman, ever present in the hearts of all. He is the refuge of all, he is the supreme goal. In him exists all that moves and breathes. In him exists all that is. He is both that which is gross and that which is subtle. Adorable is he. Beyond the ken of the senses is he. Supreme is he. Attain thou him!

He, the self-luminous, subtler than the subtlest, in whom exist all the worlds and all those that live therein—he is the imperishable Brahman. He is the principle of life. He is speech, and he is mind. He is real. He is immortal. Attain him, O my friend, the one goal to be attained!

Affix to the Upanishad, the bow incomparable, the sharp arrow of devotional worship; then, with mind absorbed and heart melted in love, draw the arrow and hit the mark—the imperishable Brahman.

OM is the bow, the arrow is the individual being, and Brahman is the target. With a tranquil heart, take aim. Lose thyself in him, even as the arrow is lost in the target.

In him are woven heaven, earth, and sky, together with the mind and all the senses. Know him, the Self alone. Give up vain talk. He is the bridge of immortality.

Within the lotus of the heart he dwells, where, like the spokes of a wheel in its hub, the nerves meet. Meditate on him as OM. Easily mayest thou cross the sea of darkness.

This Self, who understands all, who knows all, and whose glory is manifest in the universe, lives within the lotus of the heart, the bright throne of Brahman.

By the pure in heart is he known. The Self exists in man, within the lotus of the heart, and is the master of his life and of his body. With mind illumined by the power of meditation, the wise know him, the blissful, the immortal.

The knot of the heart, which is ignorance, is loosed, all doubts are dissolved, all evil effects of deeds are destroyed, when he who is both personal and impersonal is realized.

In the effulgent lotus of the heart dwells Brahman, who is

20

passionless and indivisible. He is pure, he is the light of lights. Him the knowers of the Self attain.

Him the sun does not illumine, nor the moon, nor the stars, nor the lightning—nor, verily, fires kindled upon the earth. He is the one light that gives light to all. He shining, everything shines.

This immortal Brahman is before, this immortal Brahman is behind, this immortal Brahman extends to the right and to the left, above and below. Verily, all is Brahman, and Brahman is supreme.

Like two birds of golden plumage, inseparable companions, the individual self and the immortal Self are perched on the branches of the selfsame tree. The former tastes of the sweet and bitter fruits of the tree; the latter, tasting of neither, calmly observes.

The individual self, deluded by forgetfulness of his identity with the divine Self, bewildered by his ego, grieves and is sad. But when he recognizes the worshipful Lord as his own true Self, and beholds his glory, he grieves no more.

THE *CHANDOGYA UPANISHAD*

The *Chandogya Upanishad* is an anonymous work probably composed between 500 and 400 BCE. It is one of the oldest of the *Upanishads*, and certainly the oldest to be included in this book.

The *Upanishads* form something like an appendix to the more ancient Vedic texts, claiming to reveal the true, inner meaning of the earlier texts and of the rituals described in them. The specific early Vedic text to which the *Chandogya Upanishad* is appended, the *Sama Veda*, is concerned primarily with music and the proper chanting of verses from the earliest Veda—the *Rig Veda*—in the context of rituals. The themes of song and sound and the mystical power of reflection upon them are therefore particularly prominent in this text.

A central theme of Vedanta present in all of the selections from the *Upanishads* in this volume is the relationship of identity between the reality that is at the core of one's innermost being— the Self—and Brahman, the Infinite, transcendent reality that is the basis of all existence. All of these texts therefore spring from and affirm mysticism, defined as "the yearning for direct connection to a transcendent reality." The realization of a direct connection between the Self and Brahman is presented in these texts as the highest goal and the end of all wisdom (which is also the literal meaning of *Vedanta*). This realization leads to freedom from the cycle of death and rebirth and the inevitable suffering that this cycle involves. The *Chandogya Upanishad* is no exception.

The relatively brief selection from the *Chandogya Upanishad* included here (for it is a lengthy text) begins with a discussion of duty, or *dharma*, which is contrasted with the spiritual quest for Brahman. Doing one's duty, being a good person—the activities one often associates with conventional religiosity—all of this is a good thing. Such activities "lead one to the realm of the blest." But, as we have also seen in the *Katha* and *Mundaka Upanishads*,

22

the "realm of the blest," or heaven, is a temporary abode. After the effects of the good actions that led one there—one's *karma*—have been exhausted, one dies and returns again to this world. In other words, heaven, while pleasant, is nevertheless part of the cycle of death and rebirth. Only one "who is firmly established in the knowledge of Brahman achieves immortality"—that is, freedom from the cycle of rebirth. Only one who takes up the spiritual quest, the path of mysticism, will reach the ultimate goal, beyond all material rewards.

It is then explained that Brahman is the basis of both cosmic reality and the reality of the individual person. "The light that shines above the heavens and above this world, the light that shines in the highest world, beyond which there are no others— that is the light that shines in the hearts of men." According to commentators in the various Hindu traditions, "light" here refers to consciousness. Brahman is infinite, unlimited awareness.

Brahman is both impersonal and personal—the material cause of existence ("All is Brahman") and the supreme deity ("Worship Brahman alone").

One realizes Brahman at least in part through an act of will. "A man is, above all, his will. As is his will in this life, so does he become when he departs from it." Our life takes on the form of that to which we direct our desires. One therefore attains Brahman only if one desires Brahman above all else. "He who worships him [Brahman], and puts his trust in him, shall surely attain him."

The next section, a dialogue between teacher and student (as is so often the case in the *Upanishads*), emphasizes the nature of Brahman as the Infinite. No finite goal is able to satisfy the longing of the soul. "There is no joy in the finite. Only in the Infinite is there joy." The Infinite is self-sufficient and independent, "resting in itself." It is from the Infinite that all finite goods emerge. The whole universe "issues forth from it." It is the Self. "The Self is one, and it has become all things." All that exists has emanated from Brahman.

The seeker after Brahman is urged to withdraw attention from the finite things of the world and focus inward, upon the "lotus of the heart" where Brahman dwells within as the Self. This lotus of the heart does not refer to the heart of the physical body, for this lotus "does not grow old" as the body does. Withdrawing attention from the objects of the senses and focusing within is a recurring theme of the Hindu traditions, which is also found in one of the selections from the *Yoga Sutras* found in this volume.

Another theme that this text shares with other selections found here is that of the temporary nature of the heavenly rewards achieved through Vedic ritual—a topic also seen in the selections from the *Katha* and *Mundaka Upanishads*. Interestingly, the *Chandogya Upanishad* does not simply recommend, as the *Mundaka Upanishad* does, that one give up attachment to these temporary rewards, forsaking them for the mystical quest and the pursuit of Brahman. It says, rather, that the sage who realizes Brahman *also* achieves all of the temporary rewards he might desire as well—such as a vision of his departed loved ones. "Whatsoever a knower of Brahman may desire, straightway it is his." The paradox is that one must renounce the desire for these lesser goals in order to attain them. One is reminded of the saying of Jesus, "Seek ye first the kingdom of heaven and all else will be given unto you" (Luke 12:31).

The *Chandogya Upanishad* also emphasizes the virtue of continence, or restraint of sensory impulses, as essential to attaining the true freedom of Brahman, the "world of Brahman," where one drinks from the lake of the nectar of true bliss.

Jeffery D. Long

The requirements of duty are three. The first is sacrifice, study, almsgiving; the second is austerity; the third is life as a student in the home of a teacher and the practice of continence. Together, these three lead one to the realm of the blest. But he who is firmly established in the knowledge of Brahman achieves immortality.

The light that shines above the heavens and above this world, the light that shines in the highest world, beyond which there are no others—that is the light that shines in the hearts of men.

Truly has this universe come forth from Brahman. In Brahman it lives and has its being. Assuredly, all is Brahman. Let a man, freed from the taint of passion, worship Brahman alone.

A man is, above all, his will. As is his will in this life, so does he become when he departs from it. Therefore should his will be fixed on attaining Brahman. The Self, who is to be realized by the purified mind and the illumined consciousness, whose form is light, whose thoughts are true; who, like the ether, remains pure and unattached; from whom proceed all works, all desires, all odors, all tastes; who pervades all, who is beyond the senses, and in whom there is fullness of joy forever—he is my very Self, dwelling within the lotus of my heart.

Smaller than a grain of rice is the Self; smaller than a grain of barley, smaller than a mustard seed, smaller than a canary seed, yea, smaller even than the kernel of a canary seed. Yet again is that Self, within the lotus of my heart, greater than the earth, greater than the heavens, yea, greater than all the worlds.

He from whom proceed all works, all desires, all odors, all tastes; who pervades all, who is beyond the senses, and in whom there is fullness of joy forever—he, the heart-enshrined Self, is verily Brahman. I, who worship the Self within the lotus of my heart, will attain him at death. He who worships him, and puts his trust in him, shall surely attain him.

....

"The Infinite is the source of joy. There is no joy in the finite. Only in the Infinite is there joy. Ask to know of the Infinite."

"Sir, I ask to know of it."

"Where one sees nothing but the One, hears nothing but the One, knows nothing but the One—there is the Infinite. Where one sees another, hears another, knows another—there is the finite. The Infinite is immortal, the finite is mortal."

"In what does the Infinite rest?"

"In its own glory—nay, not even in that. In the world it is said that cows and horses, elephants and gold, slaves, wives, fields, and houses are man's glory—but these are poor and finite things. How shall the Infinite rest anywhere but in itself?

"The Infinite is below, above, behind, before, to the right, to the left. I am all this. This Infinite is the Self. The Self is below, above, behind, before, to the right, to the left. I am all this. One who knows, meditates upon, and realizes the truth of the Self— such an one delights in the Self, revels in the Self, rejoices in the Self. He becomes master of himself, and master of all the worlds. Slaves are they who know not this truth.

"He who knows, meditates upon, and realizes this truth of the Self, finds that everything—primal energy, ether, fire, water, and all other elements—mind, will, speech, sacred hymns and scriptures—indeed the whole universe —issues forth from it.

"It is written: He who has realized eternal Truth does not see death, nor illness, nor pain; he sees everything as the Self, and obtains all.

"The Self is one, and it has become all things.

"When the senses are purified, the heart is purified; when the heart is purified, there is constant and unceasing remembrance of the Self; when there is constant and unceasing remembrance of the Self, all bonds are loosed and freedom is attained."

Thus the venerable Sanatkumara taught Narada, who was pure in heart, how to pass from darkness into light.

Within the city of Brahman, which is the body, there is the heart, and within the heart there is a little house. This house has the shape of a lotus, and within it dwells that which is to be sought after, inquired about, and realized.

What then is that which, dwelling within this little house, this lotus of the heart, is to be sought after, inquired about, and realized?

As large as the universe outside, even so large is the universe within the lotus of the heart. Within it are heaven and earth, the sun, the moon, the lightning, and all the stars. What is in the macrocosm is in this microcosm.

All things that exist, all beings and all desires, are in the city of Brahman; what then becomes of them when old age approaches and the body dissolves in death?

Though old age comes to the body, the lotus of the heart does not grow old. At death of the body, it does not die. The lotus of the heart, where Brahman exists in all his glory—that, and not the body, is the true city of Brahman. Brahman, dwelling therein, is untouched by any deed, ageless, deathless, free from grief, free from hunger and from thirst. His desires are right desires, and his desires are fulfilled.

As here on earth all the wealth that one earns is but transitory, so likewise transitory are the heavenly enjoyments acquired by the performance of sacrifices. Therefore those who die without having realized the Self and its right desires find no permanent happiness in any world to which they go; while those who have realized the Self and its right desires find permanent happiness everywhere.

If the sage desires to see his fathers of the spirit-world, lo, his fathers come to meet him. In their company he is happy.

And if he desires to see his mothers of the spirit-world, lo, his mothers come to meet him. In their company he is happy.

And if he desires to see his brothers of the spirit-world, lo, his brothers come to meet him. In their company he is happy.

And if he desires to see his sisters of the spirit-world, lo, his sisters come to meet him. In their company he is happy.

And if he desires to see his friends of the spirit-world, lo, his friends come to meet him. In their company he is happy.

And if he desires heavenly perfumes and garlands, lo, heavenly perfumes and garlands come to him. In their possession he is happy.

And if he desires heavenly food and drink, lo, heavenly food and drink come to him. In their possession he is happy.

And if he desires heavenly song and music, lo, heavenly song and music come to him. In their possession he is happy.

Indeed, whatsoever such a knower of Brahman may desire, straightway it is his; and having obtained it, he is exalted of men. The fulfillment of right desires is within reach of everyone, but a veil of illusion obstructs the ignorant. That is why, though they desire to see their dead, their beloved, they cannot see them.

Do we wish for our beloved, among the living or among the dead, or is there aught else for which we long, yet, for all our longing, do not obtain? Lo, all shall be ours if we but dive deep within, even to the lotus of the heart, where dwells the Lord. Yea, the object of every right desire is within our reach, though unseen, concealed by a veil of illusion.

As one not knowing that a golden treasure lies buried beneath his feet, may walk over it again and again, yet never find it, so all beings live every moment in the city of Brahman, yet never find him, because of the veil of illusion by which he is concealed.

The Self resides within the lotus of the heart. Knowing this, devoted to the Self, the sage enters daily that holy sanctuary.

Absorbed in the Self, the sage is freed from identity with the body and lives in blissful consciousness. The Self is the immortal, the fearless; the Self is Brahman. This Brahman is eternal Truth.

The Self within the heart is like a boundary which divides the world from THAT. Day and night cross not that boundary, nor old age, nor death; neither grief nor pleasure, neither good nor evil deeds. All evil shuns THAT. For THAT is free from impurity: by impurity can it never be touched.

Wherefore he who has crossed that boundary, and has realized the Self, if he is blind, ceases to be blind; if he is wounded, ceases to be wounded; if he is afflicted, ceases to be afflicted. When that boundary is crossed, night becomes day; for the world of Brahman is light itself.

And that world of Brahman is reached by those who practice continence. For the knower of eternal truth knows it through continence. And what is known as worship, that also is continence. For a man worships the Lord by continence, and thus attains him.

What is called salvation is really continence. For through continence man is freed from ignorance. And what is known as the vow of silence, that too is continence. For a man through continence realizes the Self and lives in quiet contemplation.

What people call dwelling in the forest, that is continence.

In the world of Brahman there is a lake whose waters are like nectar, and whosoever tastes thereof is straightway drunk with joy; and beside that lake is a tree which yields the juice of immortality. Into this world they cannot enter who do not practice continence.

For the world of Brahman belongs to those who practice continence. They alone enter that world and drink from that lake of nectar. For them there is freedom in all the worlds.

The *Yoga Sutras*

INTRODUCTION

The *Yoga Sutras* are a collection of short aphorisms, or *sutras*, attributed to the sage Patanjali. In its current form, this collection was most probably composed between 100 BCE and 500 CE and possibly drew upon considerably more ancient teachings and practices.

The two selections from the *Yoga Sutras* included in this volume are from a modern translation and commentary on Patanjali's aphorisms by Swami Prabhavananda (1893–1976) and Christopher Isherwood (1904–1986). Prabhavananda and Isherwood are both prominent figures associated with the Vedanta Society, an organization established in 1894 by Swami Vivekananda (1863–1902), the first Hindu spiritual teacher to bring the teachings of Vedanta, the central philosophy of Hinduism, to the western world with his famous presentation at the Parliament of the World's Religions in Chicago in 1893. This organization has done a great deal to publicize and spread Hindu thought in America and to shape contemporary perceptions of Hinduism and its contributions to mysticism and the spiritual quest. Vivekananda was a disciple of Sri Ramakrishna (1836–1886), a Hindu sage from Bengal, in the northeastern part of India, who is held in great reverence today by Hindus and non-Hindus alike for his emphasis on experiencing God directly—which is the essence of mysticism—and his teaching of the ultimate unity of all religions as paths to the mystical experience. One of the selections from the *Yoga Sutras* given in this volume cites both Ramakrishna and Vivekananda and also quotes from the Christian gospels—which is a reflection of the Vedanta Society's ideal of the truth in all religions.

Prabhavananda was a disciple of one of Ramakrishna's direct disciples and led the Vedanta Society of Southern California from 1930 until his death in 1976. Isherwood, a disciple of Prabhavananda in California, was a prominent author who collaborated with Prabhavananda on a number of translations of and commentaries upon some of the most important Hindu philosophical works, including the *Yoga Sutras*, the *Bhagavad Gita*, and the principal *Upanishads*. He also independently authored a biography of Ramakrishna, titled *Ramakrishna and His Disciples*.

Contrary to contemporary popular perceptions in the western world, the term *yoga* does not refer primarily to physical exercises or postures. Indeed, such postures form but one of the eight stages of the system of practice outlined in the *Yoga Sutras*. Yoga, in its original meaning, is cognate with the English word *yoke*, and refers to union or joining of the individual consciousness with the Infinite. Yoga's goal is, in other words, essentially identical to the goal of mysticism: "the yearning for *direct connection* to a transcendent reality." Yoga is a system for achieving this direct connection, and the *Yoga Sutras* are a "how-to" manual or guide to putting this system into practice.

The actual sutras, or aphorisms, are very compact. Texts of this kind are normally accompanied by the commentary of a living teacher, or, barring that, written commentary designed to explain and help the practitioner apply the sutras in his or her own life and practice. So even though Prabhavananda and Isherwood's commentary is new, relatively speaking, and designed for the modern practitioner, it continues an ancient tradition of making old wisdom ever new and relevant.

Prabhavananda and Isherwood's commentary is quite clear and, for the most part, self-explanatory. But it does utilize some terminology with which the beginning reader may not be familiar.

Ishwara, as the text explains, is the personal deity, or God, "the supreme ruler of the universe—its creator, sustainer, and dissolver." Ishwara, it is said, is free from *karmas*, which are the results of actions carried out in ignorance of one's ultimate identity with the highest Reality, or Brahman. Ishwara suffers no such ignorance and is therefore not in a state of bondage to karma and the cycle of death and rebirth to which karma gives rise. Ishwara is also said to be free from *samskaras*, the habits or tendencies to which ignorant beings are subject, and which lead to further action, leading to further karma and rebirth.

Ishwara is described as "Brahman seen within Prakriti." *Prakriti* is the material world, the limited realm of time and space in which the cycle of rebirth occurs. Prakriti has no independent reality but is a mere projection of Brahman, and Ishwara is Prakriti's master. When one realizes one's identity with Brahman, one sees that time and space are an illusion—that Prakriti is an appearance, or *maya*—and that Brahman, the eternal and the infinite, is alone real.

The text also elaborates upon the mantra (*mantram*) or sacred syllable OM, which is also found prominently in more ancient Hindu texts, such as the *Upanishads* (including in selections found in this volume). The chanting of a mantra, or *japa*, is explained to be an important component of the spiritual path, helping to focus one's thoughts upon God or upon the meaning of the mantra (which is often a name of God). In the course of the discussion of the "higher kind of reverie" that such practice helps one to cultivate, there is mention of *sattwa*, *rajas*, and *tamas*. These are the three qualities, or *gunas*, and are also a prominent topic of the discussion in the *Bhagavad Gita* (including one of the selections from this text found in this volume). The gunas are characteristics of Prakriti, modes of material energy that shape one's experience in the material world. *Sattwa* is a luminous quality that could be characterized as a calm yet aware state of mind (such as that one wishes to cultivate with the practice of meditation). *Rajas* is a dynamic, excited state and *tamas* is a state of rest. A calm, reflective pool of water could be said to be in a state of sattwa. A turbulent ocean during a storm is in a state of rajas. A block of ice is in a state of tamas. These qualities characterize both physical states and the states of consciousness of beings in the material world.

Jeffery D. Long

YOGA APHORISMS: *HOW TO KNOW GOD*

23. Concentration may also be attained through devotion to Ishwara.

24. Ishwara is a special kind of being, untouched by ignorance and the products of ignorance, not subject to karmas or samskaras or the results of action.

Here, for the first time, Patanjali introduces the idea of God. According to Vedanta philosophy, Ishwara is the supreme ruler of the universe—its creator, sustainer and dissolver. Brahman, the ultimate Reality, cannot properly be said to create, sustain or dissolve, since Brahman is, by definition, without attributes. Ishwara is Brahman seen within Prakriti. He corresponds, more or less, to God the Father in the Christian tradition.

What is important is the concept of devotion. Liberation, as we have already seen, can be reached without devotion to God. But this is a subtle and dangerous path, threading its way through the pitfalls of ambition and pride. Devotion to a personal ideal of God brings with it a natural inclination to humility and service. It sweetens the dryness of intellectual discrimination and calls forth the highest kind of love of which man is capable. We cannot even imagine Brahman until the moment of our liberation, but we can all imagine Ishwara, according to our different natures—for Ishwara has attributes which our minds can recognize. Ishwara is all that we can know of the Reality until we pass beyond Prakriti.

If we set ourselves to serve Ishwara, if we dedicate our actions and surrender our wills to him, we shall find that he draws us to himself. This is the grace of God, which Sri Ramakrishna compared to an ever-blowing breeze; you have only to raise your sail in order to catch it. And in the Gita, we read:

35

Whatever your action, Food or worship;
Whatever the gift
That you give to another; Whatever you vow
To the work of the spirit: Lay these also
As offerings before me.

This kind of devotion requires, perhaps, a special temperament. It is not for everybody. But to be able to feel it is a very great blessing, for it is the safest and happiest way to liberation.

Ishwara, it has been said, is God as he appears within Prakriti. But it must be remembered that Ishwara is Prakriti's ruler, not its servant. That is why Patanjali describes him as "a special kind of being." A man is the servant of Prakriti. He is subject to ignorance of his real Self (the Atman) and to the products of this ignorance—egotism, attachment to sense objects, aversion from them (which is merely attachment in reverse) and a blind clinging to his present life: the various forms of bondage which constitute misery, and which Patanjali will discuss more fully in the second chapter of his aphorisms. Ishwara is not subject to this ignorance, or to its products.

Man is subject to the laws of birth and death, the laws of karma. Ishwara is unborn, undying. Man is subject to his samskaras—the deeply rooted tendencies which drive him on to further actions and desires. Ishwara is free from samskaras and desires. He is not involved in the results of action.

Man, it is true, may become liberated. But, even in this, he differs from Ishwara—for Ishwara was never in bondage. After liberation, man is one with Brahman. But he can never become one with Ishwara. (Indeed, the desire to become Ishwara, the ruler of the universe, would be the most insane of all egotistical desires—it seems to be typified, in Christian literature, by the story of the fall of Lucifer.) In the state of union with Brahman, both Ishwara and his universe are transcended, since both are merely projections of Brahman.

25. In Him, knowledge is infinite; in others it is only a germ.

26. He was the teacher even of the earliest teachers, since He is not limited by time.

These two aphorisms deal with Ishwara's attribute of omniscience. If we admit the existence of knowledge—no matter how limited—in man, we must deduce from it the existence of infinite knowledge in God. Further, granted that everybody must have a teacher, Patanjali reasons that the teacher of the first teacher can only have been God, since he alone, being timeless, was present before teachers began.

27. The word which expresses Him is OM.

28. This word must be repeated with meditation upon its meaning.

29. Hence comes knowledge of the Atman and destruction of the obstacles to that knowledge.

"In the beginning was the Word," says the Gospel according to St. John, and "the Word was with God, and the Word was God." This statement echoes, almost exactly, a verse from the Rik Veda: "In the beginning was Brahman, with whom was the Word; and the Word was truly the supreme Brahman." The philosophy of the Word may be traced, in its various forms and modifications, down from the ancient Hindu scriptures through the teachings of Plato and the Stoics to Philo of Alexandria and the author of the Fourth Gospel. Perhaps an actual historical link can be proved to exist between all these succeeding schools of thought; perhaps it cannot. The question is not very important. Truth may be rediscovered, independently, in many different epochs and places. The power of the Word, for good and for evil, has been recognized by mankind since the dawn of history. Primitive tribes enshrined it in their taboos and secret cults. Twentieth-century cultures have prostituted it to the uses of politics and commercial advertisement.

Words and ideas are inseparable. You cannot have the idea of God without the word which expresses God. But why, necessarily, use the word OM? The Hindus reply that, because God is the basic fact of the universe, he must be represented by the most basic, the most natural, the most comprehensive of all sounds. And they claim that this sound is OM (or AUM, as it should be properly pronounced). To quote Swami Vivekananda: "The first letter, A, is the root sound, the key, pronounced without touching any part of the tongue or palate; M represents the last sound in the series, being produced by the closed lips, and the U rolls from the very root to the end of the sounding board of the mouth. Thus, OM represents the whole phenomena of sound-producing." If any of us feel that a mere argument from phonetics is insufficient to establish this claim, we should remember, also, that OM is almost certainly the most ancient word for God that has come down to us through the ages. It has been used by countless millions of worshipers—always in the most universal sense, implying no special attribute, referring to no one particular deity. If such use can confer sanctity, then OM is the most sacred word of all.

But what really matters is that we should appreciate the power of the Word in our spiritual life; and this appreciation can only come through practical experience. People who have never tried the practice of repeating the name of God are apt to scoff at it: it seems to them so empty, so mechanical. "Just repeating the same word over and over!" they exclaim scornfully. "What possible good can that do?"

The truth is that we are all inclined to flatter ourselves—despite our daily experience to the contrary—that we spend our time thinking logical, consecutive thoughts. In fact, most of us do no such thing. Consecutive thought about any one problem occupies a very small proportion of our waking hours.

More usually, we are in a state of reverie—a mental fog of disconnected sense impressions, irrelevant memories, nonsensical scraps of sentences from books and newspapers, little darting fears and resentments, physical sensations of discomfort, excite-

38

ment, or ease. If, at any given moment, we could take twenty human minds and inspect their workings, we should probably find one, or at most two, which were functioning rationally. The remaining eighteen or nineteen minds would look more like this: "Ink bottle. That time I saw Roosevelt. In love with the night mysterious. Reds veto Pact. Jimmy's trying to get my job. Mary says I'm fat. Big toe hurts. Soup good...." etc., etc. Because we do nothing to control this reverie, it is largely conditioned by external circumstances. The weather is cloudy, so our mood is sad. The sun comes out; our mood brightens. Insects begin to buzz around us, and we turn irritable and nervous. Often, it is as simple as that.

But now, if we introduce into this reverie the repetition of the name of God, we shall find that we can control our moods, despite the interference of the outside world. We are always, anyhow, repeating words in our minds—the name of a friend or an enemy, the name of an anxiety, the name of a desired object—and each of these words is surrounded by its own mental climate. Try saying "war," or "cancer," or "money," ten thousand times, and you will find that your whole mood has been changed and colored by the associations connected with that word. Similarly, the name of God will change the climate of your mind. It cannot do otherwise.

In the Hindu scriptures we often find the phrase: "To take refuge in his name." (See also the Book of Proverbs, 18:10: "The name of the Lord is a strong tower: the righteous runneth into it and is safe.") This phrase—which at first may sound rather too poetical—comes to have a very real and literal significance in our spiritual life. When the mind is so violently disturbed by pain or fear or the necessities of some physical emergency that it cannot possibly be used for meditation or even rational thought, there is still one thing that you can always do; you can repeat his name, over and over. You can hold fast to that, throughout all the tumult. Once you have really tested and proved the power of the holy Word, you will rely upon it increasingly. Through constant practice, the repetition becomes automatic. It no longer has to be consciously willed. It is rather like the thermostat on a water heater or a refrigerator. Whenever the mind reaches an undesirable "temperature" you will find that the repetition begins of itself and continues as long as it is necessary.

Mere repetition of God's name is, of course, insufficient—as Patanjali points out. We must also meditate upon its meaning. But the one process follows naturally upon the other. If we persevere in our repetition, it will lead us inevitably into meditation. Gradually, our confused reverie will give way to concentrated thought. We cannot long continue to repeat any word without beginning to think about the reality which it represents. Unless we are far advanced in spiritual practice, this concentration will not be maintained for more than a few moments; the mind will slip back into reverie again. But it will be a higher kind of reverie—a reverie dominated by sattwa rather than by rajas or tamas. And the Name, perpetually uttered within it, will be like a gentle plucking at our sleeve, demanding and finally recapturing our attention.

In India, when a disciple comes to his teacher for initiation, he is given what is called a mantram. The mantram consists of one or more holy names which the disciple is to repeat and meditate upon, throughout the rest of his life. It is regarded as very private and very sacred—the essence, as it were, of the teacher's instructions to that particular disciple, and the seed within which spiritual wisdom is passed down from one generation to another. You must never tell your mantram to any other human being. The act of repeating it is called japam. You can make japam aloud if you are alone, or silently if you are among other people. It is convenient to do this with a rosary—thus linking thought with physical action (which is one of the great advantages of all ritual) and providing a small but sufficient outlet for the nervous energy of the body, which might otherwise accumulate and disturb the mind. Most spiritual aspirants resolve to make a certain fixed amount of japam every day. The rosary serves to measure this— one bead to each repetition of the mantram—so that you are not distracted by having to count.

Needless to add, the practice of making japam is not confined to the Hindu religion. The Catholics teach it also. "Hail Mary" is a mantram. A form of mantram is also recognized by the Greek Orthodox Church. We quote here from a volume containing two remarkable books, *The Way of a Pilgrim* and *The Pilgrim Continues His Way*, which record the spiritual pilgrimage of a Russian monk during the middle of the nineteenth century.

"The continuous interior Prayer of Jesus is a constant uninterrupted calling upon the divine Name of Jesus with the lips, in the spirit, in the heart; while forming a mental picture of his constant presence, and imploring his grace, during every occupation, at all times, in all places, even during sleep. The appeal is couched in these terms, 'Lord Jesus Christ, have mercy on me.' One who accustoms himself to this appeal experiences as a result so deep a consolation and so great a need to offer the prayer always, that he can no longer live without it, and it will continue to voice itself within him of its own accord.

"Many so-called enlightened people regard this frequent offering of one and the same prayer as useless and even trifling, calling it mechanical and a thoughtless occupation of simple people. But unfortunately they do not know the secret which is revealed as a result of this mechanical exercise, they do not know how this frequent service of the lips imperceptibly becomes a genuine appeal of the heart, sinks down into the inward life, becomes a delight, becomes as it were, natural to the soul, bringing it light and nourishment and leading it on to union with God.

"St. John Chrysostom, in his teaching about prayer, speaks as follows: 'No one should give the answer that it is impossible for a man occupied with worldly cares, and who is unable to go to church, to pray always. Everywhere, wherever you may find yourself, you can set up an altar to God in your mind by means of prayer. And so it is fitting to pray at your trade, on a journey, standing at the counter or sitting at your handicraft....In such an order of life all his actions, by the power of the invocation of the Name of God, would be signalized by success, and finally he would train himself to the uninterrupted prayerful invocation of the Name of Jesus Christ. He would come to know from experience that frequency of prayer, this sole means of salvation, is a possibility for the will of man, that it is possible to pray at all times, in all circumstances and in every place, and easily to rise from frequent vocal prayer to prayer of the mind and from that to prayer of the heart, which opens up the Kingdom of God within us.'"

THE EIGHT LIMBS OF YOGA

In this selection from the *Yoga Sutras*, Patanjali lists the eight stages of the system of yoga—the practice designed to "yoke" (the literal meaning of *yoga*) the individual mind to its true Self, the Atman (also a major topic of the selections from the *Upanishads* given in this volume). One could say that the teachings of the *Upanishads* presuppose such a system—referring to its various dimensions, such as moral restraint and the withdrawal of the senses—while the *Yoga Sutras* are a presentation of the system itself.

The first stage—*yama*, or "restraint"—consists of five moral observances that are a prerequisite for the other seven stages. These are nonviolence, truthfulness, non-stealing, control of sexual desires and activities, and detachment.

The second stage—*niyama*, "observance" or "discipline"—consists of five virtues: purity, contentment, asceticism, study, and surrender to the Lord (Ishwara).

The third stage—*asana*, or posture—is where the various postures and exercises that most people today associate with yoga fit into Patanjali's system. In later yoga tradition, beginning around the tenth century CE, the fairly elaborate system of postures known as *Hatha Yoga* was developed as an aid to meditation and continues to be experimented with and added to in the modern world. Interestingly, however, all Patanjali says about posture is that one must keep one's back straight, in alignment with one's head and neck, and that one must sit in a place that is clean and comfortable. The main idea is to prevent the physical body from being a distraction to the mystical process. The various calming exercises and stretches now associated with yoga are originally intended only to aid this goal. But these exercises are now practiced by many as an end in themselves, or for physical fitness. How many people who pursue these practices have first cultivated the moral restraints and virtues of the first two stages of yoga? Or go on to the other stages?

The fourth stage is *pranayama*: control of the breath, or *prana*. This is often done through cultivating mindful awareness of the breathing process—inhaling deliberately, and then holding the breath for a short time, and then exhaling, and then pausing again for a short time before inhaling and beginning the process again. Holding one's breath for too long is not recommended, and is a frequent mistake of beginning practitioners of yoga. The idea here is *not* to try to make the pause between inhalations and exhalations as long as possible. It is to breathe deliberately and consciously—to become self-aware in the act of breathing, which is something that we normally do with no thought at all. This focuses one's consciousness.

The fifth stage is *pratyahara*, or withdrawal of the mind from sense objects. After one has focused one's awareness through the control of the breath, one begins to direct that awareness inward, and away from distracting external objects. This is compared in some Hindu texts to a turtle withdrawing its limbs into its shell. It is a theme also found in the selections in this volume from the *Upanishads*, which do not so much describe the process as presuppose it.

The sixth stage is *dharana*, or concentration. One continues to focus one's mind inwardly, but now aided by a particular object of concentration—often either a sound, like a mantra (a sacred verse, such as a name of God), or a visualization of a sacred image, or both, in combination with one another.

The seventh stage is *dhyana*, or meditation, in which one becomes absorbed fully in the object of one's concentration, with all other thoughts gradually melting away.

In the final, eighth stage—*samadhi*, or absorption in the Atman, or Self—the object of one's concentration also melts away, and consciousness merges into itself, becoming its own object. Samadhi is further divided into two sub-stages. First, there is *savikalpa samadhi*, in which there continues to be a subtle distinction between one's sense of self as subject, or experiencer, and the object of one's experience (which, at this stage of yoga, is pure consciousness itself). Then, there is *nirvikalpa samadhi*, in which even the subtle sense of individual subjectivity disappears, and there is only pure consciousness, without subject or object. This pure Self-awareness is the ultimate goal of Patanjali's system of yoga.

For more detailed information on Patanjali's *Yoga Sutras* as a whole, please see the introduction to selections from the *Yoga Sutras*.

Jeffery D. Long

Patanjali now begins a detailed description of the so-called "limbs" of yoga—the various rules and practices which we must observe in order to clear the mind of its impurities. To remove these impurities—the obstacles to knowledge of the Atman—is the sole purpose of spiritual discipline. For the knowledge itself does not have to be sought. It is already within us—unlike that mundane knowledge which must be acquired from books and experiences in the external world. When the obstacles have been removed, the ever-present Atman is immediately revealed.

29. The eight limbs of yoga are: the various forms of abstention from evildoing (yama), the various observances (niyamas), posture (asana), control of the prana (pranayama), withdrawal of the mind from sense objects (pratyahara), concentration (dharana), meditation (dhyana), and absorption in the Atman (samadhi).

The *Bhagavad Gita*

INTRODUCTION

The *Bhagavad Gita* (the "Song of the Lord" or "Song of God") was probably composed between 100 BCE and 100 CE. This eighteen-chapter segment of the sixth book of a vast Sanskrit epic called the *Mahabharata* is viewed as an authoritative scripture in its own right, particularly in the modern period, though numerous premodern commentaries were written upon it as well. Many Hindus see this text as a comprehensive summary of Hindu philosophy. As a scripture, it serves a function in contemporary Hinduism closer to that of the Bible in Christianity than do the venerable, but less popular, *Vedas*.

Occurring at the point in the *Mahabharata*'s narrative when the climactic battle of Kurukshetra is about to take place, the *Bhagavad Gita* consists of a dialogue between the hero, Arjuna, and his best friend and cousin, Krishna, who has agreed to act as Arjuna's charioteer in the battle, and who is also an *avatara*, or divine incarnation.

Deeply troubled by the moral dilemma that he faces, having to fight in a war that will require him to slay such revered persons as his grandsire Bhishma and his teacher Drona, Arjuna falls into despair. Krishna's counsel to Arjuna at this point takes the form of a conversation that ranges over a great variety of topics and views current in Indian philosophy at the time of the text's composition. Currents of thought that are discernible in the *Bhagavad Gita* include Samkhya, yoga, Vedanta, Buddhism, and Jainism, as well as an early articulation of the theistic philosophy of the *bhakti*, or devotional, movement, which became highly popular in the centuries to follow.

47

Hinduism

Later Hindu tradition gives the text an increasingly privileged status as a summary of all Hindu thought. It is often called simply "the *Gita*"—"the Song"—despite there being many texts in the *Gita* genre. With the *Upanishads* and the *Brahma Sutras*, the *Bhagavad Gita* forms part of the *Prasthana Traya*, or threefold foundation of Vedanta philosophy, upon which all the major historical Vedantic sages have commented. Mahatma Gandhi referred to this text as his "dictionary of daily reference" and cited it as a major influence on his philosophy of active engagement with the world as an important component of the spiritual quest.

The most controversial aspect of the text is its location on a battlefield, coupled with the fact that Krishna encourages Arjuna to fight in battle, rather than taking a path of nonviolence—although Krishna, somewhat paradoxically, does commend nonviolence to Arjuna as one of the virtues of an enlightened person. In one of the selections from this text in this volume, when Arjuna says to Krishna, "Why are you telling me to do these terrible deeds?" it is to this battle and the bloodshed it will entail that he is referring.

Commentators have responded to the question of violence and nonviolence in the *Bhagavad Gita* in a variety of ways: ignoring it, frankly accepting the violence entailed as a part of life in ancient India or of life in general, viewing the entire episode in terms of the symbolism that the text itself suggests—with the body as the field of battle and the real enemies being negative qualities such as ignorance, desire, and egotism—or, in the case of Gandhi, seeing the violence of the epic context as finally irrelevant to and even incompatible with the deeper spiritual message of the text, which becomes abstracted from its literary context. A related issue on which scholars disagree is whether the *Gita* is a later interpolation, inserted into the *Mahabharata* at a later date—and in disagreement with it on the issue of violence—or whether it should be seen as integral to the epic and the issue of violence merely a secondary consideration.

The central emphasis of the *Gita*'s teaching is not primarily in regard to violence, despite its setting, but in regard to mysticism

and the spiritual quest. How does one reach the ultimate goal of
Hindu thought and practice: the realization of the identity of the
Self and Brahman, which leads to liberation from the cycle of
birth, death, and rebirth? Is it through the *yoga,* or spiritual discipline, or action—performing good works and offering them as a
sacrifice at the feet of God, analogous to the sacrificial rituals of
the *Vedas*? Is it through the yoga of knowledge, the path of realization taught in the *Upanishads*? Is it through devotion to
Brahman as the personal deity, the Ishwara of the *Yoga Sutras*? Is
it through the yoga of contemplative practice and meditation? Or
is it in a combination of all of these practices that the path to the
highest bliss can be found? Various teachers and traditions within
Hinduism differ among themselves in their interpretation of the
Gita, some saying it emphasizes one or the other of the paths
listed here as the primary one, with the others playing merely supporting roles, and others arguing for a synthesis. It is a hard text
to interpret in a conclusive way, given that, whenever it is describing a specific path, it also endorses this path as the best way to the
ultimate goal. And it is also possible that even this fact is significant, and that the *Gita* is pluralistic in regard to how the spiritual
quest might be accomplished—but this is of course just one more
interpretation!

Jeffery D. Long

KARMA YOGA (WAY OF SELFLESS ACTION)

As mentioned in the general introduction to the *Bhagavad Gita*, this text is a dialogue on the battlefield of Kurukshetra, just prior to the climactic battle of the ancient Hindu epic, the *Mahabharata*, between the hero, Arjuna, and his friend, Krishna, who is also an incarnation of the divine. In the course of his advice to Arjuna, encouraging him to fight the battle before him, Krishna describes a variety of paths to God realization, the ultimate goal of Hindu thought and practice, which culminates in freedom from the cycle of death and rebirth.

In the preceding chapter, Krishna has extolled the path of knowledge of Brahman, teaching in a manner similar to that which we have seen in the selections in this volume from the *Upanishads*. In this chapter, however, Krishna makes a significant departure from the *Upanishads'* emphasis on renunciation of action, teaching a path of action that even a householder, a non-monastic practitioner with a home, family, and responsibilities, can pursue in order to reach the ultimate goal. Unlike the *Mundaka Upanishad*, the *Gita* is saying that it is an *inner* renunciation, an attitude of detachment, and not the physical giving up of worldly activity, that is effective in the spiritual quest.

Krishna first emphasizes that no one can ever truly abstain from action, "even for a moment." The very fact of being physically alive involves actions such as breathing, eating, drinking, sleeping, and so on. Krishna here articulates an insight similar in some ways to the teachings of the ancient Jain tradition of India, according to which our every moment of life involves us in some way in activity that could be seen as harmful to the environment around us, with the very space we occupy being filled with tiny organisms that are routinely destroyed by our activities. When Krishna says, "All are helplessly forced to act, by the gunas," he is referring to the three *gunas*, or qualities to nature that were men-

50

tioned in one of the selections from the *Yoga Sutras*. The gunas are a central topic of the *Bhagavad Gita*, which taps into the ancient Samkhya philosophy of Hindu thought, according to which realization involves the awareness that the Self is a distinct reality from these gunas. The gunas are characteristics of Prakriti, or modes of material energy that shape one's experience in the physical world (see the introduction to the *Yoga Sutras*, pp. 31–34).

According to Krishna, these gunas have their own inherent energy that results in their being in a state of constant motion, or constant change. One cannot end this process merely by an act of will—by trying to give up action. One must, instead, detach oneself from it, realizing that "I am not this. I am the infinite, unchanging Self."

Apart from this metaphysical basis, Krishna's advice here is also quite practical. It is simply not possible to give up all action, and to claim to do so is hypocritical. It is better, instead, to act, but selflessly—not out of desire for the results, for this only fuels the process of karma and rebirth—doing one's duty, pursuing the good not for oneself, but because it is good. Arjuna is to fight his battle in this spirit, not out of hatred for enemies or desire for the fruits of victory, but because it his duty as a warrior to fight injustice and restore justice, or *dharma*.

But this is easier said than done. How does one engage in action and also avoid the universal law of karma, which Hinduism affirms, that every action leads to an equal and opposite reaction? The lynchpin of Krishna's argument is the important claim that "The world is imprisoned in its own activity, *except when actions are performed as worship of God.*" In other words, selfless actions, done purely for the good, and as a kind of sacramental offering to God (rather than for oneself), do not have karmic effects, and do not bind one to the cycle of death and rebirth.

Krishna says that even he, as God, must engage in activity in order to sustain the world. "Suppose I were to stop?" Krishna asks rhetorically. The beings in the universe "would all be lost."

In the *Upanishads*, the action of Vedic rituals, which lead to merely temporary results, are contrasted with the fruits of renunciation and knowledge—true immortality, taking the form of liberation from death and rebirth. But Krishna refines this distinction, affirming action but also the renunciation of its temporary fruits: "The ignorant work for the fruit of their action: The wise must work also without desire, pointing man's feet to the path of his duty." It is also important, Krishna says, for the wise to grasp this teaching and not give those who are less wise the wrong impression that inaction is to be recommended: "Let the wise beware lest they bewilder the minds of the ignorant hungry for action: Let them show by example how work is holy when the heart of the work is fixed on the Highest."

One who is enlightened realizes that, in any case, it is not the Self that engages in any of this action. It is merely the gunas engaged in their perpetual play. The idea is to act while realizing one is not really doing anything.

Jeffery D. Long

ARJUNA:

But, Krishna, if you consider knowledge of Brahman superior to any sort of action, why are you telling me to do these terrible deeds?

Your statements seem to contradict each other. They confuse my mind. Tell me one definite way of reaching the highest good.

SRI KRISHNA:

I have already told you that, in this world, aspirants may find enlightenment by two different paths. For the contemplative is the path of knowledge: for the active is the path of selfless action.

Freedom from activity is never achieved by abstaining from action. Nobody can become perfect by merely ceasing to act. In fact, nobody can ever rest from his activity even for a moment. All are helplessly forced to act, by the gunas.

A man who renounces certain physical actions but still lets his mind dwell on the objects of his sensual desire, is deceiving himself. He can only be called a hypocrite. The truly admirable man controls his senses by the power of his will. All his actions are disinterested. All are directed along the path to union with Brahman.

Activity is better than inertia. Act, but with self-control. If you are lazy, you cannot even sustain your own body.

The world is imprisoned in its own activity, except when actions are performed as worship of God. Therefore you must perform every action sacramentally, and be free from all attachments to results.

In the beginning
The Lord of beings
Created all men,
To each his duty.
"Do this," He said,

"And you shall prosper.
Duty well done
Fulfils desire
Like Kamadhenu
The wish-fulfiller."
"Doing of duty
Honours the devas:
To you the devas
In turn will be gracious:
Each honouring other,
Man reaches the Highest.
Please the devas:
Your prayer will be granted."
But he who enjoys the devas' bounty
Showing no thanks,
He thieves from the devas.
Pious men eat
What the gods leave over
After the offering:
Thus they are sinless.
But those ungodly
Cooking good food
For the greed of their stomachs
Sin as they eat it.
Food quickens the life-sperm:
Food grows from the rainfall
Called down out of heaven
By sacrifice offered:
Sacrifice speaks
Through the act of the ritual.
This is the ritual
Taught by the sacred
Scriptures that spring
From the lips of the Changeless:
Know therefore that Brahman

The all-pervading
Is dwelling for ever
Within this ritual.

If a man plays no part
In the acts thus appointed
His living is evil
His joy is in lusting.
Know this, O Prince:
His life is for nothing.

But when a man has found delight and satisfaction and
peace in the Atman, then he is no longer obliged to perform any
kind of action. He has nothing to gain in this world by action,
and nothing to lose by refraining from action. He is independent
of everybody and everything. Do your duty, always; but without
attachment. That is how a man reaches the ultimate Truth; by
working without anxiety about results. In fact, Janaka and many
others reached enlightenment, simply because they did their duty
in this spirit. Your motive in working should be to set others, by
your example, on the path of duty.

Whatever a great man does, ordinary people will imitate;
they follow his example. Consider me: I am not bound by any
sort of duty. There is nothing, in all the three worlds, which I do
not already possess; nothing I have yet to acquire. But I go on
working, nevertheless. If I did not continue to work untiringly as
I do, mankind would still follow me, no matter where I led them.
Suppose I were to stop? They would all be lost. The result would
be caste-mixture and universal destruction.

The ignorant work
For the fruit of their action:
The wise must work also
Without desire
Pointing man's feet
To the path of his duty.

Let the wise beware
Lest they bewilder
The minds of the ignorant
Hungry for action:
Let them show by example
How work is holy
When the heart of the worker
Is fixed on the Highest.

Every action is really performed by the gunas. Man, deluded by his egoism, thinks: "I am the doer." But he who has the true insight into the operations of the gunas and their various functions, knows that when senses attach themselves to objects, gunas are merely attaching themselves to gunas. Knowing this, he does not become attached to his actions.

The illumined soul must not create confusion in the minds of the ignorant by refraining from work. The ignorant, in their delusion, identify the Atman with the gunas. They become tied to the senses and the action of the senses.

Shake off this fever of ignorance. Stop hoping for worldly rewards. Fix your mind on the Atman. Be free from the sense of ego. Dedicate all your actions to me. Then go forward and fight.

If a man keeps following my teaching with faith in his heart, and does not make mental reservations, he will be released from the bondage of his karma. But those who scorn my teaching, and do not follow it, are lost. They are without spiritual discrimination. All their knowledge is a delusion.

Even a wise man acts according to the tendencies of his own nature. All living creatures follow their tendencies. What use is any external restraint? The attraction and aversion which the senses feel for different objects are natural. But you must not give way to such feelings; they are obstacles.

It is better to do your own duty, however imperfectly, than to assume the duties of another person, however successfully. Prefer to die doing your own duty: the duty of another will bring you into great spiritual danger.

ARJUNA:

Krishna, what is it that makes a man do evil, even against his own will; under compulsion, as it were?

SRI KRISHNA:

The rajo-guna has two faces,
Rage and lust: the ravenous, the deadly:
Recognize these: they are your enemies.
Smoke hides fire,
Dust hides a mirror,
The womb hides the embryo:
By lust the Atman is hidden.

Lust hides the Atman in its hungry flames.
The wise man's faithful foe.
Intellect, senses and mind
Are fuel to its fire:
Thus it deludes
The dweller in the body,
Bewildering his judgment.

Therefore, Arjuna, you must first control your senses, then kill this evil thing which obstructs discriminative knowledge and realization of the Atman.

The senses are said to be higher than the sense-objects. The mind is higher than the senses. The intelligent will is higher than the mind. What is higher than the intelligent will? The Atman Itself.

You must know Him who is above the intelligent will. Get control of the mind through spiritual discrimination. Then destroy your elusive enemy, who wears the form of lust.

THE YOGA OF RENUNCIATION
(WAY OF LOVING FAITH)

As mentioned in the general introduction to the *Bhagavad Gita*, this text is a dialogue on the battlefield of Kurukshetra, just prior to the climactic battle of the ancient Hindu epic, the *Mahabharata*. In this, the final chapter of the *Gita*, the contents of the entire dialogue between the hero, Arjuna, and his friend, the divine charioteer, Krishna, are summarized.

The chapter begins with Arjuna asking Krishna to clarify the distinction between renunciation, defined as completely giving up all actions that are motivated by desire, and non-attachment, which is giving up the fruits of action. In his reply, Krishna contrasts two approaches to this issue adopted by different schools of thought in ancient India. On the one hand, Krishna says, there are those who say "that all kinds of action should be given up, because action always contains a certain measure of evil." This might refer to the Jains, mentioned in the introduction to the *Gita* as a whole, who affirm that the very act of being physically alive involves inevitable violence toward tiny microorganisms in the air and water. On the other hand, there are those who commend certain actions as not only praiseworthy, but necessary: "acts of sacrifice, almsgiving, and austerity." This may be a reference to adherents of the Brahmanical, Hindu worldview, which affirms rituals of sacrifice from its very beginning—in ancient texts such as the *Rig Veda*, which have an active, ritualistic orientation toward upholding the cosmos through acts of sacrifice to the gods, or forces of creation.

Krishna takes the side of the Brahmanical perspective—and establishes the *Gita* as a firmly orthodox Hindu text—by stating that sacrificial action must not be given up. But he also incorporates the renouncer worldview of the *Upanishads* and renouncer traditions such as Jainism and Buddhism by further stating that such action should be pursued with detachment, and not out of desire for its fruits (which is also the main theme of the third chapter of this text).

Krishna then invokes the concept of the three gunas, or modes of material nature, in stating that renunciation is of three kinds, depending upon which guna is predominant. One who realizes that the Atman, or Self, performs no action at all—that action, while it is not avoidable for an embodied being, occurs only in the realm of the material energies—is non-attached. On the other hand, one who still identifies with the body and its desires is still subject to the various effects of action, or karma: pleasant, unpleasant, and mixed. If one renounces identification with the body and its desires, however, one is no longer tied to the cycle of cause and effect that leads to rebirth. Such a person "will reap no fruit at all, either in this world or in the next."

In the next section, various types of action are contrasted based upon the guna that is predominant. A clear hierarchy is formed here, in which the worst kinds of action (and corresponding effects) are those associated with the *tamasic guna*. Somewhat better, but still conducive to suffering, is the *rajasic guna*. The *sattwic guna* is the best, and the most conducive to the higher realization that leads beyond the gunas altogether.

Krishna then affirms that the specific action that is best for a person is that which is "natural" for that person. This part of the text has been interpreted in a variety of ways by Hindu thinkers through the centuries. A conservative interpretation would identify the work that is natural for a person with the *jati*, or occupational community, into which that person was born. This is a reference to the social order that has come to be referred to as the "caste" system, according to which one takes up the occupation of one's family. If one is a male, and one's father is, say, a basket weaver, then one is expected also to take up basket weaving, probably starting as an apprentice to one's father, who also learned basket weaving from his father, who learned it from his father, who learned it from his father, and so on. And if one is female, one is expected to marry a basket weaver, be a homemaker, and raise children who will be basket weavers or wives of basket weavers.

This, however, is a stereotype and a distortion of the much more complex realities of Indian society. First, it is not only Hindus who practice such systems of occupation by birth. Christians and Muslims in India, for example, also observe this system, sometimes even more conservatively and rigidly than many Hindus. And second, many Hindus do not observe this system, and even oppose it. Even in ancient times, there were Hindus who would say, "But what if I do not want to be a basket weaver?" and Indian history, as well as Hindu scriptural literature, contains many instances of people choosing not to take up the occupation to which they were born.

For those who have questioned, challenged, or rejected this system, the "natural" duty of a person to which the *Gita* refers is interpreted more liberally, as the duty toward which one feels called, or that is ethically binding upon all people, such as the duty to be honest, or not to steal, or not to kill, except perhaps under extraordinary circumstances, like those in which Arjuna finds himself. Many contemporary Hindus see their duty in these terms, seeking to discern the destiny that is most spiritually satisfying, rather than simply following the tradition of pursuing their fathers' occupations—or, as is increasingly the case for women, seeking a fulfilling career and not limiting themselves solely to the roles of wife and mother.

Social structures, of course, change with the winds of history, being of the realm of the gunas. The *Gita*'s ideal, in any social setting, is the pursuit of action in a spirit of detachment.

Jeffery D. Long

ARJUNA:

I want to learn the truth about renunciation and non-attachment. What is the difference between these two principles?

SRI KRISHNA:

The sages tell us that renunciation means the complete giving-up of all actions which are motivated by desire. And they say that non-attachment means abandonment of the fruits of action.

Some philosophers declare that all kinds of action should be given up, because action always contains a certain measure of evil. Others say that acts of sacrifice, almsgiving and austerity should not be given up. Now you shall hear the truth of this matter.

Acts of sacrifice, almsgiving and austerity should not be given up: their performance is necessary. For sacrifice, almsgiving and austerity are a means of purification to those who rightly understand them. But even these acts must be performed without attachment or regard for their fruits. Such is my final and considered judgment.

Renunciation is said to be of three kinds. If a man, in his ignorance, renounces those actions which the scriptures ordain, his renunciation is inspired by tamas. If he abstains from any action merely because it is disagreeable, or because he fears it will cause him bodily pain, his renunciation is inspired by rajas. He will not obtain any spiritual benefit from such renunciation. But when a man performs an action which is sanctioned by the scriptures, and does it for duty's sake only, renouncing all attachment and desire for its fruits, then his renunciation is inspired by sattwa.

When a man is endowed with spiritual discrimination and illumined by knowledge of the Atman, all his doubts are dispelled. He does not shrink from doing what is disagreeable to him, nor does he long to do what is agreeable. No human being

61

can give up action altogether, but he who gives up the fruits of action is said to be non-attached.

To those who have not yet renounced the ego and its desires, action bears three kinds of fruit—pleasant, unpleasant, and a mixture of both. They will be reaped in due season. But those who have renounced ego and desire will reap no fruit at all, either in this world or in the next.

. . . .

There are three things which motivate action: knowledge, the knower and that which is known. There are three constituents of action: the instrument, the purpose and the doer. Sankhya philosophy declares that knowledge, action and doer are of three kinds only, according to the guna which predominates in each. Listen, this is their nature.

> There is that knowledge
> From sattwa proceeding
> Which knows one Being
> Deathless in every creature,
> Entire amidst all division.
>
> The knowledge that is rajas
> Knows nothing but difference:
> Many souls in many creatures,
> All various, each
> Apart from his fellow.
>
> The knowledge that is tamas
> Knows no reason:
> Its sight distorted
> Takes the part for the whole,
> Misreading Nature.
>
> The act of sacred duty,
> Done without attachment,
> Not as pleasure desired,

Not as hated compulsion,
By him who has no care
For the fruit of his action:
That act is of sattwa.

The act of weary toil
Done in despite of nature
Under the whip of lust
And the will of the ego:
That act is of rajas.

The act undertaken
In the hour of delusion
Without count of cost,
Squandering strength and treasure,
Heedless of harm to another,
By him who does not question
His power to perform it:
That act is of tamas.

The doer without desire,
Who does not boast of his deed,
Who is ardent, enduring,
Untouched by triumph,
In failure untroubled:
He is a man of sattwa.

The doer with desire,
Hot for the prize of vainglory,
Brutal, greedy and foul,
In triumph too quick to rejoice,
In failure despairing:
He is a man of rajas.

The indifferent doer
Whose heart is not in his deed,

Stupid and stubborn,
A cheat, and malicious,
The idle lover of delay,
Easily dejected:
He is a man of tamas.

There are three kinds of conscience and three kinds of determination, according to the predominance of each guna. Now listen: I will explain them fully, one by one.

A man's conscience has the nature of sattwa when it can distinguish between the paths of renunciation and worldly desire. Then it knows what actions are right or wrong, what is safe and what is dangerous, what binds the embodied spirit and what sets it free. But when the conscience cannot distinguish truly between right and wrong, or know what should and what should not be done, then it has the nature of rajas. And when the conscience is so thickly wrapped in ignorance that it mistakes wrong for right and sees everything distorted, then it has the nature of tamas.

Determination inspired by sattwa never wavers. It is strengthened by the practice of yoga. A man who has this kind of determination gains absolute control over his mind, vital energy and senses. Rajas, on the other hand, inspires that kind of determination with which a man follows the object of his desire, or seeks wealth, or does a duty, looking for reward and personal advantage. As for the determination inspired by tamas, it is nothing but obstinacy. It makes a man stubbornly refuse to shake off his dullness, fear, grief, low spirits or vanity.

....

Now you shall hear how a man may become perfect, if he devotes himself to the work which is natural to him. A man will reach perfection if he does his duty as an act of worship to the Lord, who is the source of the universe, prompting all action, everywhere present.

A man's own natural duty, even if it seems imperfectly done, is better than work not naturally his own even if this is well per-

64

formed. When a man acts according to the law of his nature, he cannot be sinning. Therefore, no one should give up his natural work, even though he does it imperfectly. For all action is involved in imperfection, like fire in smoke.

When a man has achieved non-attachment, self-mastery and freedom from desire through renunciation, he reaches union with Brahman, who is beyond all action.

…You must never tell this holy truth to anyone who lacks self-control and devotion, or who despises his teacher and mocks at me. But the man who loves me, and teaches my devotees this supreme truth of the Gita, will certainly come to me. No one can do me a higher service than this. No one on earth can be dearer to me.

And if any man meditates upon this sacred discourse of ours, I shall consider that he has worshipped me in spirit. Even if a man simply listens to these words with faith, and does not doubt them, he will be freed from his sins and reach the heaven of the righteous.

Have you listened carefully, Arjuna, to everything I have told you? Have I dispelled the delusions of your ignorance?

ARJUNA:

By your grace, O Lord, my delusions have been dispelled. My mind stands firm. Its doubts are ended. I will do your bidding.

SANJAYA:

Such were the words that thrilled my heart, that marvellous
   discourse,
Heard from the lips of the high-souled Prince and the great
   Lord Krishna,
Not with these earthly ears, but by mystic grace of Vyasa,
Thus I learned that yoga supreme from the Master of yogis.
Ever and ever again I rejoice, O King, and remember
Sacred and wonderful truths that Krishna told to his comrade.
Ever again, O King, I am glad and remember rejoicing

That most splendid of forms put on by Krishna, the Sweet
   One.
Where Lord Krishna is, and Arjuna, great among archers,
There, I know, is goodness and peace, and triumph and
   glory.
OM. Peace. Peace. Peace.

The *Brahma Sutras*

The *Brahma Sutras*, like the *Yoga Sutras*, are a collection of aphoristic writings designed for memorization by students and commentary by teachers, who use the short phrases that make up such texts as an opportunity to elaborate upon the fundamental teachings of a particular school of thought. The *Brahma Sutras* form the core text of the various Vedanta systems of philosophy. Along with the *Upanishads* and the *Bhagavad Gita*, the *Brahma Sutras* help to form the *Prasthana Traya* or "threefold foundation" of Vedanta—the three authoritative texts on which every *acharya*, or founder of a Vedantic tradition, has written a *bhashya*, or commentary. The specific commentary from which the selections given here are drawn is that of Shankara (788–820 CE), the most important teacher of the *Advaita*, or non-dualist, system of Vedanta.

Estimates of the date of composition of the *Brahma Sutras* vary. An approximate date of 200 BCE is possible, though it is also very likely that the compilation process was gradual, extending into the Common Era. In terms of relative chronology, the text must have been compiled after the composition of the major *Upanishads*, which it summarizes, but prior to the *Bhagavad Gita*, which mentions it (though this reference may or may not be to this specific text, perhaps referring generically to wisdom literature on Brahman). The *Brahma Sutras* are traditionally attributed to Badarayana, who is also identified with Veda Vyasa, the traditional author of the *Mahabharata* and compiler of the *Vedas*. As the root text of the Vedanta systems of philosophy, the verses of the *Brahma Sutras* are also known as the *Vedanta Sutras*.

The *Brahma Sutras* present an inquiry into the nature of Brahman and collect the major threads of thought on this topic found in the *Upanishads*. They are, in other words, a summary of the teachings of the *Upanishads*.

The *Upanishads* themselves do not present a single, clear system of philosophy. As a collection of inspired dialogues, they do contain certain dominant themes and ideas. But parts of them are difficult to interpret, and it is not always clear how, or even if, ideas presented in one part of one *Upanishad* can be reconciled with parts of others. According to the various forms of Vedanta, however, the *Upanishads* are authoritative scriptures and do teach a consistent doctrine. Showing that this is the case, and explaining exactly what that doctrine is, is the task that the various teachers of Vedanta have set for themselves. The *Brahma Sutras* are an early attempt to collect the core teachings of the *Upanishads* in a single, easy-to-memorize text, and form the foundation for various interpreters of the Vedanta philosophy to demonstrate the connection between their understanding of it and its authoritative writings.

The connection between what can sometimes appear as dry philosophical writing and argumentation and mysticism and the spiritual quest is not always obvious. But it is a deep and important connection. All of the various systems of Vedanta agree that a right understanding of the nature of reality is essential to the spiritual path. How can one form a direct connection to a transcendent reality absent some correct understanding of what it is that one is connecting to? As Shankara says in one the selections cited here, "one who accepts some view without examining it might be prevented from attaining the ultimate good and might also come to grief."

Although Shankara affirms the importance of reasoning in determining the nature of Brahman—the infinite, ultimate reality—he argues that reason alone does not reveal this nature in its fullness. For this, scripture is required. Shankara's argument anticipates the similar claims of the Roman Catholic scholar St. Thomas Aquinas, who lived about four centuries after Shankara, in Europe. Aquinas, like Shankara, affirms that human reason is able to reveal a good many things about the nature of ultimate reality. But revelation is needed to make certain profound truths about this reality known to the limited and finite human mind. Similarly, both Shankara and Aquinas affirm that reason is acceptable as a means of knowledge and is needed for the interpretation and correct understanding of the words of scripture. As Shankara points out, the Hindu scriptures themselves recommend the use of reason.

Scripture is needed for understanding Brahman, Shankara says, because Brahman is "not within the provenance of the senses." Though Brahman is a real entity, and as such has certain definite characteristics, these are not discernible in the same way that the traits of sensory objects are discernible. So some other means of knowledge is necessary. This means, according to Shankara, is the words of scripture: the *Vedas* and the *Upanishads*.

Elaborating upon the next verse of the *Brahma Sutras*, Shankara explains that the scripture is a reliable source of knowledge about Brahman because Brahman is the source of the scripture. Just as we trust the words of authoritative persons who know their fields well (Shankara cites, for example, the scholar Panini, an authority on Sanskrit grammar), we can trust the words of scripture because they have emerged from Brahman, which is the highest authority of all.

One of the intellectual opponents to which Shankara's arguments are directed is a group of Hindu scholars called the Purva Mimamsakas. According to their philosophy, the only meaningful statements in the Vedic scriptures are those that enjoin action. They do not, therefore, take texts like the *Upanishads* to be of great significance. Shankara's argument against this view is in his commentary on the next verse, which asserts thematic unity and harmony within the *Upanishads*, consisting of these texts' numerous references to Brahman. Shankara concludes by stating that the action being enjoined by texts like the *Upanishads* is the avoidance of suffering and the attainment of our ultimate aspiration through the realization of Brahman—a realization that can only occur on the basis of true understanding of the nature of Brahman, which, in turn, is fully known only by scripture.

Jeffery D. Long

Now that Brahman may be well known or unknown; if it is well known, there is no need to desire to know it; if on the other hand, it is unknown, it could never be desired to be known. The answer to this objection is as follows: The Brahman exists, eternal, pure, enlightened, free by nature, omniscient, and attended by all power. When the word "Brahman" is explained etymologically, it being eternal, pure and so on, are all understood, for these are in conformity with the meaning of the root brh [from which Brahman is derived]. The Brahman's existence is well known, because it is the Self of all; everyone realizes the existence of the Self, for none says, "I am not"; if the existence of the Self is not well known, the whole world of beings would have the notion "I do not exist." And the Self is the Brahman.

It may be contended that if the Brahman is well known in the world as the Self, it has already been known, and again it becomes something that need not be inquired into. It is not like that, for [although its existence in general is accepted], there are differences of opinion about its particular nature. Ordinary people and the materialists are of the view that the Self is just the body qualified by intelligence; others think that it is the intelligent sense-organs themselves that are the Self; still others, that it is the mind; some hold it as just the fleeting consciousness of the moment; some others as the void; certain others say that there is some entity, which is different from the body, etc., and which transmigrates, does, and enjoys; some consider him as the enjoyer and not as the doer; some that there is, as different from the above entity, the Lord who is omniscient and omnipotent. According to still others, it is the inner Self of the enjoyer. Thus, resorting to reasonings and texts and the semblances thereof, there are many who hold divergent views. Hence one who accepts some view without examining it might be prevented from attaining the ultimate good and might also come to grief. Therefore, by way of setting forth the inquiry into the Brahman, here is begun the discussion of the meaning of the texts of the Upanishads, aided by such ratiocination as is in conformity to Scripture and having for its fruit the Supreme Beatitude.

It has been said that the Brahman is to be inquired into; on the question as to the characteristics of that Brahman, the blessed author of the aphorisms says:

WHENCE IS THE ORIGIN...OF THIS

...Of this universe made distinct through names and forms, having many agents and enjoyers, serving as the ground of the fruits of activities attended by specific places, times, and causes, and whose nature and design cannot be conceived even in one's mind—that omniscient, omnipotent cause wherefrom the origin, maintenance, and destruction of such a universe proceed is the Brahman; such is the full meaning that is to be understood....

It is not possible to discard the Lord, characterized as above, and suppose anything else, primordial matter devoid of intelligence, atoms, nonexistence, or a person subject to the transmigratory cycle as the cause of the origin, etc., of the universe characterized above. Nor can it proceed from the very nature of things, for we require here [for production of a thing] a specific place, time, and cause.

This itself is taken by those philosophers who speak of the Lord as the cause of the universe, as an inference capable of demonstrating the existence, etc., of a Lord, different from the transmigrating individuals. And here, too, in the present aphorism, "whence, etc.," is it not the same idea that is propounded? It is not so, for the aphorisms string together the flowers of the statements in the Vedanta [Upanishads]; it is the Upanishadic statements that are cited in the form of aphorisms and examined. It is by the examination of the meaning of the scriptural texts and determining it exactly that Brahman-realization is achieved, not by inference and other sources of knowledge. The Vedantic texts that speak of the cause of the origin, etc., of the world being there, inference, which would strengthen the understanding of their meaning and would be in conformity with the Vedantic text, is not precluded from being one of the sources of knowledge; for ratiocination is accepted by scripture itself as an aid. Thus the Scripture says: "That Self is to be listened and thought over" and shows in the text "Just as an intelligent man who has been well informed would reach the Gandhara country," even so here, "he who has a teacher knows" that the Scripture takes the aid of human intellect. As far as the inquiry into the Brahman is concerned, scripture, etc., are not the sole source of knowledge as in the case of the inquiry into dharma; scripture, etc., and direct experience, etc., according to the occasion, are sources of knowledge; for the knowledge of the Brahman has for its object something that already exists and completes itself in its direct experience. In a thing that is to be *done*, there is no need for experience, and scripture, etc., may alone be the source of knowledge, for the thing to be done depends, for its very coming into being, on the person [who proposes to do it]. An act, whether mundane or ordained by scripture, may be done, may not be done at all, or may be done in a different manner; likewise, with reference to the scripture-ordained acts, the texts say: "One takes the *sodasin* cup in the *Atiratra* ritual" and also [elsewhere]: "One does not take the *sodasin* cup in the *Atiratra*"; also: "One offers oblations after sunrise" and [elsewhere] "One offers oblations before sunrise." Injunctions and prohibitions too have meaning in this sphere, as also optional rules and exceptions. But a thing as such does not admit of alternative propositions like "It is thus" and "It is not thus," "It is" and "It is not"; alternative suppositions depend on the human mind, but knowledge of the truth of a thing is not dependent on the human mind; on what then does that depend? It is solely dependent on the thing itself. In respect of a pillar the knowledge of its true nature cannot take the form, "This is either the pillar or a man or something else"; "This is a man or something else" is suppositious knowledge; "This is really a pillar" is correct knowledge, because the question depends on the nature of the thing. In this manner, the validity of knowledge in respect of objects that are already in existence depends on the things themselves.

Thus the knowledge of the Brahman too is dependent on the thing, because the knowledge refers to a thing already in existence. The objection may be raised that, in so far as the Brahman is an object already in existence, it can be surely comprehended by other means of knowledge and the discussion on the Vedantic texts becomes futile; this objection cannot hold because the Brahman is not within the provenance of the senses, the invariable relation between it and its effect is not apprehensible in its case; by nature, senses have for their object things of the world, not the Brahman. It is only when the Brahman can be the object of sense-perception that one can apprehend that there is an effect that is related to the Brahman [its cause]; when the effect alone is apprehended [by the senses], it is not possible to decide if it is related to the Brahman or to something else; therefore the present aphorism mentioning origin, etc., is not for setting forth a theistic syllogism. But then what is it for? It is to draw attention to a Vedantic text. What is the Vedantic text that is intended to be indicated in this aphorism? It is the text that begins with the words "Bhrigu, son of Varuna, approached his father Varuna with the request, 'O Blessed one, teach me the Brahman,'" and states: "That from which all these beings are born, that by which those born subsist and that into which those dying enter, that do you try to know; that is the Brahman." Of this Brahman [so characterized] the text that clinches its nature is the following: "From bliss it is that these beings are born; by bliss are those born sustained and into bliss do those dead enter." Other texts of this kind, which speak of its being by nature eternal, pure, enlightened, and free, and of its being omniscient, and of the form of the Self and the cause, are also to be cited.

By showing the Brahman as the cause of the universe it has been suggested that the Brahman is omniscient; now to reinforce that omniscience the author of the aphorisms says:

AS IT IS THE SOURCE OF THE SCRIPTURE

Of the extensive scripture [*sastra*] comprising the *Rig Veda,* etc., reinforced and elaborated by many branches of learning, illumining everything even as a lamp, and like unto one omniscient, the source [lit. womb] is the Brahman. Of a scripture of this type, of the nature of the *Rig Veda* and the like, endowed with the quality of omniscience, the origin cannot be from anything other than the omniscient one. Whatever teaching has, for purposes of elaborate exposition, come forth from an eminent personage, as the science of grammar from Panini, etc., though it is comprehensive of that branch of knowledge, it is well understood in the world that its exponent [e.g., Panini] possesses knowledge far more than what is in his work; it therefore goes without saying that unsurpassed omniscience and omnipotence is to be found in that Supreme Being from whom, as the source, issued forth, as if in sport and without any effort, like the breathing of a person, this scripture in diverse recensions, called *Rig Veda*, etc., which is the repository of all knowledge and is responsible for the distinctions into gods, animals, humans, classes, stages of life, etc.; this is borne out by scriptural texts like: "This that is called *Rig Veda* [and so on] is the breathings out of this Great Being."

Or the scripture consisting of *Rig Veda*, etc., is the source, i.e., the authoritative means of knowing this Brahman in its real form; what is meant is that it is from the authoritative source of scripture that the Brahman, the cause of the origin, etc. of the universe is known. The scriptural text concerned was cited under the previous aphorism: "That from which these things have their birth, etc." Wherefore then the present aphorism, when the Brahman being knowable from the scriptural source has already been shown by the previous aphorism, which cites scriptural texts of this class? The reply is: In the previous aphorism the scripture has not been expressly stated and one might doubt that by that aphorism, "whence, etc.," a syllogistic proof of the Brahman has been set forth; to remove such a doubt, this aphorism came in, saying, "As it has the scripture as its source."

But how is it said [as Purva Mimamsaka might contend] that the Brahman is known from scripture? It has been shown by the statement: "As the scripture has action as its purpose such texts as do not have that purport are useless," that the scripture refers to ritual action; therefore the Upanishads are useless as they do not have action as their purport; or as revealing the agent, the deity, etc., they are subservient to the texts that enjoin ritual action; or they are for enjoining some other activity like meditation. It is not possible that the Veda sets forth the nature of a thing already well established, for a thing well established becomes the object of direct perception and other sources of knowledge; and even if such a thing is set forth, there is no human objective served by it, as there is nothing there to be avoided or desired. For this very reason, texts like "He wept," lest they should become meaning-less, have been said to have meaning as recommendatory eulo-gies, according to the statement "By reason of syntactic unity with the injunctive texts, they might be for praising the injunctions." Of the Vedic texts called mantras, e.g., "Thee for nourishment," the intimate association with the ritual has been shown, as they speak of an act and its accessories; no Vedic text is seen anywhere nor can it be justified without some relation to the enjoining of an act. Such enjoining of an act is not possible in respect of the nature of a thing that is well established, for injunction has for its object an action. Therefore, by reason of revealing the nature of the agent, the deity, etc., required for the ritual, the Upanishads are complementary to the texts enjoining ritual acts. If, however, this standpoint is not accepted, out of the fear that the Upanishads represent a different context altogether, still, the Upanishads may be held to have their purport in an activity like the meditation set forth in their own texts. Therefore the Brahman is not to be known from the scriptural source. In the face of that objection it is said:

THAT, HOWEVER, IS SO BECAUSE OF TEXTUAL HARMONY

The word "however" is for warding off the *prima facie* view. That Brahman, omniscient, omnipotent, and cause of the birth, existence, and dissolution of the universe *is* known from the scripture as represented by the Upanishads. How? "Because of textual harmony." In all the Upanishads the texts are in agreement in propounding, as their main purport, this idea. For example, "Dear one! this thing Existence alone was at the beginning"; "The one without a second"; "The Self, this one only, existed at first"; "This Brahman, devoid of anything before or after, inside or outside"; "This Self, the Brahman, the all-experiencing one"; "At first there was only this Brahman, the immortal one." When it is decisively known that the purport of the words in these texts is the nature of the Brahman, and when unity is seen, to imagine a different purport is improper, as thereby one will have to give up what is expressly stated and imagine something not stated. Nor could it be concluded that their purport is to set forth the nature of the agent, deity, etc.; for there are texts like "Then whom should It see and with what?," which refute action, agent, and fruit.

Because the Brahman is a thing already well established, it cannot be held to be the object of perception by senses, etc.; for the truth that the Brahman is the Self, as set forth in the text "That thou art," cannot be known without the scripture. As regards the objection that since there is nothing here to be avoided or desired, there is no use in teaching it, it is no drawback; it is from the realization that the Self is the Brahman, devoid of things to be avoided or desired, that all miseries are ended and the aspiration of man is achieved.

TWO

CHINESE TRADITIONS

TWO

CHINESE TRADITIONS

The *Tao Te Ching* of Lao Tzu

The *Tao Te Ching* is an ancient Chinese mystical text attributed to the poet sage Lao Tzu, and is a foundational text for the Chinese mystical tradition known in the West as Taoism. Pronounced *Dao De Jing*, the title means "classic text (*Ching*) of the Way (*Tao*) and its power or virtue (*Te*)." Much like the Brahman of the *Upanishads* (the earliest of which are roughly contemporaneous with the *Tao Te Ching* of China—about the sixth century BCE), the Tao, or the Way, is the basic essence of all existence. Establishing a personal connection to this Way is fundamental to the spiritual path, the mystical search "for direct connection to a transcendent reality."

While the concept of Brahman in the *Upanishads* tends to be understood among the Indian traditions in terms that emphasize its eternal and unchanging nature, the Tao is seen more as a process of constant change. Like Brahman, the Tao is also eternal. Even if it is a process of change, it is a *constant* process—one that occurs without having a beginning or an end. Many mystics would affirm that the concepts of Brahman and Tao point to one and the same ultimate reality. The point is simply that the term *Brahman* is one that tends to evoke the idea of permanence, while "Tao" evokes a changing flow.

Like Brahman, the Tao is ultimately beyond anything that words or concepts can capture. In its fullness, the highest reality is ineffable. It can only be evoked and never fully captured. This is the gist of Lao Tzu's first aphorism: "A way that can be walked is not The Way. A name that can be named is not The Name." The Tao is all things; but it is not any one *thing* in particular. "Tao is both Named and Nameless." It encompasses all of reality: both the concrete and conceptualized, the "Named," and the infinite reality beyond the concrete and beyond concepts—the "Nameless."

"As Nameless, it is the origin of all things." The Tao that goes beyond words is the source of all particular things—named things. It is that from which all concrete reality has emerged and continues to emerge. "As Named, it is the mother of all things." Once one has a concept of the Tao—once it is named—it becomes a concrete reality like others. The particular concrete reality to which the named Tao corresponds is "the mother of all things." "Mother" is a more concrete term than "origin," evoking a very specific process of bringing new life into being from one's own body. Why not a father? As we shall see, the idea of the divine feminine is an important one in the *Tao Te Ching*—for the feminine, passive dimension of creativity is ultimately more powerful than is the aggressive "male" energy that seeks to impose its will through force. This is the Te—the power or virtue—of the Tao to which the title of the text refers: not the quick and aggressive power of fire or lightning, with their dramatic and immediate effects, but the subtle power of the water and the wind, which, in time, can wear down mountains and completely alter the character of the entire landscape.

How does one know the Tao? The *Tao Te Ching* contains strong suggestions that some kind of meditative practice is involved, as in other mystical traditions. A mind that is "free of thought, merged within itself, beholds the essence of Tao." This is suggestive of a process, such as that found in the *Yoga Sutras* of the Hindu tradition, of calming the mind and stilling the constant fluctuation of thought and emotion that characterizes our normal, conscious awareness. When the waters of the mind are calm, they reflect back to the mind the true nature of reality like a clear and polished mirror of glass. The mind in this state "beholds the essence of Tao." But "a mind filled with thought, identified with its own perceptions, beholds the mere forms of this world." The conscious mind that is in its usual state of turbulence perceives only the concrete forms that are the manifestations of the Tao, but not the essence of the Tao itself.

The Tao and the world are not two different realities, however. They are the same reality perceived through two different modes of perception. "Tao and this world seem different, but in truth they are one and the same. The only difference is in what we call them." By naming—by conceptualizing our experience in a particular way—we either perceive reality as multiple concrete manifestations of a deep, inner essence, or we perceive that essence itself. "How deep and mysterious this unity is! How profound, how great! It is the truth beyond the truth, the hidden within the hidden. It is the path to all wonder, the gate to the essence of everything!"

The remaining selections from the *Tao Te Ching* continue to unfold the basic idea summarized in the first. The next selection refers again to the divine feminine, She who is the "Hidden Creator"—the supreme concrete manifestation of the Tao in the universe, "the very face of the Absolute." This selection also emphasizes another important Taoist theme, namely, the immanence of the divine presence in creation—in nature. "Listen to Her voice. Hear it echo through creation." Nature, and we ourselves as parts of it, are already perfect, for we are manifestations of the Tao. We have simply forgotten who and what we truly are. But the Tao can draw us back to itself, by the power (Te) manifested in the divine. "Without fail, She reveals her presence. Without fail, She brings us to our own perfection."

Verse 42 refers to the Chinese concept of the twin polarities of energy that make up the world: yin and yang, or passive and aggressive energies. Verse 66 depicts a wise ruler, or Sage, who rules his kingdom according to the same principles by which the Tao acts as the underlying flow of existence. And finally, verse 67, in a striking anticipation of later Christian concepts in the West, emphasizes the character of the Tao as love.

Jeffery D. Long

VERSE 1

A way that can be walked
　　is not The Way
A name that can be named
　　is not The Name

Tao is both Named and Nameless
As Nameless, it is the origin of all things
As Named, it is the mother of all things

A mind free of thought,
　　merged within itself,
　　beholds the essence of Tao
A mind filled with thought,
　　identified with its own perceptions,
　　beholds the mere forms of this world

Tao and this world seem different
　　but in truth they are one and the same
The only difference is in what we call them

How deep and mysterious this unity is
　　How profound, how great!
It is the truth beyond the truth,
　　the hidden within the hidden
It is the path to all wonder,
　　the gate to the essence of everything!

VERSE 6

Endlessly creating
Endlessly pulsating

The Spirit of the Valley never dies
She is called the Hidden Creator

Although She becomes the whole universe
    Her immaculate purity is never lost
Although She assumes countless forms
    Her true identity remains intact
Whatever we see or don't see
Whatever exists or doesn't exist
Is nothing but the creation of this Supreme Power

Tao is limitless, unborn, eternal—
    It can only be reached through the Hidden Creator
She is the very face of the Absolute
The gate to the source of all things eternal

Listen to Her voice
    Hear it echo through creation
Without fail, She reveals her presence
Without fail, She brings us to our own perfection

VERSE 42

Tao gives life to the one
The one gives life to the two
The two give life to the three
The three give life to ten thousand things

All beings support *yin* and embrace *yang*
    and the interplay of these two forces
    fills the universe
Yet only at the still-point,
    between the breathing in and the breathing out,
    can one capture these two in perfect harmony

People suffer at the thought of being
    without parents, without food, or without worth

Yet this is the very way that
    kings and lords once described themselves

Who knows what fate may bring—
    one day your loss may be your fortune
    one day your fortune may be your loss

The age-old lesson that others teach, I also teach—
    "As you plant, so you reap"
    "As you live, so you die"
Know this to be the foundation of my teachings

VERSE 66

Why do the hundred rivers
    turn and rush toward the sea?
Because it naturally stays below them

He who wishes to rule over the people
    must speak as if below them
He who wishes to lead the people
    must walk as if behind them
So the Sage rules over the people
    but he does not weigh them down
He leads the people
    but he does not block their way

The Sage stays low
    so the world never tires of exalting him
He remains a servant
    so the world never tires of making him its king

VERSE 67

All the world talks about my Tao
    with such familiarity—
What folly!

Tao is not something found at the marketplace
    or passed on from father to son
It is not something gained by knowing
    or lost by forgetting
If Tao were like this
It would have been lost and forgotten long ago

I have three treasures that I cherish and hold dear
    the first is love
    the second is moderation
    the third is humility
With love one is fearless
With moderation one is abundant
With humility one can fill the highest position
Now if one is fearless but has no love
    abundant but has no moderation
    rises up but has no humility
Surely he is doomed

Love vanquishes all attackers
It is impregnable in defense
When Heaven wants to protect someone
    does it send an army?
No, it protects him with love

Chuang Tzu

The Taoist sage Chuang Tzu lived in the fourth century BCE, roughly two centuries after the great master Lao Tzu, to whom is attributed the wisdom of the *Tao Te Ching*, and Confucius (551–479 BCE), founder of the tradition that bears his name.

Chuang Tzu lived during a very troubled era of Chinese history known to scholars as the Period of Warring States. During this period, the feudal sociopolitical order of China was in a state of disarray. Rival warlords and gangs of bandits roamed the land in a constant struggle for supremacy and common people lived in a state of deep insecurity and fear. This period of social breakdown was just beginning in the time of Lao Tzu and Confucius, and the philosophies of Taoism and Confucianism can each be seen as a type of response to the crisis of ancient Chinese society.

As is evident in the selections from the *Tao Te Ching* given in this volume, Lao Tzu recommended a mystical path—a path of withdrawal from worldly concerns in search of a deeper harmony with the fundamental nature of things. It would be an error, though, to see Lao Tzu only as a mystic. Rather, comparably perhaps to a modern figure such as Mahatma Gandhi, Lao Tzu believed that a ruler who was informed by the philosophy of the Tao, such as the Sage of verse 66 of his classic text, could evoke in society the same harmony that underlies nature itself: that the Te, or power, of the Way—the Tao—properly channeled and understood, could transform society. Put in more modern terms, Lao Tzu believed that love could save the world.

Confucius, on the other hand, took a highly pragmatic approach, although he was no less idealistic in his aspirations than Lao Tzu. Confucius emphasized the transformation of the person through education. If people were acculturated from an early age to

87

the values of respect and harmony that held Chinese society together when it was at its height—in the golden age of the ancient Chinese historical annals that Confucius loved to contemplate—then the society would naturally move toward the path of virtue and away from the kind of social disintegration that was the fruit of the selfish pursuit of power and pleasure on the part of the noble classes: disintegration that led to the Period of Warring States.

A couple of centuries removed from both Lao Tzu and Confucius, and deep in the Period of Warring States, the writings of Chuang Tzu reveal a far more cynical outlook, a far less optimistic approach to the problems of life, than that found in the *Tao Te Ching* or in the *Analects* of Confucius. And yet Chuang Tzu, like Lao Tzu before him, has deep faith in the Tao and is motivated by a profound sense of the transformative power of the wisdom of the Way. Although a Taoist, Chuang Tzu frequently utilizes Confucius as one of the characters in his writings, often putting Taoist teaching in his mouth. At the same time, the students of Confucius are often figures of ridicule for Chuang Tzu, being overly preoccupied with the details of social etiquette and missing out on their deeper meaning or spirit, very much in the way that Christ is depicted ridiculing the strict observances of the Pharisees in some verses of the Gospels.

The first selection from Chuang Tzu depicts a conversation between Yen Hui, a favorite disciple of Confucius, and Confucius himself. Historically, Yen Hui was greatly admired by Confucius as a poor man who, despite his poverty, had become highly noble of character and well educated through diligence and hard work. In many ways, he embodied Confucian ideals. It is said that Confucius hoped that Yen Hui would be his successor. Tragically, however, Yen Hui fell ill and died. This loss was devastating to Confucius, who is said to have wept bitterly on learning of the passing of his best student.

As depicted by Chuang Tzu, Yen Hui wishes to take the permission of Confucius to go teach the ruler of the kingdom of Wei, who has many personal faults. In fact, it was long an aspiration of

Confucius that he and his disciples would advise the rulers of China and show them the path to virtue. In this conversation, however, Confucius gives Yen Hui very typically Taoist advice: to transform himself, rather than seeking to change the rulers of this world. Only through this self-transformation can one hope to transform others. He instructs Yen Hui to practice "the fasting of the mind," giving up his sense of separate ego, or self. "Listening stops with the ears, the mind stops with recognition, but spirit is empty and waits on all things. The Way gathers in emptiness alone. Emptiness is the fasting of the mind." Much as in the Buddhist tradition, with its strong emphasis on detachment from the sense of self, Yen Hui says, "Before I heard this, I was certain that I was Hui. But now that I have heard it, there is no more Hui. Can this be called emptiness?" Confucius replies, "That's all there is to it." Only through this emptiness, the passive energy of the Tao, can Yen Hui succeed.

Confucius goes on to speak of his own work, and argues for a state of equanimity in the midst of both victory and defeat, success and failure. "To suffer no harm whether you succeed or not—only the man who has virtue can do that." This is not unlike the idea of detachment from the fruits of action taught in the *Bhagavad Gita* of Hinduism. Chuang Tzu also depicts Confucius as saying, "To serve your own mind so that sadness or joy do not sway or move it; to understand what you can do nothing about and to be content with it as with fate—this is the perfection of virtue." Again, this emphasis on maintaining equanimity in the face of both success and failure reflects the era in which Chuang Tzu lived, when the people of China suffered greatly. Rather than being optimistic about transforming his society (though this aspiration is not altogether absent even in his writings), he recommends that one transform oneself. We may not be able to control what happens in our surroundings, try though we must to do what is right. But we can control how we respond to our circumstances, by cultivating harmony with the Way.

Jeffery D. Long

89

FOUR

IN THE WORLD OF MEN

YEN HUI WENT TO SEE Confucius and asked permission to take a trip.

"Where are you going?"

"I'm going to Wei."

"What will you do there?"

"I have heard that the ruler of Wei is very young. He acts in an independent manner, thinks little of how he rules his state, and fails to see his faults. It is nothing to him to lead his people into peril, and his dead are reckoned by swampfuls like so much grass. His people have nowhere to turn. I have heard you say, Master, 'Leave the state that is well ordered and go to the state in chaos! At the doctor's gate are many sick men.' I want to use these words as my standard, in hopes that I can restore his state to health."

"Ah," said Confucius, "you will probably go and get yourself executed, that's all. The Way doesn't want things mixed in with it. When it becomes a mixture, it becomes many ways; with many ways, there is a lot of bustle; and where there is a lot of bustle, there is trouble—trouble that has no remedy! The Perfect Man of ancient times made sure that he had it in himself before he tried to give it to others. When you're not even sure what you've got in yourself, how do you have time to bother about what some tyrant is doing?

"Do you know what it is that destroys virtue, and where wisdom comes from? Virtue is destroyed by fame, and wisdom comes out of wrangling. Fame is something to beat people down with, and wisdom is a device for wrangling. Both are evil weapons—not the sort of thing to bring you success. Though your virtue may be great and your good faith unassailable, if you do not understand men's spirits, though your fame may be wide and you do not strive with others, if you do not understand men's

90

minds, but instead appear before a tyrant and force him to listen to sermons on benevolence and righteousness, measures and standards—this is simply using other men's bad points to parade your own excellence. You will be called a plaguer of others. He who plagues others will be plagued in turn. You will probably be plagued by this man.

"And suppose he is the kind who actually delights in worthy men and hates the unworthy—then why does he need you to try to make him any different? You had best keep your advice to yourself! Kings and dukes always lord it over others and fight to win the argument. You will find your eyes growing dazed, your color changing, your mouth working to invent excuses, your attitude becoming more and more humble, until in your mind you end by supporting him. This is to pile fire on fire, to add water to water, and is called 'increasing the excessive.' If you give in at the beginning, there is no place to stop. Since your fervent advice is almost certain not to be believed, you are bound to die if you come into the presence of a tyrant.

"In ancient times Chieh put Kuan Lung-feng to death and Chou put Prince Pi Kan to death. Both Kuan Lung-feng and Prince Pi Kan were scrupulous in their conduct, bent down to comfort and aid the common people, and used their positions as ministers to oppose their superiors. Therefore their rulers, Chieh and Chou, utilized their scrupulous conduct as a means to trap them, for they were too fond of good fame. In ancient times Yao attacked Ts'ung-chih and Hsu-ao, and Yu attacked Yu-hu, and these states were left empty and unpeopled, their rulers cut down. It was because they employed their armies constantly and never ceased their search for gain. All were seekers of fame or gain— have you alone not heard of them? Even the sages cannot cope with men who are after fame or gain, much less a person like you!

"However, you must have some plan in mind. Come, tell me what it is."

Yen Hui said, "If I am grave and empty-hearted, diligent and of one mind, won't that do?"

"Goodness, how could that do? You may put on a fine outward show and seem very impressive, but you can't avoid having an uncertain look on your face, any more than an ordinary man can. And then you try to gauge this man's feelings and seek to influence his mind. But with him, what is called 'the virtue that advances a little each day' would not succeed, much less a great display of virtue! He will stick fast to his position and never be converted. Though he may make outward signs of agreement, inwardly he will not give it a thought! How could such an approach succeed?"

"Well then, suppose I am inwardly direct, outwardly compliant, and do my work through the examples of antiquity? By being inwardly direct, I can be the companion of Heaven. Being a companion of Heaven, I know that the Son of Heaven and I are equally the sons of Heaven. Then why would I use my words to try to get men to praise me, or try to get them not to praise me? A man like this, people call The Child. This is what I mean by being a companion of Heaven.

"By being outwardly compliant, I can be a companion of men. Lifting up the tablet, kneeling, bowing, crouching down—this is the etiquette of a minister. Everybody does it, so why shouldn't I? If I do what other people do, they can hardly criticize me. This is what I mean by being a companion of men.

"By doing my work through the examples of antiquity, I can be the companion of ancient times. Though my words may in fact be lessons and reproaches, they belong to ancient times and not to me. In this way, though I may be blunt, I cannot be blamed. This is what I mean by being a companion of antiquity. If I go about it in this way, will it do?"

Confucius said, "Goodness, how could that do? You have too many policies and plans and you haven't seen what is needed. You will probably get off without incurring any blame, yes. But that will be as far as it goes. How do you think you can actually convert him? You are still making the mind your teacher!"

Yen Hui said, "I have nothing more to offer. May I ask the proper way?"

"You must fast!" said Confucius. "I will tell you what that means. Do you think it is easy to do anything while you have [a mind]? If you do, Bright Heaven will not sanction you."

Yen Hui said, "My family is poor. I haven't drunk wine or eaten any strong foods for several months. So can I be considered as having fasted?"

"That is the fasting one does before a sacrifice, not the fasting of the mind."

"May I ask what the fasting of the mind is?"

Confucius said, "Make your will one! Don't listen with your ears, listen with your mind. No, don't listen with your mind, but listen with your spirit. Listening stops with the ears, the mind stops with recognition, but spirit is empty and waits on all things. The Way gathers in emptiness alone. Emptiness is the fasting of the mind."

Yen Hui said, "Before I heard this, I was certain that I was Hui. But now that I have heard it, there is no more Hui. Can this be called emptiness?"

"That's all there is to it," said Confucius. "Now I will tell you. You may go and play in his bird cage, but never be moved by fame. If he listens, then sing; if not, keep still. Have no gate, no opening, but make oneness your house and live with what cannot be avoided. Then you will be close to success.

"It is easy to keep from walking; the hard thing is to walk without touching the ground. It is easy to cheat when you work for men, but hard to cheat when you work for Heaven. You have heard of flying with wings, but you have never heard of flying without wings. You have heard of the knowledge that knows, but you have never heard of the knowledge that does not know. Look into that closed room, the empty chamber where brightness is born! Fortune and blessing gather where there is stillness. But if you do not keep still—this is what is called sitting but racing around. Let your ears and eyes communicate with what is inside,

93

and put mind and knowledge on the outside. Then even gods and spirits will come to dwell, not to speak of men! This is the changing of the ten thousand things, the bond of Yu and Shun, the constant practice of Fu Hsi and Chi Ch'u. How much more should it be a rule for lesser men!"

Tzu-kao, duke of She, who was being sent on a mission to Ch'i, consulted Confucius. "The king is sending me on a very important mission. Ch'i will probably treat me with great honor but will be in no hurry to do anything more. Even a commoner cannot be forced to act, much less one of the feudal lords. I am very worried about it. You once said to me, 'In all affairs, whether large or small, there are few men who reach a happy conclusion except through the Way. If you do not succeed, you are bound to suffer from the judgment of men. If you do succeed, you are bound to suffer from the yin and yang. To suffer no harm whether you succeed or not—only the man who has virtue can do that.' I am a man who eats plain food that is simply cooked, so that no one ever complains of the heat in my kitchens. Yet this morning I received my orders from the king and by evening I am gulping ice water—do you suppose I have developed some kind of internal fever? I have not even gone to Ch'i to see what the situation is like and already I am suffering from the yin and yang. And if I do not succeed, I am bound to suffer from the judgment of men. I will have both worries. As a minister, I am not capable of carrying out this mission. But perhaps you have some advice you can give me..."

Confucius said, "In the world, there are two great decrees: one is fate and the other is duty. That a son should love his parents is fate—you cannot erase this from his heart. That a subject should serve his ruler is duty—there is no place he can go and be without his ruler, no place he can escape to between heaven and earth. These are called the great decrees. Therefore, to serve your parents and be content to follow them anywhere—this is the perfection of filial piety. To serve your ruler and be content to do anything for him—this is the peak of loyalty. And to serve your own mind so that sadness or joy do not sway or move it; to understand

94

what you can do nothing about and to be content with it as with fate—this is the perfection of virtue. As a subject and a son, you are bound to find things you cannot avoid. If you act in accordance with the state of affairs and forget about yourself, then what leisure will you have to love life and hate death? Act in this way and you will be all right.

"I want to tell you something else I have learned. In all human relations, if the two parties are living close to each other, they may form a bond through personal trust. But if they are far apart, they must use words to communicate their loyalty, and words must be transmitted by someone. To transmit words that are either pleasing to both parties or infuriating to both parties is one of the most difficult things in the world. Where both parties are pleased, there must be some exaggeration of the good points; and where both parties are angered, there must be some exaggeration of the bad points. Anything that smacks of exaggeration is irresponsible. Where there is irresponsibility, no one will trust what is said, and when that happens, the man who is transmitting the words will be in danger. Therefore the aphorism says, 'Transmit the established facts; do not transmit words of exaggeration.' If you do that, you will probably come out all right.

"When men get together to pit their strength in games of skill, they start off in a light and friendly mood, but usually end up in a dark and angry one, and if they go on too long they start resorting to various underhanded tricks. When men meet at some ceremony to drink, they start off in an orderly manner, but usually end up in disorder, and if they go on too long they start indulging in various irregular amusements. It is the same with all things. What starts out being sincere usually ends up being deceitful. What was simple in the beginning acquires monstrous proportions in the end.

"Words are like wind and waves; actions are a matter of gain and loss. Wind and waves are easily moved; questions of gain and loss easily lead to danger. Hence anger arises from no other cause than clever words and one-sided speeches. When animals face death, they do not care what cries they make; their breath comes in gasps and a wild fierceness is born in their hearts. [Men, too,] if you press them too hard, are bound to answer you with ill-natured hearts, though they do not know why they do so. If they themselves do not understand why they behave like this, then who knows where it will end?

"Therefore the aphorism says, 'Do not deviate from your orders; do not press for completion.' To go beyond the limit is excess; to deviate from orders or press for completion is a dangerous thing. A good completion takes a long time; a bad completion cannot be changed later. Can you afford to be careless?

"Just go along with things and let your mind move freely. Resign yourself to what cannot be avoided and nourish what is within you—this is best. What more do you have to do to fulfill your mission? Nothing is as good as following orders (obeying fate)—that's how difficult it is!"

Yen Ho, who had been appointed tutor to the crown prince, son of Duke Ling of Wei, went to consult Ch'u Po-yu. "Here is this man who by nature is lacking in virtue. If I let him go on with his unruliness I will endanger the state. If I try to impose some rule on him, I will endanger myself. He knows enough to recognize the faults of others, but he doesn't know his own faults. What can I do with a man like this?"

"A very good question," said Ch'u Po-yu. "Be careful, be on your guard, and make sure that you yourself are in the right! In your actions it is best to follow along with him, and in your mind it is best to harmonize with him. However, these two courses involve certain dangers. Though you follow along, you don't want to be pulled into his doings, and though you harmonize, you don't want to be drawn out too far. If in your actions you follow along to the extent of being pulled in with him, then you will be overthrown, destroyed, wiped out, and brought to your knees. If in your mind you harmonize to the extent of being drawn out, then you will be talked about, named, blamed, and condemned. If he wants to be a child, be a child with him. If he wants to follow erratic ways, follow erratic ways with him. If he wants to be reckless, be reckless with him. Understand him thoroughly, and lead him to the point where he is without fault.

"Don't you know about the praying mantis that waved its arms angrily in front of an approaching carriage, unaware that they were incapable of stopping it? Such was the high opinion it had of its talents. Be careful, be on your guard! If you offend him by parading your store of talents, you will be in danger!

"Don't you know how the tiger trainer goes about it? He doesn't dare give the tiger any living thing to eat for fear it will learn the taste of fury by killing it. He doesn't dare give it any whole thing to eat for fear it will learn the taste of fury by tearing it apart. He gauges the state of the tiger's appetite and thoroughly understands its fierce disposition. Tigers are a different breed from men, and yet you can train them to be gentle with their keepers by following along with them. The men who get killed are the ones who go against them.

"The horse lover will use a fine box to catch the dung and a giant clam shell to catch the stale. But if a mosquito or a fly lights on the horse and he slaps it at the wrong time, then the horse will break the bit, hurt its head, and bang its chest. The horse lover tries to think of everything, but his affection leads him into error. Can you afford to be careless?"

Carpenter Shih went to Ch'i and, when he got to Crooked Shaft, he saw a serrate oak standing by the village shrine. It was broad enough to shelter several thousand oxen and measured a hundred spans around, towering above the hills. The lowest branches were eighty feet from the ground, and a dozen or so of them could have been made into boats. There were so many sightseers that the place looked like a fair, but the carpenter didn't even glance around and went on his way without stopping. His apprentice stood staring for a long time and then ran after Carpenter Shih and said, "Since I first took up my ax and followed you, Master, I have never seen timber as beautiful as this. But you don't even bother to look, and go right on without stopping. Why is that?"

"Forget it—say no more!" said the carpenter. "It's a worthless tree! Make boats out of it and they'd sink; make coffins and they'd rot in no time; make vessels and they'd break at once. Use it for doors and it would sweat sap like pine; use it for posts and the worms would eat them up. It's not a timber tree —there's nothing it can be used for. That's how it got to be that old!"

After Carpenter Shih had returned home, the oak tree appeared to him in a dream and said, "What are you comparing me with? Are you comparing me with those useful trees? The cherry apple, the pear, the orange, the citron, the rest of those fructiferous trees and shrubs—as soon as their fruit is ripe, they are torn apart and subjected to abuse. Their big limbs are broken off, their little limbs are yanked around. Their utility makes life miserable for them, and so they don't get to finish out the years Heaven gave them, but are cut off in mid-journey. They bring it on themselves—the pulling and tearing of the common mob. And it's the same way with all other things.

"As for me, I've been trying a long time to be of no use, and though I almost died, I've finally got it. This is of great use to me. If I had been of some use, would I ever have grown this large? Moreover you and I are both of us things. What's the point of this—things condemning things? You, a worthless man about to die—how do you know I'm a worthless tree?"

When Carpenter Shih woke up, he reported his dream. His apprentice said, "If it's so intent on being of no use, what's it doing there at the village shrine?"

"Shhh! Say no more! It's only resting there. If we carp and criticize, it will merely conclude that we don't understand it. Even if it weren't at the shrine, do you suppose it would be cut down? It protects itself in a different way from ordinary people. If you try to judge it by conventional standards, you'll be way off!"

Tzu-ch'i of Nan-po was wandering around the Hill of Shang when he saw a huge tree there, different from all the rest. A thousand teams of horses could have taken shelter under it and its shade would have covered them all. Tzu-ch'i said, "What tree is this? It must certainly have some extraordinary usefulness!" But, looking up, he saw that the smaller limbs were gnarled and twisted, unfit for beams or rafters, and looking down, he saw that the trunk was pitted and rotten and could not be used for coffins. He licked one of the leaves and it blistered his mouth and made it sore. He sniffed the odor and it was enough to make a man drunk for three days. "It turns out to be a completely unusable tree," said Tzu-ch'i, "and so it has been able to grow this big. Aha!—it is this unusableness that the Holy Man makes use of!"

The region of Ching-shih in Sung is fine for growing catalpas, cypresses, and mulberries. But those that are more than one or two arm-lengths around are cut down for people who want monkey perches; those that are three or four spans around are cut down for the ridgepoles of tall roofs; and those that are seven or eight spans are cut down for the families of nobles or rich merchants who want side boards for coffins. So they never get to live out the years Heaven gave them, but are cut down in mid-journey by axes. This is the danger of being usable. In the Chieh sacrifice, oxen with white foreheads. Following Ma Hsü-lun, I read *mien* (roof) in place of Ming. Pigs with turned-up snouts, and men with piles cannot be offered to the river. This is something all the shamans know, and hence they consider them inauspicious creatures. But the Holy Man for the same reason considers them highly auspicious.

There's Crippled Shu—chin stuck down in his navel, shoulders up above his head, pigtail pointing at the sky, his five organs on the top, his two thighs pressing his ribs. By sewing and washing, he gets enough to fill his mouth; by handling a winnow and sifting out the good grain, he makes enough to feed ten people. When the authorities call out the troops, he stands in the crowd waving good-by; when they get up a big work party, they pass him over because he's a chronic invalid. And when they are doling out grain to the ailing, he gets three big measures and ten bundles of firewood. With a crippled body, he's still able to look after himself and finish out the years Heaven gave him. How much better, then, if he had crippled virtue!

When Confucius visited Ch'u, Chieh Yu, the madman of Ch'u, wandered by his gate crying, "Phoenix, phoenix, how his virtue failed! The future you cannot wait for; the past you cannot pursue. When the world has the Way, the sage succeeds; when the world is without the Way, the sage survives. In times like the present, we do well to escape penalty. Good fortune is light as a feather, but nobody knows how to hold it up. Misfortune is heavy as the earth, but nobody knows how to stay out of its way. Leave off, leave off—this teaching men virtue! Dangerous, dangerous—to mark off the ground and run! Fool, fool—don't spoil my walking! I walk a crooked way—don't step on my feet. The mountain trees do themselves harm; the grease in the torch burns itself up. The cinnamon can be eaten and so it gets cut down; the lacquer tree can be used and so it gets hacked apart. All men know the use of the useful, but nobody knows the use of the useless!"

NIEH CH'ILEH WAS QUESTIONING Wang Ni. Four times he asked a question and four times Wang Ni said he didn't know. Nieh Ch'ileh proceeded to hop around in great glee and went and told Master P'u-i. Master P'u-i said, "Are you just now finding that out? The clansman Yu-yii was no match for the clansman T'ai. The clansman Yu-yii still held on to benevolence and worked to win men over. He won men over all right, but he never got out into [the realm of] 'not-man.' The clansman T'ai, now—he lay down peaceful and easy; he woke up wide-eyed and blank. Sometimes he thought he was a horse; sometimes he thought he was a cow. His understanding was truly trustworthy; his virtue was perfectly true. He never entered [the realm of] 'not-man!'"

Chien Wu went to see the madman Chieh Yii. Chieh Yii said, "What was Chung Shih telling you the other day?"

Chien Wu said, "He told me that the ruler of men should devise his own principles, standards, ceremonies, and regulations, and then there will be no one who will fail to obey him and be transformed by them."

The madman Chieh Yu said, "This is bogus virtue! To try to govern the world like this is like trying to walk the ocean, to drill through a river, or to make a mosquito shoulder a mountain! When the sage governs, does he govern what is on the outside? He makes sure of himself first, and then he acts. He makes absolutely certain that things can do what they are supposed to do, that is all. The bird flies high in the sky where it can escape the danger of stringed arrows. The field mouse burrows deep down under the sacred hill where it won't have to worry about men digging and smoking it out. Have you got less sense than these two little creatures?"

T'ien Ken was wandering on the sunny side of Yin Mountain. When he reached the banks of the Liao River, he happened to meet a Nameless Man. He questioned the man, saying, "Please may I ask how to rule the world?"

The Nameless Man said, "Get away from me, you peasant! What kind of a dreary question is that! I'm just about to set off with the Creator. And if I get bored with that, then I'll ride on the Light-and-Lissome Bird out beyond the six directions, wandering in the village of Not-Even-Anything and living in the Broad-and-Borderless field. What business do you have coming with this talk of governing the world and disturbing my mind?"

But T'ien Ken repeated his question. The Nameless Man said, "Let your mind wander in simplicity, blend your spirit with the vastness, follow along with things the way they are, and make no room for personal views—then the world will be governed."

Yang Tzu-chu went to see Lao Tan and said, "Here is a man swift as an echo, strong as a beam, with a wonderfully clear understanding of the principles of things, studying the Way without ever letting up—a man like this could compare with an enlightened king, couldn't he?"

Lao Tan said, "In comparison to the sage, a man like this is a drudging slave, a craftsman bound to his calling, wearing out his body, grieving his mind. They say it is the beautiful markings of the tiger and the leopard that call out the hunters, the nimbleness of the monkey and the ability of the dog to catch rats that make them end up chained. A man like this—how could he compare to an enlightened king?"

Yang Tzu-chu, much taken aback, said, "May I venture to ask about the government of the enlightened king?"

Lao Tan said, "The government of the enlightened king? His achievements blanket the world but appear not to be his own doing. His transforming influence touches the ten thousand things but the people do not depend on him. With him there is no promotion or praise—he lets everything find its own enjoyment. He takes his stand on what cannot be fathomed and wanders where there is nothing at all."

In Cheng there was a shaman of the gods named Chi Hsien. He could tell whether men would live or die, survive or perish, be fortunate or unfortunate, live a long time or die young, and he would predict the year, month, week, and day as though he were a god himself. When the people of Cheng saw him, they dropped everything and ran out of his way. Lieh Tzu went to see him and was completely intoxicated. Returning, he said to Hu Tzu, "I used to think, Master, that your Way was perfect. But now I see there is something even higher!"

Hu Tzu said, "I have already showed you all the outward forms, but I haven't yet showed you the substance—and do you really think you have mastered this Way of mine? There may be a flock of hens but, if there is no rooster, how can they lay fertile eggs? You take what you know of the Way and wave it in the face of the world, expecting to be believed! This is the reason men can see right through you. Try bringing your shaman along next time and letting him get a look at me."

The next day Lieh Tzu brought the shaman to see Hu Tzu. When they had left the room, the shaman said, "I'm so sorry—your master is dying! There's no life left in him—he won't last the week. I saw something very strange—something like wet ashes!"

Lieh Tzu went back into the room, weeping and drenching the collar of his robe with tears, and reported this to Hu Tzu.

Hu Tzu said, "Just now I appeared to him with the Pattern of Earth—still and silent, nothing moving, nothing standing up. He probably saw in me the Workings of Virtue Closed Off. Try bringing him around again."

The next day the two came to see Hu Tzu again, and when they had left the room, the shaman said to Lieh Tzu, "It certainly was lucky that your master met me! He's going to get better—he has all the signs of life! I could see the stirring of what had been closed off!"

Lieh Tzu went in and reported this to Hu Tzu.

Hu Tzu said, "Just now I appeared to him as Heaven and Earth—no name or substance to it, but still the workings, coming up from the heels. He probably saw in me the Workings of the Good One. Try bringing him again."

The next day the two came to see Hu Tzu again, and when they had left the room, the shaman said to Lieh Tzu, "Your master is never the same! I have no way to physiognomize him! If he will try to steady himself, then I will come and examine him again."

Lieh Tzu went in and reported this to Hu Tzu.

Hu Tzu said, "Just now I appeared to him as the Great Vastness Where Nothing Wins Out. He probably saw in me the Workings of the Balanced Breaths. Where the swirling waves gather there is an abyss; where the still waters gather there is an abyss; where the running waters gather there is an abyss. The abyss has nine names and I have shown him three. Try bringing him again."

The next day the two came to see Hu Tzu again, but before the shaman had even come to a halt before Hu Tzu, his wits left him and he fled.

"Run after him!" said Hu Tzu, but though Lieh Tzu ran after him, he could not catch up. Returning, he reported to Hu Tzu, "He's vanished! He's disappeared! I couldn't catch up with him."

Hu Tzu said, "Just now I appeared to him as Not Yet Emerged from My Source. I came at him empty, wriggling and turning, not knowing anything about 'who' or 'what,' now dipping and bending, now flowing in waves—that's why he ran away."

After this, Lieh Tzu concluded that he had never really begun to learn anything. He went home and for three years did not go out. He replaced his wife at the stove, fed the pigs as though he were feeding people, and showed no preferences in the things he did. He got rid of the carving and polishing and returned to plainness, letting his body stand alone like a clod. In the midst of entanglement he remained sealed, and in this oneness he ended his life.

Do not be an embodier of fame; do not be a storehouse of schemes; do not be an undertaker of projects; do not be a proprietor of wisdom. Embody to the fullest what has no end and wander where there is no trail. Hold on to all that you have received from Heaven but do not think you have gotten anything. Be empty, that is all. The Perfect Man uses his mind like a mirror—going after nothing, welcoming nothing, responding but not storing. Therefore he can win out over things and not hurt himself.

The emperor of the South Sea was called Shu [Brief], the emperor of the North Sea was called Hu [Sudden], and the emperor of the central region was called Hun-tun [Chaos]. Shu and Hu from time to time came together for a meeting in the territory of Hun-tun, and Hun-tun treated them very generously. Shu and Hu discussed how they could repay his kindness. "All men," they said, "have seven openings so they can see, hear, eat, and breathe. But Hun-tun alone doesn't have any. Let's trying boring him some!"

Every day they bored another hole, and on the seventh day Hun-tun died.

THREE

BUDDHISM

The Dhammapada

The Dhammapada, which loosely means "Verses of the Teaching," is a canonical collection of 423 verses of accessible, ethical advice, arranged thematically into twenty-six chapters. *The Dhammapada* can be found within a collection of discourses called the *Khuddakanikāya* (the Group of Small Texts), itself part of the *Suttapiṭaka*, the "basket of sermons" that Buddhists of the Theravada lineage attribute to the historical Buddha, discourses preserved in a South Asian language called Pāli. Theravada Buddhism is the dominant form of Buddhism in Sri Lanka, Thailand, Myanmar (Burma), Cambodia, and Laos.

A voluminous commentary on *The Dhammapada* from the fifth century CE not only asserts that the Buddha spoke all of the verses that appear in *The Dhammapada*, but it even narrates the circumstances under which he spoke them. With that said, modern scholars do not believe all of the verses to be actual utterances of the Buddha, though it certainly is possible that some of them do date back to his time. More likely, the verses of *The Dhammapada* are instances of a much larger, loose body of ethical advice that circulated throughout South Asia before the Common Era, both inside and outside of Buddhist communities. These verses were memorized in various local languages and eventually committed to writing.

In fact, three collections similar to *The Dhammapada*, albeit written in different languages, are extant. While these collections contain many of the same verses and chapter names as *The Dhammapada*, they also contain significant divergences. Some verses in *The Dhammapada* can also be found in non-Buddhist works from South Asia, including the great epic the *Mahābhārata*.

Regardless of the complex origins of *The Dhammapada*, its

influence in the Theravada Buddhist world is perfectly clear. Buddhist teachers cite its words in their sermons, students commonly commit its verses to memory, and politicians even quote its maxims in their speeches. The collection has also gained popularity in Europe and the United States and has been translated into English countless times over the past 150 years.

The verses of *The Dhammapada* are essentially ethical aphorisms that touch upon diverse topics, such as happiness and suffering, sin and virtue, anger, craving and violence, old age, and rebirth. Some verses also give pithy instructions on how to train on the Buddhist path, such as those calling for the cultivation of mindful awareness, for example.

The verses that follow make up three of the twenty-six chapters, or groups (*vagga* in Pāli), that appear in the canonical Pāli recension. The first two chapters of *The Dhammapada* are included here: the first is a series of coupled verses, and the second contains verses about the importance of being diligently mindful of one's sensory experiences, one's thoughts, and one's actions. The final chapter in our selection is the ninth chapter of *The Dhammapada*, which comments on positive and negative thoughts and actions.

The ninth chapter also introduces us to the idea of karma, a South Asian theory of cause and effect that spans many of the region's religions. The theory of karma stipulates that all actions, whether mental, verbal, or physical actions, necessarily bring about effects. Subjects often experience the effects of their actions in the distant future, however, even in their future rebirths. Positive actions in the present bring about positive results in the future, while negative actions bring about negative ones. Being generous with others may lead you to be reborn in a land full of wealth and plenty, for example, while being miserly may lead you to be reborn as a being with insatiable desires.

As a diverse collection of maxims, *The Dhammapada* does not articulate a singular version of the spiritual path or the spiritual quest. Still, it does introduce us to a number of important Buddhist approaches to achieving a better life. First and foremost,

The Dhammapada

the verses of *The Dhammapada* repeatedly remind us that it is important to commit positive actions in this lifetime in order to assure good rebirths in the future. While the Buddha taught his disciples to strive to liberate themselves altogether from the cycle of rebirth caused by karma, the vast majority of Buddhists in the world do not actively aspire to achieve liberation. In order to assure themselves a positive future, it therefore becomes all the more crucial to do positive actions and refrain from negative ones.

But *The Dhammapada* also contains instructions for those in the Theravada tradition who do strive for liberation. For example, its verses preach the importance of protecting oneself from the danger of the passions—the harmful tendency to grow attached to things that one likes and become angry at those things that one does not like. These habits not only cause negative effects in future lifetimes, but they are at the very source of our suffering in the present life. One way that monks can protect themselves from these passions is to cultivate mindful awareness, referenced here in the second chapter on "watchfulness" (*appamāda*). Mindfulness (*sati*) of one's thoughts, impulses, and actions at every moment is the first step toward preventing negative tendencies from arising.

Joshua Schapiro

1. CONTRARY WAYS

1 What we are today comes from our thoughts of yesterday, and our present thoughts build our life of tomorrow: our life is the creation of our mind.

If a man speaks or acts with an impure mind, suffering follows him as the wheel of the cart follows the beast that draws the cart.

2 What we are today comes from our thoughts of yesterday, and our present thoughts build our life of tomorrow: our life is the creation of our mind.

If a man speaks or acts with a pure mind, joy follows him as his own shadow.

3 "He insulted me, he hurt me, he defeated me, he robbed me." Those who think such thoughts will not be free from hate.

4 "He insulted me, he hurt me, he defeated me, he robbed me. " Those who think not such thoughts will be free from hate.

5 For hate is not conquered by hate: hate is conquered by love. This is a law eternal.

6 Many do not know that we are here in this world to live in harmony. Those who know this do not fight against each other.

7 He who lives only for pleasures, and whose soul is not in harmony, who considers not the food he eats, is idle and has not the power of virtue—such a man is moved by MARA, is moved by selfish temptations, even as a weak tree is shaken by the wind.

8 But he who lives not for pleasures, and whose soul is in self-harmony, who eats or fasts with moderation, and has faith and the power of virtue—this man is not moved by temptations, as a great rock is not shaken by the wind.

9 If a man puts on the pure yellow robe with a soul which is impure, without self-harmony and truth, he is not worthy of the holy robe.

10 But he who is pure from sin and whose soul is strong in virtue, who has self-harmony and truth, he is worthy of the holy robe.

11 Those who think the unreal is, and think the Real is not, they shall never reach the Truth, lost in the path of wrong thought.

12 But those who know the Real is, and know the unreal is not, they shall indeed reach the Truth, safe on the path of right thought.

13 Even as rain breaks through an ill-thatched house, passions will break through an ill-guarded mind.

14 But even as rain breaks not through a well-thatched house, passions break not through a well-guarded mind.

15 He suffers in this world, and he suffers in the next world the man who does evil suffers in both worlds. He suffers, he suffers and mourns when he sees the wrong he has done.

16 He is happy in this world and he is happy in the next world: the man who does good is happy in both worlds. He is glad, he feels great gladness when he sees the good he has done.

17 He sorrows in this world, and he sorrows in the next world: the man who does evil sorrows in both worlds. 'I have done evil', thus he laments, and more he laments on the path of sorrow.

18 He rejoices in this world, and he rejoices in the next world: the man who does good rejoices in both worlds. 'I have done good', thus he rejoices, and more he rejoices on the path of joy.

19 If a man speaks many holy words but he speaks and does not, this thoughtless man cannot enjoy the life of holiness: he is like a cowherd who counts the cows of his master.

20 Whereas if a man speaks but a few holy words and yet he lives the life of those words, free from passion and hate and illusion—with right vision and a mind free, craving for nothing both now and hereafter—the life of this man is a life of holiness.

2. WATCHFULNESS

21 Watchfulness is the path of immortality: unwatchfulness is the path of death. Those who are watchful never die: those who do not watch are already as dead.

22 Those who with a clear mind have seen this truth, those who are wise and ever-watchful, they feel the joy of watchfulness, the joy of the path of the Great.

23 And those who in high thought and in deep contemplation with ever-living power advance on the path, they in the end reach NIRVANA, the peace supreme and infinite joy.

24 The man who arises in faith, who ever remembers his high purpose, whose work is pure, and who carefully considers his work, who in self-possession lives the life of perfection, and who ever, for ever, is watchful, that man shall arise in glory.

25 By arising in faith and watchfulness, by self-possession and self-harmony, the wise man makes an island for his soul which many waters cannot overflow.

26 Men who are foolish and ignorant are careless and never watchful; but the man who lives in watchfulness considers it his greatest treasure.

27 Never surrender to carelessness; never sink into weak pleasures and lust. Those who are watchful, in deep contemplation, reach in the end the joy supreme.

28 The wise man who by watchfulness conquers thoughtlessness is as one who free from sorrows ascends the palace of wisdom and there, from its high terrace, sees those in sorrow below; even as a wise strong man on the holy mountain might behold the many unwise far down below on the plain.

29 Watchful amongst the unwatchful, awake amongst those who sleep, the wise man like a swift horse runs his race, outrunning those who are slow.

30 It was by watchfulness that Indra became the chief of the gods, and thus the gods praise the watchful, and thoughtlessness is ever despised.

31 The monk who has the joy of watchfulness and who looks with fear on thoughtlessness, he goes on his path like a fire, burning all obstacles both great and small.

32 The monk who has the joy of watchfulness, and who

looks with fear on thoughtlessness, he can never be deprived of his victory and he is near NIRVANA.

9. GOOD AND EVIL

116 Make haste and do what is good; keep your mind away from evil. If a man is slow in doing good, his mind finds pleasure in evil.

117 If a man does something wrong, let him not do it again and again. Let him not find pleasure in his sin. Painful is the accumulation of wrongdoings.

118 If a man does something good, let him do it again and again. Let him find joy in his good work. Joyful is the accumulation of good work.

119 A man may find pleasure in evil as long as his evil has not given fruit; but when the fruit of evil comes then that man finds evil indeed.

120 A man may find pain in doing good as long as his good has not given fruit; but when the fruit of good comes then that man finds good indeed.

121 Hold not a sin of little worth, thinking "this is little to me." The falling of drops of water will in time fill a water-jar. Even so the foolish man becomes full of evil, although he gather it little by little.

122 Hold not a deed of little worth, thinking "this is little to me." The falling of drops of water will in time fill a water-jar. Even so the wise man becomes full of good, although he gather it little by little.

123 Let a man avoid the dangers of evil even as a merchant carrying much wealth, but with a small escort, avoids the dangers of the road, or as a man who loves his life avoids the drinking of poison.

124 As a man who has no wound on his hand cannot be hurt by the poison he may carry in his hand, since poison hurts not where there is no wound, the man who has no evil cannot be hurt by evil.

125 The fool who does evil to a man who is good, to a man who is pure and free from sin, the evil returns to him like the dust thrown against the wind.

126 Some people are born on this earth; those who do evil are reborn in hell; the righteous go to heaven; but those who are pure reach NIRVANA.

127 Neither in the sky, nor deep in the ocean, nor in a mountain-cave, nor anywhere, can a man be free from the evil he has done.

128 Neither in the sky, nor deep in the ocean, nor in a mountain-cave, nor anywhere, can a man be free from the power of death.

The Heart Sūtra

The Heart of the Perfection of Wisdom Sūtra, here translated in its entirety, belongs to an important group of Sanskrit scriptures associated with Mahāyāna Buddhism. Mahāyāna (meaning the "Great Vehicle") is a movement that developed in the early centuries of the Common Era in parts of modern-day India, Pakistan, and Afghanistan, and along the Silk Route in Central Asia. The Mahāyāna eventually spread to China, Japan, Korea, and Vietnam, Tibet, and Mongolia. As will be discussed shortly, we find some of the most important philosophical ideas of Mahāyāna Buddhism in The Heart Sūtra.

The Perfection of Wisdom Sūtras (the Prajñāpāramitāsūtrās), of which The Heart Sūtra is one, are teachings traditionally claimed to have been given by the historical Buddha with the help of nearly enlightened beings called Bodhisattvas. Bodhisattvas are religious heroes of the Mahāyāna who have dedicated themselves to helping liberate all beings from the cycle of suffering and rebirth. "Sūtra" is the genre label Buddhists give to texts that contain teachings either spoken by the Buddha or spoken in his presence (though the word means something slightly different in reference to Hindu compositions).

Perfection of Wisdom scholar Edward Conze counts some forty Perfection of Wisdom Sūtras of varying length, with long versions comprising eight thousand, eighteen thousand, twenty-five thousand, and one hundred thousand lines, as well as shorter versions in twenty-five lines (The Heart Sūtra), and even a version in one single syllable (A). Exact dating of the Perfection of Wisdom literature is difficult, though versions probably began to appear slightly before the Common Era. The Heart Sūtra was composed no later than 400 CE, the approximate date of its first translation into Chinese, though that translation is of a shorter version of the text than the one presented here. It should be noted that one scholar has hypothesized that *The Heart Sūtra* was originally composed in Chinese and only later translated back into Sanskrit.

The Perfection of Wisdom Sūtras preach the truth of "emptiness," the idea that all phenomena, physical or mental, are without true reality—meaning that they lack permanence and independence. So, for example, one might say that a table is "empty" in as much as it does not truly exist as an independent phenomenon. It is constructed of parts (a flat top and legs), which are themselves constructed of parts. Apart from the parts, there is no truly existing whole; there is only an idea of "table." Even this idea of "table" is dependent on other things, such as human minds to have the thought "table," and a language (such as English) within which to articulate the idea "table." Ultimately, the chain of dependence—a table being dependent on its parts, those parts being dependent on other parts—is endless. There is absolutely nothing that we can point to that is truly, independently real, and most certainly not our "selves." The Perfection of Wisdom Sūtras do not elaborate on the meaning of emptiness in this manner, however. Rather, they contain long lists wherein the existence of various familiar Buddhist phenomena is negated.

The Perfection of Wisdom Sūtras contend that a thorough understanding of emptiness, an understanding that they name "the perfection of wisdom," is the key to attaining liberation. The spiritual quest thereby becomes a process of understanding the "empty" nature of reality by means of philosophically deconstructing the world around us and applying techniques of meditative concentration that allow this new understanding to be perfected. Paradoxically, the very idea of "liberation from suffering," normally taken to be the goal of the Buddhist path, is one of the deceptive concepts that must be overcome in order to achieve perfect wisdom. As *The Heart Sūtra* plainly states, there is no suffering and no "stopping" that suffering. Still, only a few lines later *The Heart Sūtra* speaks of beings realizing "perfect enlightenment."

The Heart Sūtra opens with a description of the Bodhisattva Avalokita, a Bodhisattva noted for his unbounded compassion, in deep meditation on the perfection of wisdom. The ensuing dialogue between Avalokita and a disciple of the Buddha named Śāriputra consists of a thorough deconstruction of various traditional categories used by Buddhists to explain the phenomena of everyday experience. The first items to be deconstructed are the five heaps or aggregates. These heaps, one physical and four mental, are traditional categories meant to encapsulate all of the constituent parts of a sentient being. Avalokita explains that each of these five (form or matter, feelings, perceptions, impulses, and consciousness) are empty, meaning they lack any true reality. The sense organs, the consciousnesses that accompany those organs (such as sight, hearing, smell, and so on), and the objects of the senses are also empty of any true reality. In fact, all of the phenomena that the Buddha talked about in order to help beings escape from suffering are also empty. The twelve links of dependent origination—categories the Buddha used to explain how ignorance and suffering perpetuate themselves over the course of multiple rebirths—are all empty of true existence. Even the Buddha's famous Four Noble Truths are empty!

Because of its terse statements about emptiness, *The Heart Sūtra* and the other Perfection of Wisdom Sūtras have been interpreted in diverse ways by Buddhist philosophers and practitioners in cultures throughout Asia, from India, Tibet, and Mongolia, to China, Japan, Korea, and Vietnam. While many commentaries focus on exploring the ideas of emptiness, including the contemporary commentaries by Thich Nhat Hanh and the Dalai Lama listed in the bibliography, other commentaries treat the Perfection of Wisdom Sūtras as sources for hidden instructions about the structure of the path to enlightenment.

In addition to being a source for religious profundities, *The Heart Sūtra* also acts as a popular prayer and is chanted throughout the Mahāyāna Buddhist world. One scholar even claims the text to be the single most commonly recited scripture in all of Asian Buddhism. Calligraphic renderings of *The Heart Sūtra* are also quite common.

Joshua Schapiro

I. The invocation

Homage to the Perfection of Wisdom, the lovely, the holy!

II. The prologue

Avalokita, the holy Lord and Bodhisattva, was moving in the deep course of the wisdom which has gone beyond. He looked down from on high, he beheld but five heaps, and he saw that in their own-being they were empty.

III. The dialectics of emptiness.
First stage

Here, O Sariputra, form is emptiness, and the very emptiness is form; emptiness does not differ from form, form does not differ from emptiness; whatever is form, that is emptiness, whatever is emptiness, that is form. The same is true of feelings, perceptions, impulses, and consciousness.

IV. The dialectics of emptiness.
Second stage

Here, O Sariputra, all dharmas are marked with emptiness; they are not produced or stopped, not defiled or immaculate, not deficient or complete.

V. The dialectics of emptiness.
Third stage

Therefore, O Sariputra, in emptiness there is no form, nor feeling, nor perception, nor impulse, nor consciousness; no eye, ear, nose, tongue, body, mind; no forms, sounds, smells, tastes, touchables or objects of mind; no sight-organ-element, and so forth, until we come to: no mind-consciousness-element; there is no ignorance, no extinction of ignorance, and so forth, until we come to: there is no decay and death, no extinction of decay and death; there is no suffering, no origination, no stopping, no path; there is no cognition, no attainment, and no non-attainment.

VI. The concrete embodiment and practical basis of emptiness

Therefore, O Sariputra, it is because of his indifference to any kind of personal attainment that a Bodhisattva, through having relied on the perfection of wisdom, dwells without thought-coverings. In the absence of thought-coverings he has not been made to tremble, he has overcome what can upset, and in the end he attains to Nirvana.

VII. Full emptiness is the basis also of Buddhahood

All those who appear as Buddhas in the three periods of time fully awake to the utmost, right and perfect enlightenment because they have relied on the perfection of wisdom.

VIII. The teaching brought within reach of the comparatively unenlightened

Therefore one should know the Prajñaparamita as the great spell, the spell of great knowledge, the utmost spell, the unequalled spell, allayer of all suffering, in truth—for what could go wrong? By the Prajñaparamita has this spell been delivered. It runs like this: Gone, Gone, Gone beyond, Gone altogether beyond, O what an awakening, All Hail!

This completes the Heart of Perfect Wisdom.

The Lotus Sūtra

The following selection is among the most famous passages in all of Mahāyāna literature, residing in perhaps the most influential text in all of East Asian Buddhism, *The Lotus Sūtra*. Committed to writing in a form of Sanskrit sometimes called "Hybrid-Buddhist Sanskrit," *The Lotus Sūtra* is a Mahāyāna scripture from some time in the first two centuries of the Common Era, with its first translation into Chinese coming in 286 CE.

Over time, *The Lotus Sūtra* became a wildly popular and influential text, particularly in East Asia, with references to its narrative episodes commonly appearing in Buddhist literature and art. *The Lotus Sūtra* is the central scripture in the Chinese Tian Tai tradition (*Tendai* Buddhism in Japan), which is based on the teachings of sixth-century master Zhiyi that were systematized in the eighth century by Zhanran. It is also the paramount scripture for the Japanese Nichiren tradition, founded by a Tendai-trained monk named Nichiren (1222–1282), who taught disciples to chant the title of *The Lotus Sūtra*, a practice called *daimoku*. An offshoot of Nichiren Buddhism called Soka Gakkai has been growing in the United States since the 1960s.

The Lotus Sūtra has likely always been an object of devotional practice. The text of *The Lotus Sūtra* calls for its own worship, promising great benefits to those who honor it. Along with other early Mahāyāna scriptures, some scholars thus believe *The Lotus Sūtra* to have participated in a "cult of the book" wherein written documents like *The Lotus Sūtra* were worshipped as powerful, holy objects, much as were the large reliquaries of the Buddha's remains, called *stūpas*, that one finds throughout the Buddhist world. Not surprisingly, preaching, writing out, and worshipping the scripture eventually became common practices in East Asia.

The later chapters of *The Lotus Sūtra* also describe devotional practices directed at great Bodhisattvas, particularly toward the Bodhisattva of compassion (and hero of *The Heart Sūtra*) Avalokiteśvara (*Guanyin* in Chinese, *Kannon* in Japanese). These practices have become quite popular in their own right.

The Lotus Sūtra employs a number of distinct kinds of narrative exposition. As is the case with our excerpt, most of the narrative units in the *Lotus Sūtra* are expounded in prose and then recapitulated in verse. The text contains a host of prophecies about the future enlightenment of people ranging from such obvious candidates as Bodhisattvas to surprising ones such as Devadatta—a competitor to the historical Buddha who repeatedly attempted to assassinate him. But *The Lotus Sūtra* most famously tells parables about the nature of Mahāyāna Buddhism and the importance of skillful means—flexible teaching techniques that take into consideration the different needs and intellectual capacities of audience members.

Much of *The Lotus Sūtra* is devoted to three interlinking ideas. First, the aforementioned idea of skillful means; second, the existence of a single path, called the One Vehicle (*ekayāna*), that encapsulates all of the different paths taught, and skillful means employed, by the Buddha (here called the Tathāgata); third, the superiority of *The Lotus Sūtra* itself as the most complete, all-encapsulating teaching of the Buddha, particularly given its delivery shortly before his death.

The Lotus Sūtra introduces the ubiquitous Mahāyāna idea that there are three distinct vehicles to liberation: the vehicle of the *Śrāvakas* (disciples or "hearers"), the vehicle of the *Pratyekabuddhas* (solitary individuals who attain liberation on their own and do not return to the world to teach others), and the vehicle of the Bodhisattvas (otherwise known as the Mahāyāna). Each of the vehicles is itself a "skillful means" to lead its followers to liberation. According to the idea of the One Vehicle, followers of all three vehicles eventually make it to the same place: perfect enlightenment. Other Mahāyāna scriptures do not take the same universalistic approach, however. The text is also ambiguous as to whether or not the One Vehicle is synonymous with the Mahāyāna.

The parable that follows tells of a father whose children are stuck in a burning house (symbolizing the world of suffering). In order to get his children out of the house, the father promises each child a toy cart specifically to his or her liking: a bullock cart for one, a goat cart for another, and a deer cart for a third. These toy carts represent the different paths that the Buddha teaches to his disciples in order to coax them out of the cycle of suffering and rebirth. Once the children escape the house, the father gives all of them identical toys—grand, jewel-adorned bullock carts, which represent, of course, the One Vehicle. Not only does this famous parable give an account of the workings of skillful means and describe the relationship of the three (or four) vehicles to liberation, but it also enacts *The Lotus Sūtra*'s own skillful means. The parable itself is a skillful way to teach its audience about the Buddha's teachings.

While *The Lotus Sūtra* is short on explicit instructions for pursuing the spiritual quest (beyond its repeated calls for its audience to recite *The Lotus Sūtra* and devote themselves to it), it nonetheless lays out an accessible and influential map of how seemingly contradictory spiritual paths can relate to one another. In this vision, different Buddhist paths are all skillful means, catering to the specific needs of their constituencies.

Generations of Buddhists have also produced manifold interpretations of the text and have developed robust approaches to the spiritual path grounded on the authority of *The Lotus Sūtra*. Ironically, some of these interpretations, most notably those of Nichiren, the founder of Nichiren Buddhism, are dismissive of all competing versions of the Buddhist path.

Joshua Schapiro

24. After paying honour to many kotis of Buddhas, making strenuous efforts in the course of duty, and after having produced in thyself the ten powers, thou shalt reach supreme, perfect enlightenment.

25. Within a period inconceivable and immense there shall be an Æon rich in jewels (or, the Æon jewel-rich), and a sphere named Viraga, the pure field of the highest of men;

26. And its ground will consist of lapis lazuli, and be set off with gold threads; it will have hundreds of jewel trees, very beautiful, and covered with blossoms and fruits.

27. Bodhisattvas of good memory, able in showing the course of duty which they have been taught under hundreds of Buddhas, will come to be born in that field.

28. And the afore-mentioned Gina, then in his last bodily existence, shall, after passing the state of prince royal, renounce sensual pleasures, leave home (to become a wandering ascetic), and thereafter reach the supreme and the highest enlightenment.

29. The lifetime of that Gina will be precisely twelve intermediate kalpas, and the life of men will then last eight intermediate kalpas.

30. After the extinction of the Tathigata the true law will continue thirty-two Æons in full, for the benefit of the world, including the gods.

31. When the true law shall have come to an end, its counterfeit will stand for thirty-two intermediate kalpas. The dispersed relics of the holy one will always be honoured by men and gods.

32. Such will be the fate of that Lord. Rejoice, O son of Sâri, for it is thou who shalt be that most excellent of men, so unsurpassed.

33. The four classes of the audience, monks, nuns, lay devotees male and female, gods, Nagas, goblins, Gandharvas, demons, Garudas, Kinnaras, great serpents, men and beings not human, on hearing the announcement of the venerable Sâriputra's destiny to

supreme, perfect enlightenment, were so pleased, glad, charmed, thrilling with delight and joy, that they covered the Lord severally with their own robes, while Indra the chief of gods, Brahma Sahâmpati, besides hundred thousands of kotis of other divine beings, covered him with heavenly garments and bestrewed him with flowers of heaven, Mandâravas and great Mandâravas. High aloft they whirled celestial clothes and struck hundred thousands of celestial musical instruments and cymbals, high in the sky; and after pouring a great rain of flowers they uttered these words: The wheel of the law has been put in motion by the Lord, the first time at Benares at Rishipatana in the Deer-park; to-day has the Lord again put in motion the supreme wheel of the law.

34. Let us suppose the following case, Sâriputra. In a certain village, town, borough, province, kingdom, or capital, there was a certain housekeeper, old, aged, decrepit, very advanced in years, rich, wealthy, opulent; he had a great house, high, spacious, built a long time ago and old, inhabited by some two, three, four, or five hundred living beings. The house had but one door, and a thatch; its terraces were tottering, the bases of its pillars rotten, the coverings and plaster of the walls loose. On a sudden the whole house was from every side put in conflagration by a mass of fire. Let us suppose that the man had many little boys, say five, or ten, or even twenty, and that he himself had come out of the house.

35. Now, Sâriputra, that man, on seeing the house from every side wrapt in a blaze by a great mass of fire, got afraid, frightened, anxious in his mind, and made the following reflection: I myself am able to come out from the burning house through the door, quickly and safely, without being touched or scorched by that great mass of fire; but my children, those young boys, are staying in the burning house, playing, amusing, and diverting themselves with all sorts of sports. They do not perceive, nor know, nor understand, nor mind that the house is on fire, and do not get afraid. Though scorched by that great mass of fire, and affected with such a mass of pain, they do not mind the pain, nor do they conceive the idea of escaping.

36. The man, Sâriputra, is strong, has powerful arms, and (so) he makes this reflection: I am strong, and have powerful arms; why, let me gather all my little boys and take them to my breast to effect their escape from the house. A second reflection then presented itself to his mind: This house has but one opening; the door is shut; and those boys, fickle, unsteady, and childlike as they are, will, it is to be feared, run hither and thither, and come to grief and disaster in this mass of fire. Therefore I will warn them. So resolved, he calls to the boys: Come, my children; the house is burning with a mass of fire; come, lest ye be burnt in that mass of fire, and come to grief and disaster. But the ignorant boys do not heed the words of him who is their well-wisher; they are not afraid, not alarmed, and feel no misgiving; they do not care, nor fly, nor even know nor understand the purport of the word 'burning;' on the contrary, they run hither and thither, walk about, and repeatedly look at their father; all, because they are so ignorant.

37. Then the man is going to reflect thus: The house is burning, is blazing by a mass of fire. It is to be feared that myself as well as my children will come to grief and disaster. Let me therefore by some skilful means get the boys out of the house. The man knows the disposition of the boys, and has a clear perception of their inclinations. Now these boys happen to have many and manifold toys to play with, pretty, nice, pleasant, dear, amusing, and precious. The man, knowing the disposition of the boys, says to them: My children, your toys, which are so pretty, precious, and admirable, which you are so loth to miss, which are so various and multifarious, (such as) bullock-carts, goat-carts, deer-carts, which are so pretty, nice, dear, and precious to you, have all been put by me outside the house-door for you to play with. Come, run out, leave the house; to each of you I shall give what he wants.

He, the Tathâgata, endowed with Buddha-knowledge, forces, absence of hesitation, uncommon properties, and mighty by magical power, is the father of the world, who has reached the highest perfection in the knowledge of skilful means, who is most merciful, long-suffering, benevolent, compassionate. He appears in this triple world, which is like a house the roof and shelter whereof are decayed, (a house) burning by a mass of misery, in order to deliver from affection, hatred, and delusion the beings subject to birth, old age, disease, death, grief, wailing, pain, melancholy, despondency, the dark enveloping mists of ignorance, in order to rouse them to supreme and perfect enlightenment. Once born, he sees how the creatures are burnt, tormented, vexed, distressed by birth, old age, disease, death, grief, wailing, pain, melancholy, despondency; how for the sake of enjoyments, and prompted by sensual desires, they severally suffer various pains. In consequence both of what in this world they are seeking and what they have acquired, they will in a future state suffer various pains, in hell, in the brute creation, in the realm of Yama; suffer such pains as poverty in the world of gods or men, union with hateful persons or things, and separation from the beloved ones. And whilst incessantly whirling in that mass of evils they are sporting, playing, diverting themselves; they do not fear, nor dread, nor are they seized with terror; they do not know, nor mind; they are not startled, do not try to escape, but are enjoying themselves in that triple world which is like unto a burning house, and run hither and thither. Though overwhelmed by that mass of evil, they do not conceive the idea that they must beware of it.

38. Under such circumstances, Sâriputra, the Tathâgata reflects thus: Verily, I am the father of these beings; I must save them from this mass of evil, and bestow on them the immense, inconceivable bliss of Buddha-knowledge, wherewith they shall sport, play, and divert themselves, wherein they shall find their rest.

Then, Sâriputra, the Tathâgata reflects thus: If, in the conviction of my possessing the power of knowledge and magical faculties, I manifest to these beings the knowledge, forces, and absence of hesitation of the Tathâgata, without availing myself of some device, these beings will not escape. For they are attached to the pleasures of the five senses, to worldly pleasures; they will not be freed from birth, old age, disease, death, grief, wailing, pain, melancholy, despondency, by which they are burnt, tormented, vexed, distressed. Unless they are forced to leave the triple world which is like a house the shelter and roof whereof is in a blaze, how are they to get acquainted with Buddha-knowledge?

Now, Sâriputra, even as that man with powerful arms, without using the strength of his arms, attracts his children out of the burning house by an able device, and afterwards gives them magnificent, great carts, so, Sâriputra, the Tathâgata, the Arhat, &c., possessed of knowledge and freedom from all hesitation, without using them, in order to attract the creatures out of the triple world which is like a burning house with decayed roof and shelter, shows, by his knowledge of able devices, three vehicles, viz. the vehicle of the disciples, the vehicle of the Pratyekabuddhas, and the vehicle of the Bodhisattvas. By means of these three vehicles he attracts the creatures and speaks to them thus: Do not delight in this triple world, which is like a burning house, in these miserable forms, sounds, odours, flavours, and contacts. For in delighting in this triple world ye are burnt, heated, inflamed with the thirst inseparable from the pleasures of the five senses. Fly from this triple world; betake yourselves to the three vehicles: the vehicle of the disciples, the vehicle of the Pratyekabuddhas, the vehicle of the Bodhisattvas. I give you my pledge for it, that I shall give you these three vehicles; make an effort to run out of this triple world. And to attract them I say: These vehicles are grand, praised by the Aryas, and provided with most pleasant things; with such you are to sport, play, and divert yourselves in a noble manner. Ye will feel the great delight of the faculties, powers, constituents of Bodhi, meditations, the (eight) degrees of emancipation, self-concentration, and the results of self-concentration, and ye will become greatly happy and cheerful.

Now, Sâriputra, the beings who have become wise have faith in the Tathâgata, the father of the world, and consequently apply themselves to his commandments. Amongst them there are some who, wishing to follow the dictate of an authoritative voice, apply themselves to the commandment of the Tathâgata to acquire the knowledge of the four great truths, for the sake of their own complete Nirvâna.

These one may say to be those who, coveting the vehicle of the disciples, fly from the triple world, just as some of the boys will fly from that burning house, prompted by a desire of getting a cart yoked with deer. Other beings desirous of the science without a master, of self-restraint and tranquillity, apply themselves to the commandment of the Tathâgata to learn to understand causes and effects, for the sake of their own complete Nirvâna. These one may say to be those who, coveting the vehicle of the Pratyekabuddhas, fly from the triple world, just as some of the boys fly from the burning house, prompted by the desire of getting a cart yoked with goats. Others again desirous of the knowledge of the all-knowing, the knowledge of Buddha, the knowledge of the self-born one, the science without a master, apply themselves to the commandment of the Tathâgata to learn to understand the knowledge, powers, and freedom from hesitation of the Tathâgata, for the sake of the common weal and happiness, out of compassion to the world, for the benefit, weal, and happiness of the world at large, both gods and men, for the sake of the complete Nirvâna of all beings. These one may say to be those who, coveting the great vehicle, fly from the triple world. Therefore they are called Bodhisattvas Mahâsattvas. They may be likened to those among the boys who have fled from the burning house prompted by the desire of getting a cart yoked with bullocks.

In the same manner, Sâriputra, as that man, on seeing his children escaped from the burning house and knowing them safely and happily rescued and out of danger, in the consciousness of his great wealth, gives the boys one single grand cart; so, too, Sâriputra, the Tathâgata, the Arhat, &c., on seeing many kotis of beings recovered from the triple world, released from sorrow, fear, terror, and calamity, having escaped owing to the command of the Tathâgata, delivered from all fears, calamities, and difficulties, and having reached the bliss of Nirvâna, so, too, Sâriputra, the Tathâgata, the Arhat, &c., considering that he possesses great wealth of knowledge, power, and absence of hesitation, and that all beings are his children, leads them by no other vehicle but the Buddha-vehicle to full development. But he does not teach a particular Nirvâna for each being; he causes all beings to reach complete Nirvâna by means of the complete Nirvâna of the Tathâgata. And those beings, Sâriputra, who are delivered from the triple world, to them the Tathâgata gives as toys to amuse themselves with the lofty pleasures of the Aryas, the pleasures of meditation, emancipation, self-concentration, and its results; (toys) all of the same kind. Even as that man, Sâriputra, cannot be said to have told a falsehood for having held out to those boys the prospect of three vehicles and given to all of them but one great vehicle, a magnificent vehicle made of seven precious substances, decorated with all sorts of ornaments, a vehicle of one kind, the most egregious of all, so, too, Sâriputra, the Tathâgata, the Arhat, &c., tells no falsehood when by an able device he first holds forth three vehicles and afterwards leads all to complete Nirvâna by the one great vehicle. For the Tathâgata, Sâriputra, who is rich in treasures and storehouses of abundant knowledge, powers, and absence of hesitation, is able to teach all beings the law which is connected with the knowledge of the all-knowing. In this way, Sâriputra, one has to understand how the Tathâgata by an able device and direction shows but one vehicle, the great vehicle.

And on that occasion the Lord uttered the following stanzas:

39. A man has an old house, large, but very infirm; its terraces are decaying and the columns rotten at their bases.

40. The windows and balconies are partly ruined, the wall as well as its coverings and plaster decaying; the coping shows rents from age; the thatch is everywhere pierced with holes.

41. It is inhabited by no less than five hundred beings; containing many cells and closets filled with excrements and disgusting.

42. Its roof-rafters are wholly ruined; the walls and partitions crumbling away; kotis of vultures nestle in it, as well as doves, owls, and other birds.

43. There are in every corner dreadful snakes, most venomous and horrible; scorpions and mice of all sorts; it is the abode of very wicked creatures of every description.

44. Further, one may meet in it here and there beings not belonging to the human race. It is defiled with excrement and urine, and teeming with worms, insects, and fire-flies; it resounds from the howling of dogs and jackals.

45. In it are horrible hyenas that are wont to devour human carcasses; many dogs and jackals greedily seeking the matter of corpses.

Perfection of Wisdom as the Middle Way

The following dense excerpt comes from a massive tract entitled "The Great Treatise on the Perfection of Wisdom" (Sanskrit *Mahā-prajñāpāramitā-upadeśa*, Chinese *Da zhi du lun*). The work, extant only in Chinese, is an early fifth-century translation of a Sanskrit work purportedly written by seminal Mahāyāna philosopher Nāgārjuna. Nāgārjuna, who, modern scholars generally agree, lived in Southern India around the second century, composed a number of demanding treatises that endeavor to prove the emptiness of all phenomena by systematically demonstrating the absurdity of all possible claims to the contrary. The philosophical procedures therein are called Madhyamaka, meaning "that which is in the middle." The connection between the concepts of "the middle" and "emptiness" will be explored shortly.

The Chinese and Tibetan communities who inherited Nāgārjuna's writings understand him to have systematized the religio-philosophical approach articulated in the Perfection of Wisdom literature (as exemplified by *The Heart Sūtra*). To the point, legend tells of Nāgārjuna retrieving the Perfection of Wisdom Sūtras from the kingdom of the *nāgas* (snake or dragon-like beings who live underground or in bodies of water), where the scriptures had been safely kept since the time of the Buddha. The Chinese and Tibetan traditions each ascribe an overlapping but distinct set of texts to Nāgārjuna, however. Moreover, contemporary scholars tend to be suspicious of the attribution of many of these works to Nāgārjuna, including "The Great Treatise on the Perfection of Wisdom." Some have suggested that Kumārajīva (344–413), the monk-scholar who translated "The Great Treatise on the Perfection of Wisdom" into Chinese, may have even participated in the composition of the text, though there is no scholarly consensus about its authorship.

Kumārajīva was himself a figure of enormous import in bringing Mahāyāna scriptures and Madhyamaka treatises to China. Originally from the kingdom of Kucha in the Tarim Basin, Kumārajīva settled in the capital of Chang'an in 402 CE after being taken to China as a prisoner of war some years earlier. Over the ensuing decade or so, Kumārajīva oversaw the translation of as many as three hundred Buddhist works into Chinese, including both *The Lotus Sūtra* and *The Heart Sūtra*. Kumārajīva's spiritual descendants established what came to be called the "Three Treatise" (*san lun* in Chinese) school of Chinese Buddhist thought, so named because of its exegetical focus on three Madhyamaka works—two by Nāgārjuna and a third by Nāgārjuna's disciple Aryadeva.

The brief excerpt that follows develops an important principle of Madhyamaka: the middle way. The idea of the middle way appears in the very first sermon of the Buddha, where it refers to the Buddha's insistence that his followers neither excessively deny themselves everyday needs, like food and sleep, nor excessively indulge in sensory pleasures. The successful spiritual traveler, the Buddha teaches, must cleave a middle way between the two extremes of ascetic denial and indulgence. In our excerpt, however, the middle way applies to understanding the nature of reality. The text calls on us to reject false conceptual extremes of all sorts, including ideas like permanence and impermanence, materiality and immateriality, defilement and purity.

Buddhist philosophers and exegetes have developed a variety of ways of parsing the philosophical ideas referenced in our passage. With that said, some tentative suggestions are in order. The primary polarity denied by Nāgārjuna and his interpreters is the pair "existence/nonexistence." So, when Buddhist philosophers claim that something is "empty," they mean that it neither exists nor does not exist. How so? Take the example of a table. A table does not exist as we think that it does, in so much as it does not exist independently of its parts; nor does it exist independently of our idea of a "table," as explained in the introduction to *The Heart Sūtra*. Yet, the table also does not *not exist*. It would be false to claim that when we point to a table, there is a *nothing* there. "*Nothing*" is another false idea—another false projection of our minds onto reality. We would therefore be incorrect to posit either an *existent* table, or the *nonexistence* of that table. In this way, the table neither exists nor does not exist. An understanding of the table that rejects both the extremes of existence and nonexistence is true to the middle way. Such an understanding is called *prajñāpāramitā*, or "the perfection of wisdom."

How does the philosophical principle of the middle way relate to the spiritual quest? Buddhists across the Mahāyāna world have developed a variety of approaches for cultivating "the perfection of wisdom." To generalize, however, it might be suggested that Buddhist practitioners strive to generate a state of mind wherein two things are accomplished simultaneously. First, the habitual tendency to mistakenly latch on to supposedly existent phenomena is eliminated. These mistaken phenomena might be material objects (like tables), mental ideas (like "liberation"), or some combination of the two (like "me" and "mine"). Second, conceptual thinking—which always entails embracing a conceptual extreme of one sort or another—is altogether eliminated. An enlightened state of mind is therefore one that is capable of cutting through our misconceptions about the world while staying concept-free. As our passage teaches, to abide in the absence of any extreme is the perfection of wisdom (*prajñāpāramitā*)...but only if one can avoid the trap of identifying this mental state as the perfection of wisdom and all other mental states as not the perfection of wisdom.

Joshua Schapiro

135

NĀGĀRUNA'S PHILOSPHY AS PRESENTED IN *THE MAHĀ-PRAJÑĀPĀRAMITĀ-SĀSTRA*

Eternal is one extreme, evanescent is another. Abandoning these two extremes to fare on the Middle Way, this is *prajñāpāramitā*. Similarly permanence and impermanence, pain and pleasure, non-substantial and substantial, self and not-self, etc. (also become extremes when exclusively embraced). Materiality is one extreme, immateriality is another. Visibility is one extreme, invisibility is another; resisting is one extreme, non-resisting is another; composite is one extreme, in-composite is another; defiled is one extreme, undefiled is another; mundane is one extreme, transmundane is another. The same is the case with all forms of duality. (All these could be turned into extremes when exclusively embraced.) Ignorance is one extreme, extinction of ignorance is another; birth and death is one extreme, cessation of birth and death is another; that all things are existent is one extreme, that all things are non-existent are another. Abandoning these two extremes to fare on the Middle Way, this is *prajñāpāramitā*. Bodhisattva is one extreme, the six *pāramitās* is another; the Buddha is one extreme, the *bodhi* is another. Abandoning these two extremes to fare on the Middle Way, this is *prajñāpāramitā*. To put the matter briefly, the six internal senses are one extreme, the six external objects are another; abandoning these two extremes to fare on the Middle Way, this is *prajñāpāramitā*. That this is *prajñāpāramitā* is one extreme; that this is not *prajñāpāramitā* is another extreme; to abandon these two extremes and to fare on the Middle Way, this is *prajñāpāramitā*.

The Practice of Meditation

The following two chapters of meditation instruction come from a renowned Sanskrit narrative poem by second-century poet Aśvaghoṣa entitled the *Saundarananda*. The title, meaning "Handsome Nanda," also alludes to the names of two of the story's chief characters, the half-brother of the Buddha named Nanda and his wife Sundarī. Aśvaghoṣa—who also authored what is perhaps the best-known account of the Buddha's life written in India, called the *Buddhacarita*, or "Acts of the Buddha"—is an early exemplar of Sanskrit *kāvya*, an ornate form of high literature composed in India by Buddhist, Hindu, and Jain authors. *Kāvya* constitutes one of the world's great literary traditions, having not only inspired poets from around the world (including Goethe), but also having spawned an exceedingly sophisticated tradition of literary aesthetics. The *Saundarananda* is a wonderful example of the *kāvya* tradition whose popularity is confirmed by the existence of numerous South Asian sculptures depicting its scenes.

Little is known about Aśvaghoṣa's life, though he probably flourished in the first century of the Common Era. Aśvaghoṣa supposedly was raised in a Brahman family only to convert to Buddhism later in life. One scholar has pointed to Aśvaghoṣa's facility with Brahmanical lore and the presence of conversion episodes in his two great *kāvya* as evidence for the veracity of this story. Legend has it that after being captured by the forces of the great Kushan King Kaniṣka, Aśvaghoṣa instructed the king about the teachings of the Buddha. As with the case of Nāgārjuna, the Chinese and Tibetan traditions attribute a number of religious treatises to Aśvaghoṣa, though it is unlikely that these works were composed by the author of the *Buddhacarita* and *Saundarananda*.

While the *Buddhacarita* recounts the story of the Buddha's journey from being a pampered prince, to a wandering ascetic, to an enlightened teacher, the *Saundarananda* tells the story of the conversion and eventual liberation of the Buddha's half-brother and reluctant disciple, Nanda. As the story goes, Nanda and his wife Sundarī miss the Buddha's triumphant return to his former kingdom Kapilavastu because they are at home absorbed in each other's love. Realizing that he has failed to properly greet his half-brother, Nanda becomes ashamed and sets out to make things right. Upon catching up to the Buddha, Nanda is begrudgingly initiated into the Buddha's order of monks. After Nanda debates one of the Buddha's disciples over the value of life as a celibate monk, the Buddha decides to take Nanda to visit one of the heavenly paradises. There, Nanda witnesses the magnificence of the female residents and acknowledges their superiority in beauty to his wife, Sundarī. Nanda agrees to engage in the austerities that the Buddha teaches in order to win himself rebirth in a heavenly realm and thereby enjoy its beautiful women.

After a lengthy conversation with another of the Buddha's disciples, however, Nanda comes to realize that the rewards of liberation are preferable to rebirth in heaven. Nanda again seeks out the Buddha, who now gives him instructions on how to achieve liberation, some of which are contained in the excerpt that follows. After receiving these instructions, Nanda meditates, achieves realization, and becomes a teacher of the Buddhist path, with his wife soon following in his footsteps and becoming a disciple herself.

The instructions contained in the *Saundarananda* constitute a relatively early written rendering of the path to liberation. They preach the importance of disciplining oneself by controlling the senses and strictly monitoring one's eating and sleeping. They also contain meditation instructions on how to deal with dangerous emotions such as anger, how to respond to obsessive thoughts about one's family and friends, how to control one's breath, how to reflect on death, and how to properly understand the nature of reality.

The following excerpt exposes us to themes common in Buddhist spiritual instructions. The instructions are practical, giving suggestions for how to manage eating and sleeping. They display a concern for the middle way—namely, a path to liberation that entails neither excessive asceticism nor excessive indulgence. The instructions preach mindfulness of one's actions: calling on practitioners to be keenly aware of all movements when sitting, walking, and standing. They also contain ample metaphors for "guarding" one's mind, thereby displaying the tendency in early Buddhist teachings to treat the outside world as dangerous (because of the human tendency to react harmfully to sensory stimulations). Note, for example, how the instructions compare life to a battlefield! The instructions also preach the importance of single-pointed concentration—the technique of focusing all of one's attention on a single object of meditation, such as the tip of one's nose. Such skill in concentration is essential for successfully internalizing the Buddha's observations about the nature of reality. The instructions also contain plentiful references to fundamental Buddhist teachings about the pervasiveness of suffering in the world (notice the familiar reference to the world as a burning house in verse 14.30) and the ever-looming certainty of death.

Joshua Schapiro

CANTO XIV
THE FIRST STEPS

1. Then, closing-up the dam of the senses with the sluice-gate of attention, learn exact measure in the eating of food for the sake of mystic meditation and of freedom from disease.

2. For food taken in excessive quantities impedes the intake and outflow of the breath, induces lassitude and drowsiness and destroys enterprise.

3. And as too much food conduces to disaster, so eating too little leads to loss of capacity.

4. Deficiency of food drains *away* the substance of the body with its brilliance, energy, activity and strength.

5. As the scales fall with too heavy a weight, rise with too light a one and remain level with the proper one, so is it with the body and its nourishment.

6. Therefore you should eat carefully considering your requirements, and should not measure out to yourself too much or too little under the influence of pride.

7. For the fire of the body, if loaded with heavy food, dies down like a small fire covered all at once with a great load of fuel.

8. Complete abstinence from food too is not recommended, for he who refrains from food is extinguished like a fire without fuel.

9. Since no creature drawing breath can exist without food, therefore to take food is not wrong, but a choice of foods is prohibited,

10. Since living beings are not so much attached to any other single object as to superfine food. Know the reason for this teaching.

11. As a wounded man applies salve to his wound to heal it, so food is to be taken to destroy hunger by the man desirous of emancipation.

12. And as the axle of a chariot is greased to enable it to bear a load, so the wise man employs food to enable his life to continue.

13. As parents on a journey, grievous though they would find it, would eat the flesh of their children to enable them to cross the desert,

14. So food should be eaten with circumspection, not to obtain splendour or beauty of form or out of intoxication or wantonness.

15. For food is intended for the support of the body; like a prop for the support of a weak dwelling that is falling down.

16. As a man will construct a boat with great labour and even carry it, not because he loves it, but simply in order to cross a great flood,

17. So men of insight support the body by the usual means, not out of love for it, but simply to cross the flood of suffering.

18. Just as a man who is being oppressed, gives in grief to an enemy, not out of devotion to him or of desire for anything, but merely to preserve his life,

19. So the Yoga adept tenders food to his body merely to suppress hunger, not out of gluttony or devotion to it.

20. After passing the day self-controlled in the restraint of your mind, you should shake off drowsiness and spend the night to in the practice of Yoga.

21. And do not deem your consciousness to be then properly conscious, when during that consciousness drowsiness may make itself felt in your heart.

22. When overcome, by drowsiness, always apply to your mind the principles of energy and steadfastness, of strength and courage.

23. You should repeat aloud those Scriptures you have studied, and you should teach them to others and reflect on them yourself.

24. In order to keep always awake, wet your face with water, look round in all directions and fix your gaze on the stars.

25. Walk about or sit down at night, keeping your mind from wandering and your senses directed inwards, steady and under control.

26. Drowsiness has no hold on a man affected by fear, love or grief. Therefore practice these three feelings when drowsiness assails you.

27. You should foster fear of the approach' of death, love in marriage with the Law and grief at the boundless sufferings from birth.

28. This and the like, my friend, is the course to be followed to keep awake. For what wise man would let his life become unproductive by lying down to sleep.

29. It is no more fitting for the wise man who desires to escape from the great danger to sleep in neglect of the snakes of the vices than for a man to sleep in neglect of snakes in his house.

30. For since the world of the living is blazing with the fires of death, disease, and old age, who would lie down in it without agitation, any more than in a burning house?

31. Therefore recognising sleep to be mental darkness; do not let it overtake you while the *vices*, like armed foes, are still unquelled.

32. But after passing the first of the three night-watches in activity, you should lie down to rest your body in full control of yourself.

33. Lie with tranquil mind on your right side; keeping present the idea of light and bearing watchfulness in your heart.

34. Rise up in the third watch and, either walking or sitting, practise Yoga again in purity of mind with your senses under guard.

35. Then fully conscious of all your actions, fix your attention on your sitting, moving, standing, looking, speaking and so on.

36. The man, whose attention is directed towards the door (of his actions) like a doorkeeper towards his door, is not molested by the vices, any more than a guarded town is attacked by its foes.

37. No sin is produced in him whose attention is fixed on

his body. It guards his thoughts in all circumstances, as a nurse guards a child.

38. But he who licks the *armour* of attention is a target for the vices, as the unarmed man is a target on the battlefield for the enemy.

39. The mind which is not guarded by attention is to be recognised as unprotected, like a sightless man walking over uneven ground without a guide.

40. Loss of attention is the reason that men are attached to what is calamitous and averse from their proper aims and fail to take alarm in the presence of danger.

41. And it is attention which, like a herdsman after his scattered vows, goes after all the virtues, discipline, etc., where they are, each in its own domain.

42. Lost is the everlasting good for him whose attention is distracted; it is within the grasp of him whose attention is directed to his body.

43. Where is the noble plan for him who lacks attention? And he who has not the noble plan has lost the holy Path.

44. He who has lost the holy Path has lost the place where death is not; and he who has lost that place is not delivered from suffering.

45. Therefore when moving, you should think 'I am moving', and when standing, 'I am standing', keeping your attention fixed on these and the like occasions.

46. Thus, my friend, betake yourself to a seat or couch, suitable for Yoga, solitary and free from noise ; for by first making the body solitary it is easy to attain discrimination of Mind.

47. For the man filled with passion, who has not attained tranquillity of the feelings and does not adopt the solitary method, fails to find the Path and is hurt like a man walking on very thorny ground.

48. If an enquiring man has not visualised the truth and is surrounded by the varied manifestations of sensual objects, he

cannot easily restrain his mind, just as a crop-eating bull is not easily to be kept out of a field of corn.

49. But as the brightly shining fire, when not fanned by the wind, dies down, so the thoughts, when not subject to any stimulus, come to rest with little trouble in solitude.

50. That man is to be considered successful who rejoices in solitude and avoids contact with others like a thorn, eating in any place whatever there is and wearing any clothes whatsoever, living anywhere sufficient to himself; for his mind is made up and he knows the taste of the bliss of tranquillity.

51. If a man live, pure with tranquil heart and indifferent to the opposites, in a solitary place in the world which delights in the opposites and has its heart disturbed by sensual objects, then he drinks the draught of wisdom as if it were nectar, and with heart appeased he reaches discrimination and deplores the world which is subject to attachment and greedy for sensual objects.

52. If he continually rejoices living alone in a deserted place, if he avoids intercourse with the sources of sin, as if they were enemies, and if living sufficient to himself he drinks the water of ecstasy, then he enjoys a happiness greater than the realm of the Lord of the thirty gods could give him.

CANTO XV
EMPTYING THE MIND

1. Taking up the best posture of meditation in some solitary place, setting your body upright and keeping your attention present,

2. You should make your wandering mind wholly intent on an object such as the tip of your nose or your forehead or the space between the brows.

3. If that fever of the mind, namely, the thought of passion, should molest you, it must not be tolerated but must be shaken off like dust which has lodged on one's clothes.

4. Although you have cast off the passions through insight, you must destroy them by their opposite, as darkness by light.

5. There remains a latent tendency towards them, like a fire covered up with ashes; it must be quenched by meditation, my friend, like fire by water.

6. For they become active again from that tendency, like shoots from a seed; by destroying it they would cease to exist, just as there are no shoots when the seed is destroyed.

7. Realise therefore what sufferings are caused by the passions in their acquisition, etc. to those subject to them and cut them off, root and all, like enemies who style themselves friends.

8. For the passions should be killed like poisonous snakes, being impermanent, of their nature subject to loss, empty of real value, the causes of calamity and shared by many others (who may deprive you of them).

9. They lead to suffering in the quest for them, but not to tranquillity in their retention. They lead to great grief in the losing, but to no satisfaction in the consummation.

10. He is lost who considers satisfaction to lie in great wealth, success to consist in reaching Paradise and pleasure to be born from the passions.

11. Take heed not to fix your attention in this world on the passions, which are unstable, unreal, hollow and uncertain; the pleasure which they give is but a product of the imagination.

12. Should your mind be troubled by malevolence or the desire to hurt, it should *be made calm* by their counteragent, as muddied water is made clear by a jewel.

13. Know their counteragents to be benevolence and compassion; for there is ever an opposition between them as between light and darkness.

14. He who has given up evil ways and yet in whom malevolence is active throws dirt over himself, as an elephant throws dirt over his body after his bath.

15. For what religious man, instinct with compassion, would

cause further suffering to mortals already suffering from disease, death, old age, etc.

16. A man may or may not cause hurt to another by his malevolent mind in this world, but in either case the mind of the man of malevolent thoughts is forthwith burned up.

17. Therefore you should cultivate thoughts of benevolence and compassion towards all beings, not of malevolence or the desire to hurt.

18. For through habit a man's thoughts become inclined to whatever he reflects on continually.

19. Therefore you should abandon evil and think only of what is good; for it will redound to your advantage in this world and to the attainment of the supreme goal.

20. For evil thoughts gain in a strength by being cherished in the heart and breed disaster alike for oneself and for others.

21. They lead not only to one's own ruin by placing an obstacle in the way of the highest good, but also to the ruin of others' devotion by destruction of the state of grace.

22. Moreover you should practise concentration in the workings of your mind, but in no circumstances should you think evil thoughts, my friend.

23. For the thought that works in the mind towards enjoyment of threefold passion both fails to attain excellence and also conduces to bondage.

24. A defiled state of mind involves delusion, resulting in the destruction of others and in one's own sinfulness, and leads to Hell.

25. Therefore do not destroy yourself by evil thoughts, when you are well-armed and adorned with the *jewels*, like a man who in digging up the ground casts earth in his well-armed and bejewelled body.

26. Just as an ignoramus would burn costly aloe wood like ordinary fuel, so by not following the plan one would destroy one's existence here as a human being.

27. And the man who, passing over the Law that leads to final beatitude, should cultivate evil thoughts is like the man who should pass over the jewels and take away lumps of earth from a jewel-island.

28. The man who, having obtained the state of a human being, should follow sin and not good is like a man who should go to the Himalayas and eat poison and not health-giving herbs.

29. You should understand this and should cast out thoughts by their counteragents, as a wedge is driven not from a cleft in a log by a slender counter-wedge.

The Tibetan Book of the Dead

The primary source for the following death instructions is a composition entitled "Liberation upon Hearing in the Bardo," commonly referred to as *The Tibetan Book of the Dead*. Traditionally believed to have been composed by a mythic figure of the eighth century, the instructions were discovered by a visionary named Karma Lingpa in the fourteenth century before being standardized in the seventeenth century and printed in the eighteenth century.

The Tibetan Book of the Dead is an example of a Tibetan "treasure text." Tibetans believe that the majority of these treasure texts were actually composed and hidden by Padmasambhava, a legendary hero of the eighth century who ensured Buddhism's acceptance in Tibet by conquering and converting local spirits. Beginning around the eleventh century, Tibetans began to find these compositions hidden behind rocks or in caves, often written in code on small scraps of yellow paper; sometimes Padmasambhava's teachings even appeared directly in the treasure discoverer's mind. While rival Tibetan religious leaders and polemicists have often disputed the authority of treasure revelations, the practice of discovering treasures continues to this day.

Karma Lingpa found the materials that were expanded into *The Tibetan Book of the Dead* on a small mountain peak in Southeast Tibet. The primary use of the "Liberation upon Hearing" eventually became liturgical, however. Lamas (Tibetan Buddhist teachers) chant the text in the homes of recently deceased persons with the hope that the instructions will guide the deceased person's mind to a good rebirth. Because of its ritual import, a written or printed edition of the *Book of the Dead* is considered to be powerful in its own right.

Buddhism

Unlike some Buddhist cultures, in which people understand rebirth to occur immediately following death, Tibetans conceive of an intermediary state, called the "*bardo*," where one's mental continuum resides for up to forty-nine days before being reborn into one of the six realms of existence (as a human, an animal, a hungry ghost, a hell-dweller, a god, or a jealous god). Rebirth occurs because one's karmic deeds (past actions, thoughts, and emotions) create imprints on one's mind-stream. In the *bardo*, these imprints, parsed here as "dispositions," manifest in an attraction to one of the six realms. So, as our selection describes, someone with a disposition toward envy may be reborn as a jealous god (Sanskrit: *asura*). Before rebirth, however, the dead experience a series of visions projected by their own minds. These visions captured the imagination of twentieth-century investigators of the subconscious such as Carl Jung and Timothy Leary, both of whom played roles in popularizing of the so-called *Tibetan Book of the Dead* in the English-speaking world.

Tibetan Buddhists consider the *bardo* experience to be a valuable opportunity for liberation from the cycle of rebirth, making it a uniquely important moment on the spiritual path. Because one's mind travels free of a physical body in the *bardo* state, one almost literally comes face to face with one's own mind in its subtlest form. Of course, most people are distracted by the various scary experiences described in the following passage, such as mentally projected images of wrathful deities, and are unable to recognize in them the workings of their own minds. Given the proper training during one's life, however, a practitioner can conceivably recognize the mind in the *bardo* for what it is: entirely empty (nonsubstantial, never produced nor destroyed) yet still miraculously capable of perceptions. As one Tibetan tradition called the Great Perfection (*rdzogs chen*) commonly puts it, one's mind is by nature empty yet luminous. By recognizing this empty yet luminous nature of one's own mind in the *bardo*, one achieves liberation instantaneously.

Here we might note one prevalent strategy for achieving enlightenment in Tibetan traditions: the simultaneous recogni-

150

tion of the emptiness of the mind (its lack of substantiality, independence, or essence) and its "luminous" capacity (exemplified by the experience of one's mind as bright light). This "luminosity" captures the capacity for the mind, despite its ultimately empty nature, to generate our experience of the phenomenal world: sights, sounds, smells, thoughts, and so on. If one can face one's empty yet luminous mind without fear or attachment, two primary causes of suffering, then one has taken a huge step toward liberation.

The excerpt that follows is actually a summation of Tibetan materials, compiled by scholar Edward Conze and based on well-known English and French translations by other scholars. Conze's summary, while a simplification of complex material, nonetheless introduces us to important Tibetan ideas about death and rebirth, the possibility of liberation, and the power of the mind.

Joshua Schapiro

LIFE AFTER DEATH, AND 'THE BOOK OF THE DEAD'

This is what the Lama reads to the dying person:

Preamble

I now transmit to you the profound teachings which I have myself received from my Teacher, and, through him, from the long line of initiated Gurus. Pay attention to it now, and do not allow yourself to be distracted by other thoughts! Remain lucid and calm, and bear in mind what you hear! If you suffer, do not give in to the pain! If restful numbness overtakes you, if you swoon away, into a peaceful forgetting—do not surrender yourself to that! Remain watchful and alert!

The factors which made up the person known as E.C. are about to disperse. Your mental activities are separating themselves from your body, and they are about to enter the intermediary state. Rouse your energy, so that you may enter this state self-possessed and in full consciousness!

The moment of death, and the clear light of Pure Reality

First of all there will appear to you, swifter than lightning, the luminous splendour of the colourless light of Emptiness, and that will surround you on all sides. Terrified, you will want to flee from the radiance, and you may well lose consciousness. Try to submerge yourself in that light, giving up all belief in a separate self, all attachment to your illusory ego. Recognize that the boundless Light of this true Reality is your own true self, and you shall be saved!

Few, however, are those who, having missed salvation during their life on earth, can attain it during this brief instant which passes so quickly. The overwhelming majority are shocked into unconsciousness by the terror they feel.

The emergence of a subtle body

If you miss salvation at that moment, you will be forced to have a number of further dreams, both pleasant and unpleasant. Even they offer you a chance to gain understanding, as long as you remain vigilant and alert. A few days after death there suddenly emerges a subtle illusory dream-body, also known as the 'mental body'. It is impregnated with the after-effects of your past desires, endowed with all sense-faculties, and has the power of unimpeded motion. It can go right through rocks, hills, boulders, and walls, and in an instant it can traverse any distance. Even after the physical sense-organs are dissolved, sights, sounds, smells, tastes, and touches will be perceived, and ideas will be formed. These are the result of the energy still residing in the six kinds of consciousness, the after-effects of what you did with your body and mind in the past. But you must know that all you perceive is a mere vision, a mere illusion, and does not reflect any really existing objects. Have no fear, and form no attachment! View it all even mindedly, without like or dislike!

The experience of the spiritual realities

Three and a half days after your death, Buddhas and Bodhisattvas will for seven days appear to you in their benign and peaceful aspect. Their light will shine upon you, but it will be so radiant that you will scarcely be able to look at it. Wonderful and delightful though they are, the Buddhas may nevertheless frighten you. Do not give in to your fright! Do not run away! Serenely contemplate the spectacle before you! Overcome your fear, and feel no desire! Realize that these are the rays of the grace or the Buddhas, who come to receive you into their Buddha-realms. Pray to them with intense faith and humility, and, in a halo of rainbow light, you will merge into the heart of the divine Father-Mother, and take up your abode in one of the realms of the Buddhas. Thereby you may still at this moment win you salvation.

But if you miss it, you will next, for another seven days, be confronted with the angry deities, and the Guardians of the Faith, surrounded by their followers in tumultuous array, many of them in the form of animals which you have never seen in the life you left. Bathed in multicoloured light they stand before you, threatening you and barring your passage.

Loud are their voices, with which they shout, 'Hit him! Hit him! Kill him! Kill him!' is what you have to hear, because you turned a deaf ear to the saving truths of religion! All these forms are strange to you, you do not recognize them for what they are. They terrify you beyond words, and yet it is you who have created the. Do not give in to your fright, resist your mental confusion! All this is unreal, and what you see are the contents of your own mind in conflict with itself. All these terrifying deities, witches, and demons around you—fear them not, flee them not! They are but the benevolent Buddhas and Bodhisattvas, changed in their outward aspect. In you alone are the five wisdoms, the source of the benign spirits! In you alone are the five poisons, the source of the angry spirits! It is from your own mind therefore that all this has sprung. What you see here is but the reflection of the contents of your own mind the Mirror of the Void. If at this point you should manage to understand that, the shock of this insight will stun you your subtle body will disperse into a rainbow, and you will find yourself in paradise among the angels.

Seeking rebirth

But if you fail to grasp the meaning of what you taught, if you still continue to feel a desire to exist as an individual, then you are now doomed to again re-enter the wheel of becoming.

The judgement

You are now before Yama, Kin of the Dead. In vain will you try to lie, and to deny or conceal the evil deeds you have done.

The Judge holds up before you the shining mirror of Karma, wherein all your deeds are reflected. But again you have to deal with dream in ages, which you yourself have made, and which you project outside, without recognizing them as your own work. The mirror in which Yama seems to read your past is your own memory, and also his judgement is your own. It is you yourself who pronounce your own judgement, which in its turn determines your next rebirth.

No terrible God pushes you into it; you go there quite on your own. The shapes of the frightening monsters who take hold of you, place a rope round your neck and drag you along, are just an illusion which you create from the forces within you. Know that apart from these karmic forces there is no Judge of the Dead, no gods, and no demons. Knowing that, you will be free!

The desire for rebirth

At this juncture you will realize that you are dead. You will think, 'I am dead! What shall I do?' and you will feel as miserable as a fish out of water on red-hot embers. Your consciousness, having no object on which to rest, will be like a feather tossed about by the wind, riding on the horse of breath. At about that time the fierce wind of karma, terrific and hard to bear, will drive you onwards, from behind, in dreadful gusts. And after a while the thought will occur to you, 'O what would I not give to possess a body!' But because you can at first find no place for you to enter into, you will be dissatisfied and have the sensation of being squeezed into cracks and crevices amidst rocks and boulders.

The dawning of the lights of the six places of rebirth

Then there will shine upon you the lights of the six places of rebirth. The light of the place in which you will be reborn will shine most prominently, but it is your own karmic disposition which decides about your choice. The rays of lights which will guide you to the various worlds will seem to you restful and friendly compared with the blinding flash of light which met you at first.

If you have deserved it by your good deeds, a white light will guide you into one of the heavens, and for a while you will have some happiness among the gods. Habits of envy and ambition will attract you to the red light, which leads to rebirth among the warlike Asuras, forever agitated by anger and envy. If you feel drawn to a blue light, you will find yourself again a human being, and well you remember how little happiness that brought you! If you had a heavy and dull mind, you will choose the green light, which leads you to the world of animals, unhappy because insecure and excluded from the knowledge which brings salvation. A ray of dull yellow will lead you to the world of the ghosts, and, finally, a ray of the colour of darkish smoke into the hells. Try to desist, if you can! Think of the Buddhas and Bodhisattvas! Recall that all these visions are unreal, control your mind, feel amity towards all that lives! And do not be afraid! You alone are the source of all these different rays. In you alone they exist, and so do the worlds to which they lead. Feel not attracted or repelled, but remain even minded and calm!

Reincarnation

If so far you have been deaf to the teaching, listen to it now! An overpowering craving will come over you for the sense-experiences which you remember having had in the past, and which through your lack of sense-organs you cannot now have. Your desire for rebirth becomes more and more urgent; it becomes a real torment to you. This desire now racks you; you do not, however, experience it for what it is, but feel it as a deep thirst which parches you as you wander along, harassed, among deserts of burning sands. Whenever you try to take some rest, monstrous forms rise up before you. Some have animal heads on human bodies, others are gigantic birds with huge wings and claws. Their howlings and their whips drive you on, and then a hurricane carries you along, with those demonic beings in hot pursuit. Greatly anxious, you will look for a safe place of refuge.

Everywhere around you, you will see animals and humans in the act of sexual intercourse. You envy them, and the sight attracts you. If your karmic coefficients destine you to become a male, you feel attracted to the females and you hate the males you see. If you are destined to become a female, you will feel love for the males and hatred for the females you see. Do not go near the couples you see, do not try to interpose yourself between them, do not try to take the place of one of them! The feeling which you would then experience would make you faint away, just at the moment when egg and sperm are about to unite. And afterwards you will find that you have been conceived as a human being or as an animal.

Letter to Lord Nakamura

Bassui Tokushō (1327–1387), author of the *Letter to Lord Nakamura*, was a popular Zen teacher of the Rinzai lineage, one of the three largest lineages recognized by Zen Buddhists. Zen Buddhism is the Japanese continuation of Chinese Chan Buddhism, itself a Mahāyāna sect that developed in the late sixth century. Due to the work of a handful of skilled Japanese visitors to the United States in the mid-twentieth century and the writings of their talented students, Zen is probably the most well known form of Buddhism in the United States today (though it is not the one with the greatest number of adherents).

Living during a time of intense civil unrest in Japan, Bassui built a reputation as a skillful teacher while residing at his temple and hermitage Kogaku-ji, near Mount Fuji. Bassui is known to have expressed his skepticism about the institutional Buddhism of his day, having criticized popular ceremonies wherein large masses of people would temporarily become monks, for example. Before moving to Kogaku-ji, Bassui spent much of his life in relative isolation, making pilgrimages, and practicing and studying in forests, hills, and mountains surrounding temples. In addition to authoring a well-known collection of instructions to his disciples entitled "Mud and Water from Enzan," Bassui also wrote many instructional letters, one of which is the *Letter to Lord Nakamura*. Bassui composed his dharma instructions, given to both monks and laity, in an easily understood style.

The *Letter to Nakamura* exemplifies Bassui's approach to the spiritual quest. He instructs his students to search obsessively for the nature of their mind, with the assumption being that one's mind is itself naturally enlightened. This idea of "original enlightenment" (*hongaku* in Japanese)—that our minds are naturally

159

unchanging, pure, and already enlightened—is a crucial concept in Japanese Buddhism that developed in the Tendai tradition in the eleventh century. Given "original enlightenment," practitioners do not need to *transform* themselves from impure, suffering beings to pure, liberated ones. The path to spiritual realization rather entails *discovering* one's already enlightened nature.

True to this idea, Bassui returns time and again to the theme of discovering one's originally enlightened mind. The mind, as he explains, has no location, being neither within our bodies, without, nor in between. Bassui is obsessed with searching for this mind, which he understands to be that which truly experiences sensory perception. He frequently refers to the mind as the "Master" who sees and hears, and he prods his disciples to look for what it is that hears.

Biographical accounts of Bassui's life attest to his lifelong cultivation of doubt and uncertainty about accepted ideas in his culture. Not surprisingly, then, Bassui teaches that doubt is essential to the spiritual journey. Obsessive doubt, which provokes an "existential quandary" in the words of one scholar, has long been an experience cultivated by Chan students.

Persistent, doubt-filled searching is not the whole story, however. Bassui also teaches that enlightenment entails a certain kind of understanding of one's mind, an understanding that is free from any conceptual thought (a theme that we explored in connection to the "Perfection of Wisdom as the Middle Way" selection). One develops such an understanding through meditation (*zazen* in Japanese), sometimes through the application of the technique of non-abiding (not allowing the mind to settle on any single object). The *Letter to Nakamura* contains some of Bassui's instructions on how to meditate properly, which well-encapsulate the natural harmony between doubt-filled searching and resting in non-conceptuality: "[n]either loathe nor be charmed by any of your thoughts. With your mind turned inward, look steadily into their source and the delusive feelings and perceptions in which they are rooted will evaporate."

Letter to Lord Nakamura

The *Letter to Nakamura* also contains a short, enigmatic dialogue between a Zen master named Baso and a layman named Ho. This dialogue is an example of an important literary form called a *kōan* (*gong'an* in Chinese). *Kōans*, or "public cases," are literary records of past interactions between enlightened masters and their disciples. These records have historically served a whole range of functions but are often used as the content of meditative contemplation for Zen students. With that said, the proper way to study these dialogues has often been debated by Zen Buddhists. Bassui, for example, criticized some of his peers for their overly intellectual approach to *kōan* study. The *Letter to Nakamura* gives us a view of what one approach to *kōan* interpretation looks like.

The translation that follows is by famous twentieth-century Zen teacher Philip Kapleau (b. 1912). Kapleau was a student of controversial but influential Zen teacher Hakuun Yasutani (1885–1973) in Japan. After studying in Japan for eleven years, Kapleau moved to Rochester, New York, and opened a Buddhist practice center that is still thriving today. His *The Three Pillars of Zen*, wherein this translation originally appears, was first published in 1965. Notable for its inclusion of intimate spiritual interviews between Hakuun Yasutani and his students, it remains one of the best-selling English introductions to Zen Buddhism.

Joshua Schapiro

3 / TO LORD NAKAMURA, GOVERNOR OF AKI PROVINCE /

You ask me how to practice Zen with reference to this phrase from a sutra: "Mind, having no fixed abode, should flow forth." There is no express method for attaining enlightenment. If you but look into your Self-nature directly, not allowing yourself to be deflected, the Mind flower will come into bloom. Hence the sutra says: "Mind, having no fixed abode, should flow forth." Thousands of words spoken directly by Buddhas and Patriarchs add up to this one phrase. Mind is the True-nature of things, transcending all forms. The True-nature is the Way. The Way is Buddha. Buddha is Mind. Mind is not within or without or in between. It is not being or nothingness or non-being or non-nothingness or Buddha or mind or matter. So it is called the abodeless Mind. This Mind sees colors with the eyes, hears sounds with the ears. Look for this master directly!

A Zen master [Rinzai] of old says: "One's body, composed of the four primal elements, can't hear or understand this preaching. The spleen or stomach or liver or gall bladder can't hear or understand this preaching. Empty-space can't understand it. Then what does hear and understand?" Strive to perceive directly. If your mind remains attached to any form or feeling whatsoever, or is affected by logical reasoning or conceptual thinking, you are as far from true realization as heaven is from earth.

How can you cut off at a stroke the sufferings of birth-and-death? As soon as you consider how to advance, you get lost in reasoning; but if you quit you are adverse to the highest path. To be able neither to advance nor to quit is to be a "breathing corpse." If in spite of this dilemma you empty your mind of all thoughts and push on with your zazen, you are bound to enlighten yourself and apprehend the phrase "Mind, having no fixed abode, should flow forth." Instantly you will grasp the sense of all Zen dialogue as well as the profound and subtle meaning of the countless sutras.

The layman Ho asked Baso: "What is it that transcends everything in the universe?" Baso answered: "I will tell you after you have drunk up the waters of the West River in one gulp. Ho instantly became deeply enlightened. See here, what does this mean? Does it explain the phrase "Mind, having no fixed abode, should flow forth," or does it point to the very one reading this? If you still don't comprehend, go back to questioning, "What is hearing now?" Find out this very moment! The problem of birth-and-death is momentous, and the world moves fast. Make the most of time, for it waits for no one.

Your own Mind is intrinsically Buddha. Buddhas are those who have realized this. Those who haven't are the so-called ordinary sentient beings. Sleeping and working, standing and sitting, ask yourself, "What is my own Mind?" looking into the source from which your thoughts arise. What is this subject that right now perceives, thinks, moves, works, goes forth, or returns? To know it you must intensely absorb yourself in the question. But even though you do not realize it in this life, beyond a doubt you will in the next because of your present efforts.

In your zazen think in terms of neither good nor evil. Don't try to stop thoughts from arising, only ask yourself: "What is my own Mind?" Now, even when your questioning goes deeper and deeper you will get no answer until finally you will reach a cul-de-sac, your thinking totally checked. You won't find anything within that can be called "I" or "Mind." But who is it that understands all this? Continue to probe more deeply yet and the mind that perceives there is nothing will vanish; you will no longer be aware of questioning but only of emptiness. When awareness of even emptiness disappears, you will realize there is no Buddha outside Mind and no Mind outside Buddha. Now for the first time you will discover that when you do not hear with your ears you are truly hearing, and when you do not see with your eyes you are

163

really seeing Buddhas of the past, present, and future. But don't cling to any of this, just experience it for yourself!

See here, what is your own Mind? Everyone's Original-nature is not less than Buddha. But since men doubt this and search for Buddha and Truth outside their Mind, they fail to attain enlightenment, being helplessly driven within cycles of birth-and-death, entangled in karma both good and bad. The source of all karma bondage is delusion, i.e., the thoughts, feelings, and perceptions [stemming from ignorance]. Rid yourself of them and you are emancipated. Just as ash covering a charcoal fire is dispersed when the fire is fanned, so these delusions vanish once you realize your Self-nature.

During zazen neither loathe nor be charmed by any of your thoughts. With your mind turned inward, look steadily into their source and the delusive feelings and perceptions in which they are rooted will evaporate. This is not yet Self-realization, however, even though your mind becomes bright and empty like the sky, you have awareness of neither inner nor outer, and all the ten quarters seem clear and luminous. To take this for realization is to mistake a mirage for reality. Now ever more intensely search this mind of yours which hears. Your physical body, composed of the four basic elements, is like a phantom, without reality, yet apart from this body there is no mind. The empty-space of ten quarters can neither see nor hear; still, something within you does hear and distinguish sounds. Who or what is it? When this question totally ignites you, distinctions of good and evil, awareness of being or emptiness, vanish like a light extinguished on a dark night. Though you are no longer consciously aware of yourself; still you can hear and know you exist. Try as you will to discover the subject hearing, your efforts will fail and you will find yourself at an impasse. All at once your mind will burst into great enlightenment and you will feel as though you have risen from the dead, laughing loudly and clapping your hands in delight. Now for the first time you will know that Mind itself is Buddha. Were someone to ask, "What does one's Buddha-mind look like?"

I would answer: "In the trees fish play, in the deep sea birds are flying." What does this mean? If you don't understand it, look into your own Mind and ask yourself: "What is he, this master who sees and hears?"

Make the most of time: it waits for no one.

FOUR

JUDAISM

Song of Songs

The *Song of Songs* is an appropriate selection with which to begin a discussion of Jewish spirituality and mysticism.

On the one hand, this lush series of love poems traditionally ascribed to King Solomon is found within the Hebrew Bible. As such, the *Song of Songs* is part of mainstream Jewish—and Christian—religion and spirituality, rather than a highly esoteric guide for finding one's way into a deeper relationship with God than that typically offered by everyday religion to its practitioners. The intensity of spiritual relationship expressed in this text became part of the canon at precisely the time when Judaism and Christianity were contending not only with each other but with paganism on the topic of how best to understand divinity and relate to it.

On the other hand, precisely because this is love poetry, with imagery that some might consider rather graphic for a text that is supposed to be part of divinely inspired canon—"Let him kiss me with the kisses of his mouth!...My beloved is to me a bag of myrrh that lies between my breasts....Upon my bed at night I sought him whom my soul loves...How beautiful you are my love...your lips are like a crimson thread...your two breasts are like two fawns, twins of a gazelle...my beloved thrust his hand into the opening, and my inmost being yearned for him..."—the *Song of Songs* found its way into the Hebrew Bible rather late. It was one of the last texts to be accepted into the Jewish canon.

That acceptance was made possible only through the inspired thinking of Rabbi Akiva, perhaps the preeminent Jewish leader of the early second century, but also renowned, according to tradition, as a successful practitioner of esoteric communication with God: a mystic. Akiva convinced his fellow rabbis that the *Song of Songs* is an extended allegory of the love relationship between God and the People Israel: the Jewish people. Thus it asserts the spiritual "correctness" of Judaism against diverse challenges to that assertion.

As such, the details of the text that might under other circumstances be considered even pornographic become merely vivid expressions of the spiritual passion that governs the relationship between Jews and God. That relationship is analogized to the relationship between a groom and his bride, the lover and the beloved.

Of course, within the mystical traditions that variously connect Jewish thinking with that found in Christianity as well as in Islam, Hinduism, and other faiths, the sort of imagery offered in the *Song of Songs* could be, and became, a perfect vehicle for expressing both the goal of the mystic and the condition of having achieved that goal. For the mystic seeks absolute and perfect union with God, like the lover and the beloved.

Paradoxically, one aspect of the Jewish mystical tradition (primarily the earlier, *Merkavah* aspect) emphasizes the awesome distance of God from us and the inconceivable difficulty for the aspiring mystic in trying to overcome that distance in order to merge with God. The other aspect (primarily the kabbalistic aspect) of the tradition emphasizes God's loving closeness to us, God's abiding and never wavering presence among us.

So the *Song of Songs* offers itself as an early allegorical articulation of that proximity. Moreover, in being a part of the canon and therefore expressing the very words of God as they have been inspired to the writer, be it King Solomon or any other analogous figure from the era of Israelite-Judaean prophecy, it also presents the opportunity for contemplating—it demands an interpretive focus upon—the poem's contents. Both the overall message of union between lovers—the sought-for union between mystic/ lover and God/beloved, in which they cease to be separate but become united as one being—and the ins and outs of every word, every syllable, the spaces between the letters, the sounds they represent, and the shapes they assume on the printed page: all of these tiny and larger details are inherent grist for the mystical mill.

Not surprisingly, focus on the *Song of Songs* serves not only as a stepping-off point for Jewish mysticism as it seeks means and modes through which to express the ineffable, but also presents itself along parallel lines to early Christian mystical writings as an object of intense interest. Thus figures such as Origen and St. Augustine wrote commentaries on the text in which its role as an articulation of seeking and achieving oneness with God was emphasized.

Ori Z. Soltes

1The Song of Songs, which is Solomon's.

²Let him kiss me with the kisses of his mouth!
For your love is better than wine,
³ your anointing oils are fragrant,
your name is perfume poured out;
    therefore the maidens love you.
⁴Draw me after you, let us make haste.
    The king has brought me into his chambers.
We will exult and rejoice in you;
    we will extol your love more than wine;
    rightly do they love you.

⁵I am black and beautiful,
    O daughters of Jerusalem,
like the tents of Kedar,
    like the curtains of Solomon.
⁶Do not gaze at me because I am dark,
    because the sun has gazed on me.
My mother's sons were angry with me;
    they made me keeper of the vineyards,
    but my own vineyard I have not kept!
⁷Tell me, you whom my soul loves,
    where you pasture your flock,
    where you make it lie down at noon;
for why should I be like one who is veiled
    beside the flocks of your companions?

⁸If you do not know,
    O fairest among women,
follow the tracks of the flock,
    and pasture your kids
    beside the shepherds' tents.

⁹I compare you, my love,
    to a mare among Pharaoh's chariots.
¹⁰Your cheeks are comely with ornaments,
    your neck with strings of jewels.
¹¹We will make you ornaments of gold,
    studded with silver.

¹²While the king was on his couch,
    my nard gave forth its fragrance.
¹³My beloved is to me a bag of myrrh
    that lies between my breasts.
¹⁴My beloved is to me a cluster of henna blossoms
    in the vineyards of En-gedi.

¹⁵Ah, you are beautiful, my love;
    ah, you are beautiful;
    your eyes are doves.
¹⁶Ah, you are beautiful, my beloved,
    truly lovely.
Our couch is green;
¹⁷ the beams of our house are cedar,
    our rafters are pine.

2I am a rose of Sharon,
    a lily of the valleys.

²As a lily among brambles,
    so is my love among maidens.

³As an apple tree among the trees of the wood,
    so is my beloved among young men.
With great delight I sat in his shadow,
    and his fruit was sweet to my taste.
⁴He brought me to the banqueting house,
    and his intention towards me was love.

⁵Sustain me with raisins,
   refresh me with apples;
   for I am faint with love.
⁶O that his left hand were under my head,
   and that his right hand embraced me!
⁷I adjure you, O daughters of Jerusalem,
   by the gazelles or the wild does:
do not stir up or awaken love
   until it is ready!

⁸The voice of my beloved!
   Look, he comes,
leaping upon the mountains,
   bounding over the hills.
⁹My beloved is like a gazelle
   or a young stag.
Look, there he stands
   behind our wall,
gazing in at the windows,
   looking through the lattice.
¹⁰My beloved speaks and says to me:
'Arise, my love, my fair one,
   and come away;
¹¹for now the winter is past,
   the rain is over and gone.
¹²The flowers appear on the earth;
   the time of singing has come,
and the voice of the turtle-dove
   is heard in our land.
¹³The fig tree puts forth its figs,
   and the vines are in blossom;
   they give forth fragrance.
Arise, my love, my fair one,
   and come away.

[14]O my dove, in the clefts of the rock,
  in the covert of the cliff,
let me see your face,
  let me hear your voice;
for your voice is sweet,
  and your face is lovely.
[15]Catch us the foxes,
  the little foxes,
that ruin the vineyards—
  for our vineyards are in blossom.'

[16]My beloved is mine and I am his;
  he pastures his flock among the lilies.
[17]Until the day breathes
  and the shadows flee,
turn, my beloved, be like a gazelle
  or a young stag on the cleft mountains.

3Upon my bed at night
  I sought him whom my soul loves;
I sought him, but found him not;
  I called him, but he gave no answer.
[2]'I will rise now and go about the city,
  in the streets and in the squares;
I will seek him whom my soul loves.'
  I sought him, but found him not.
[3]The sentinels found me,
  as they went about in the city.
'Have you seen him whom my soul loves?'
[4]Scarcely had I passed them,
  when I found him whom my soul loves.
I held him, and would not let him go
    until I brought him into my mother's house,
    and into the chamber of her that conceived me.
[5]I adjure you, O daughters of Jerusalem,
  by the gazelles or the wild does:

do not stir up or awaken love
   until it is ready!

⁶What is that coming up from the wilderness,
   like a column of smoke,
perfumed with myrrh and frankincense,
   with all the fragrant powders of the merchant?
⁷Look, it is the litter of Solomon!
Around it are sixty mighty men
   of the mighty men of Israel,
⁸all equipped with swords
   and expert in war,
each with his sword at his thigh
   because of alarms by night.
⁹King Solomon made himself a palanquin
   from the wood of Lebanon.
¹⁰He made its posts of silver,
   its back of gold, its seat of purple;
its interior was inlaid with love.
   Daughters of Jerusalem,
¹¹ come out.
Look, O daughters of Zion,
   at King Solomon,
at the crown with which his mother crowned him
   on the day of his wedding,
   on the day of the gladness of his heart.

4How beautiful you are, my love,
   how very beautiful!
Your eyes are doves
   behind your veil.
Your hair is like a flock of goats,
   moving down the slopes of Gilead.
²Your teeth are like a flock of shorn ewes
   that have come up from the washing,

all of which bear twins,
   and not one among them is bereaved.
³Your lips are like a crimson thread,
   and your mouth is lovely.
Your cheeks are like halves of a pomegranate
   behind your veil.
⁴Your neck is like the tower of David,
   built in courses;
on it hang a thousand bucklers,
   all of them shields of warriors.
⁵Your two breasts are like two fawns,
   twins of a gazelle,
   that feed among the lilies.
⁶Until the day breathes
   and the shadows flee,
I will hasten to the mountain of myrrh
   and the hill of frankincense.
⁷You are altogether beautiful, my love;
   there is no flaw in you.
⁸Come with me from Lebanon, my bride;
   come with me from Lebanon.
Depart from the peak of Amana,
   from the peak of Senir and Hermon,
from the dens of lions,
   from the mountains of leopards.

⁹You have ravished my heart, my sister, my bride,
   you have ravished my heart with a glance of your eyes,
   with one jewel of your necklace.
¹⁰How sweet is your love, my sister, my bride!
   how much better is your love than wine,
   and the fragrance of your oils than any spice!
¹¹Your lips distil nectar, my bride;
   honey and milk are under your tongue;
   the scent of your garments is like the scent of Lebanon.

¹²A garden locked is my sister, my bride,
    a garden locked, a fountain sealed.
¹³Your channel is an orchard of pomegranates
    with all choicest fruits,
    henna with nard,
¹⁴nard and saffron, calamus and cinnamon,
    with all trees of frankincense,
myrrh and aloes,
    with all chief spices—
¹⁵a garden fountain, a well of living water,
    and flowing streams from Lebanon.

¹⁶Awake, O north wind,
    and come, O south wind!
Blow upon my garden
    that its fragrance may be wafted abroad.
Let my beloved come to his garden,
    and eat its choicest fruits.

5I come to my garden, my sister, my bride;
    I gather my myrrh with my spice,
    I eat my honeycomb with my honey,
    I drink my wine with my milk.

Eat, friends, drink,
    and be drunk with love.

²I slept, but my heart was awake.
Listen! my beloved is knocking.
'Open to me, my sister, my love,
    my dove, my perfect one;
for my head is wet with dew,
    my locks with the drops of the night.'
³I had put off my garment;
    how could I put it on again?

I had bathed my feet;
    how could I soil them?
⁴My beloved thrust his hand into the opening,
    and my inmost being yearned for him.
⁵I arose to open to my beloved,
    and my hands dripped with myrrh,
my fingers with liquid myrrh,
    upon the handles of the bolt.
⁶I opened to my beloved,
    but my beloved had turned and was gone.
My soul failed me when he spoke.
I sought him, but did not find him;
    I called him, but he gave no answer.
⁷Making their rounds in the city
    the sentinels found me;
they beat me, they wounded me,
    they took away my mantle,
    those sentinels of the walls.
⁸I adjure you, O daughters of Jerusalem,
    if you find my beloved,
tell him this:
    I am faint with love.

⁹What is your beloved more than another beloved,
    O fairest among women?
What is your beloved more than another beloved,
    that you thus adjure us?

¹⁰My beloved is all radiant and ruddy,
    distinguished among ten thousand.
¹¹His head is the finest gold;
    his locks are wavy,
    black as a raven.
¹²His eyes are like doves
    beside springs of water,

bathed in milk,
   fitly set.
[13]His cheeks are like beds of spices,
   yielding fragrance.
His lips are lilies,
   distilling liquid myrrh.
[14]His arms are rounded gold,
   set with jewels.
His body is ivory work,
   encrusted with sapphires.
[15]His legs are alabaster columns,
   set upon bases of gold.
His appearance is like Lebanon,
   choice as the cedars.
[16]His speech is most sweet,
   and he is altogether desirable.
This is my beloved and this is my friend,
   O daughters of Jerusalem.

6Where has your beloved gone,
   O fairest among women?
Which way has your beloved turned,
   that we may seek him with you?

[2]My beloved has gone down to his garden,
   to the beds of spices,
to pasture his flock in the gardens,
   and to gather lilies.
[3]I am my beloved's and my beloved is mine;
   he pastures his flock among the lilies.

[4]You are beautiful as Tirzah, my love,
   comely as Jerusalem,
   terrible as an army with banners.
[5]Turn away your eyes from me,
   for they overwhelm me!

Your hair is like a flock of goats,
     moving down the slopes of Gilead.
⁶Your teeth are like a flock of ewes,
     that have come up from the washing;
all of them bear twins,
     and not one among them is bereaved.
⁷Your cheeks are like halves of a pomegranate
     behind your veil.
⁸There are sixty queens and eighty concubines,
     and maidens without number.
⁹My dove, my perfect one, is the only one,
     the darling of her mother,
     flawless to her that bore her.
The maidens saw her and called her happy;
     the queens and concubines also, and they praised her.
¹⁰'Who is this that looks forth like the dawn,
     fair as the moon, bright as the sun,
     terrible as an army with banners?'

¹¹I went down to the nut orchard,
     to look at the blossoms of the valley,
to see whether the vines had budded,
     whether the pomegranates were in bloom.
¹²Before I was aware, my fancy set me
     in a chariot beside my prince.

¹³Return, return, O Shulammite!
     Return, return, that we may look upon you.

Why should you look upon the Shulammite,
     as upon a dance before two armies?

7How graceful are your feet in sandals,
     O queenly maiden!
Your rounded thighs are like jewels,
     the work of a master hand.

²Your navel is a rounded bowl
    that never lacks mixed wine.
Your belly is a heap of wheat,
    encircled with lilies.
³Your two breasts are like two fawns,
    twins of a gazelle.
⁴Your neck is like an ivory tower.
Your eyes are pools in Heshbon,
    by the gate of Bath-rabbim.
Your nose is like a tower of Lebanon,
    overlooking Damascus.
⁵Your head crowns you like Carmel,
    and your flowing locks are like purple;
    a king is held captive in the tresses.

⁶How fair and pleasant you are,
    O loved one, delectable maiden!
⁷You are stately as a palm tree,
    and your breasts are like its clusters.
⁸I say I will climb the palm tree
    and lay hold of its branches.
O may your breasts be like clusters of the vine,
    and the scent of your breath like apples,
⁹and your kisses like the best wine
    that goes down smoothly,
    gliding over lips and teeth.

¹⁰I am my beloved's,
    and his desire is for me.
¹¹Come, my beloved,
    let us go forth into the fields,
    and lodge in the villages;
¹²let us go out early to the vineyards,
    and see whether the vines have budded,
whether the grape blossoms have opened
    and the pomegranates are in bloom.

There I will give you my love.
¹³The mandrakes give forth fragrance,
　　and over our doors are all choice fruits,
new as well as old,
　　which I have laid up for you, O my beloved.

8O that you were like a brother to me,
　　who nursed at my mother's breast!
If I met you outside, I would kiss you,
　　and no one would despise me.
²I would lead you and bring you
　　into the house of my mother,
　　and into the chamber of the one who bore me.
I would give you spiced wine to drink,
　　the juice of my pomegranates.
³O that his left hand were under my head,
　　and that his right hand embraced me!
⁴I adjure you, O daughters of Jerusalem,
　　do not stir up or awaken love
　　until it is ready!

⁵Who is that coming up from the wilderness,
　　leaning upon her beloved?

Under the apple tree I awakened you.
There your mother was in labour with you;
　　there she who bore you was in labour.

⁶Set me as a seal upon your heart,
　　as a seal upon your arm;
for love is strong as death,
　　passion fierce as the grave.
Its flashes are flashes of fire,
　　a raging flame.
⁷Many waters cannot quench love,
　　neither can floods drown it.

If one offered for love
    all the wealth of one's house,
    it would be utterly scorned.

8We have a little sister,
    and she has no breasts.
What shall we do for our sister,
    on the day when she is spoken for?
9If she is a wall,
    we will build upon her a battlement of silver;
but if she is a door,
    we will enclose her with boards of cedar.
10I was a wall,
    and my breasts were like towers;
then I was in his eyes
    as one who brings peace.
11Solomon had a vineyard at Baal-hamon;
    he entrusted the vineyard to keepers;
    each one was to bring for its fruit a thousand pieces of
        silver.
12My vineyard, my very own, is for myself;
    you, O Solomon, may have the thousand,
    and the keepers of the fruit two hundred!

13O you who dwell in the gardens,
    my companions are listening for your voice;
    let me hear it.

14Make haste, my beloved,
    and be like a gazelle
or a young stag
    upon the mountains of spices!

Philo of Alexandria

Philo (ca. 25 BCE–50 CE) lived in the syncretistic world of Roman-period Alexandria, Egypt. During the latter part of his life, particularly interesting questions arose with regard to spiritual convictions and ambitions. Very early Judaism and Christianity—twin siblings in the process of springing separately from the Israelite-Judaean parent—were just beginning to compete with each other and with a diversity of pagan traditions regarding how to understand what divinity is and to how to achieve spiritual oneness with it. Philo, loyal to the Judaean tradition but enthralled with Hellenistic thought, particularly its Platonic and Stoic elements, studied diverse spiritual traditions, in part with an eye toward validating Judaism's Torah in its relationship to the rationalist exploration of the world posed by the Greco-Roman pagan philosophical tradition.

Philo clearly believed that the Torah had been authored by God—not just every word but every letter and (since he was almost certainly reading it in Greek and not in Hebrew) every accent mark. But he understood much of the Torah text to be allegorical, intended by God not to be understood literally. Thus he perceived true scriptural meanings to be hidden beneath the surface. This mode of thinking afforded a range of possible connections to Greek thought.

Plato understood ultimate reality to reside in the realm of Forms or Ideas, and saw everything in our reality as limited to a condition of becoming. He also argued that the Forms—Justice, Piety, "Tableness," "Chairness" in their essences—are all but inaccessible to us. So if Plato as a rationalist could also be understood to be a spiritualist, why couldn't the Torah as the consummate spiritual guide be subject to rationalist interpretation? Several generations after Plato, the Stoics introduced the idea of *logos*—"reason"—as part of the creative process: reason activates inert preexistent matter to shape the universe. It would not require much of a jump for Philo to construe *logos* as referring to the divine act of saying the world into being: "And God said, let there be…"

More broadly, inspired by the possibilities for synthesis between Greek and Judaean ideas, Philo became interested in exploring the diversity of groups whose members sought esoteric knowledge—*gnosis* is the Greek term that they used—of the reality beyond our own that might be associated with bringing ours into existence.

Thus the first part of our Philo selection focuses on a group known as *Therapeutae* ("healers"). Philo lauds these spiritual practitioners for their capacity to heal souls "mastered by grievous and virtually incurable diseases." He had just finished discussing the Essenes: groups of Judaeans who withdrew from the mainstream community and lived extremely ascetic lives in order more effectively to focus on a relationship with the God of Israel at a time when religious leaders in Jerusalem had become factionalized and excessively politicized. His turn to the *Therapeutae* is offered in comparison both with the Essenes and with a range of pagan groups.

The *Therapeutae* dwell in places that allow them the tranquility to seek oneness with the One God, like the Essenes, albeit the Essenes dwell out in the wilderness. Philo compares them to spiritually inferior pagan groups "who revere the elements," applying "divine" names to them, and to the Egyptians and their multitudes of gods. He discusses the lifestyle of the *Therapeutae* in some detail, from their rejection of material wealth to their abandonment of the sorts of family connections that define the lives of ordinary people—not out of misanthropy but out of a desire for an untrammeled engagement of God.

It is that engagement that Philo pursues in his consideration of mysticism in the next part of our selection: "the question for God, best of all existing things, the incomparable, the Cause of all." What follows is a series of passages from different writings of Philo that share a focus on God: a description of the desire for oneness with God and modes of attachment to God; discussion of the mode of accessing God who is beyond ordinary senses without that most distinctive of human attributes, speech.

Philo's discussions interweave the issue of the human soul in its relationship with God with that of the perception of the entire universe accorded to the soul through that relationship. He ties this layered discussion to the reference to *logos*, as the ultimate extrusion of God into what takes shape as the universe. The mystic whose mind becomes embedded within and completely filled with the *ultimate* Mind (God) enjoys perfect equanimity, and is in a position to help improve the world.

Ori Z. Soltes

THE CONTEMPLATIVE LIFE

Introduction

In this treatise Philo presents an encomiastic account of an ascetic community devoted to the contemplative life with which he had personal acquaintance. Having placed the Therapeutae ("healers" or "worshipers"), the name by which this sect was known, not far from Alexandria, where he himself lived, it is clear that he could not have invented them. Utopias are usually located at remote distances, safe from any effort at verification. As for the relationship of the Therapeutae to the Essenes, the consensus is that, although originating from the same root, they nevertheless represent separate developments. The scholar Geza Vermes believes, however, that there is a close bond between them, and he interprets the opening sentence of the treatise as implying that the Therapeutae were contemplative Essenes.

Although considerably more ascetic than the Essenes, the Therapeutae are not extreme ascetics and do not practice mortifications. They do not live in the true desert, and seek only the philosophical tranquillity that will lead them to a mystic vision of the one God. Philo sharply contrasts their sober banquets with their pagan counterparts and ends his account with a vivid and highly enthusiastic depiction of their festive symposia and night vigils, which included edifying disquisitions on questions of Holy Writ and culminated with choral hymns in a wide variety of modes and the gradual blending of their male and female choirs into one.

THE CONTEMPLATIVE LIFE OR SUPPLIANTS

Mode of Exposition

I. After discussing the Essenes who zealously cultivated the active life, and excelled in all or, to put it more acceptably, in most of its spheres, I shall now proceed at once, following the sequence demanded by the treatment of this subject, to say what is fitting concerning those who have espoused the life of contemplation. I will add nothing of my own for the sake of embellishment, as is customarily done by all poets and historians through a dearth of noble life-styles in the subjects they treat, but shall absolutely hold to the truth itself, in the face of which I well know even the most eloquent orator would abandon the effort. We must nevertheless struggle through and bring the contest to its close, for the grandeur of these men's virtue ought not mute the tongue of those who hold that nothing excellent should be passed over in silence.

Explanation of the Name Therapeutae

The vocation of these philosophers is disclosed at once by their name, for they are called, according to the true meaning or etymology of the words, Therapeutae and Therapeutrides [literally, "healers," male and female], either insofar as they profess an art of healing better than that practiced in the cities—for the latter cures only the body, while theirs treats also souls mastered by grievous and virtually incurable diseases, inflicted by pleasures and lusts, mental pains and fears, by acts of greed, folly, and injustice, and the endless multitude of the other mental disturbances and vices—or else they are so called because they have been taught by nature and the holy laws to worship the Existent who is better than the Good, purer than the One, and more primal then the Monad.

Incomparable Superiority of the Therapeutae

Who among those who profess piety may properly be compared with these? Can we compare those who revere the elements, earth, water, air, fire? To these elements different names have been assigned by different people, some, for example, calling fire Hephaestus, presumably because of its kindling the air Hera because it is elevated (ai'pco) and rises to a height; water Poseidon perhaps because it is potable (oróc), and earth Demeter, inasmuch as it appears to be the mother of all plants and animals. These names, however, are the inventions of Sophists, whereas the elements are lifeless matter, incapable of self-movement and laid down by the Artificer as a substrate for every sort of form and quality. What of those who worship the finished products of creation, sun, moon, or the other stars wandering or fixed, or the entire heaven and universe? But these too did not come to be of themselves, but through a craftsman most perfect in his knowledge.

What of those who worship the demigods? Surely this is even a matter for ridicule. How could the same being be both immortal and mortal, not to mention that the very source of their generation is open to reproach, infected as it is with youthful debauchery that they impiously dare to attribute to the blessed and divine powers, supposing that the thrice blessed beings who have no share in any passion were mad after mortal women and mated with them?

What of the worshipers of carved images and statues? Their substance is stone and wood, till a short while ago utterly shapeless. Quarrymen and woodcutters cut them out of their congenital structure while their kindred and cognate parts have become urns and footbasins and some other vessels of a yet ignobler sort, which serve for use in darkness rather than in the light.

As for the gods of the Egyptians, even to mention them is indecent. The Egyptians have advanced to divine honors brute animals, not only of the tame sort but also beasts of the utmost savagery, from every sublunar species; from land creatures the lion, from those of the water the native crocodile, from those that roam the air the kite and the Egyptian ibis. And although they see these animals begotten, in need of nourishment, insatiate in their eating, crammed with ordure, venom spraying and man-devouring, the prey of all sorts of diseases, and perishing not only by a natural but often by a violent death, they make obeisance to them, they the civilized to the untamed and wild, the rational to the irrational, they who are akin to the Deity to those not even on a par with [the ape-like] Thersites, the lords and masters of creation to the naturally subservient and slavish.

II. Since these men infect with their folly not only their fellow-countrymen but also the neighboring peoples, let them remain incurable, bereft of vision, the most necessary of all the senses. And I do not mean the vision of the body, but that of the soul, through which alone the true and false are recognized. But let the sect of the Therapeutae, taught in advance to exercise their sight, aim at the vision of the Existent, and soar above the sense-perceptible sun and never abandon this post which leads to perfect happiness. And those who come to this service neither through force of habit nor on the advice or exhortation of others but because they have been ravished by a heavenly passion are possessed like Bacchants and Corybants until they behold the object of their longing.

Renunciation of Property

Then, through their yearning for the deathless and blessed life, believing that their mortal existence is already over, they leave their property to their sons or daughters or even to other kinsfolk, freely making them their heirs in advance, while those who have no kinsfolk bestow them on comrades and friends. For it was right that those who have received in ready form the wealth that has sight should surrender the blind wealth to those still mentally blind. The Greeks celebrate Anaxagoras and Democritus because, smitten with the desire for philosophy, they allowed their property to be laid waste by sheep. I too myself admire these men who showed themselves superior to wealth, but how much better are those who did not allow their lands to become feeding grounds for cattle but supplied the needs of men, whether kinsfolk or friends, and so converted their indigence into affluence. For the former was a thoughtless act, not to say "mad," speaking of men whom Greece admired, but the latter was a sober act, precisely arranged, and with exceeding good sense. What more does an enemy force do than to ravage their opponents' land and cut down its trees, in order to force their surrender through a shortage of necessaries? This is what Democritus did to those of his own blood, preparing for them artificial want and poverty, not perhaps maliciously but through not taking thought and careful consideration for the interest of others. How much better and more admirable are they who, influenced by no lesser impulse toward philosophy, preferred magnanimity to negligence and cheerfully gave away their property instead of destroying it, in this way benefiting both others and themselves, others by furnishing them with plentiful resources, themselves by their devotion to philosophy. For the management of wealth and possessions is time-consuming, and it is well to husband one's time since according to the physician Hippocrates, "life is short but art is long." Homer, too, it seems to me, hints at this in the Iliad at the beginning of the thirteenth book in the following verses:

> And the Mysians who fight at close quarters, and the
> illustrious Hippomolgoi, drinkers of mare's milk, hav-
> ing no fixed subsistence, most righteous of men.

The idea conveyed is that the effort to gain a livelihood and make money breeds injustice through the inequality entailed, while the opposite principle of action begets justice through equality, in accordance with which nature's wealth is delimited and thus surpasses the wealth derived through empty imaginings.

Rejection of Family and City Life

So when they have given up possession of their property, with nothing further to entice them, they flee without turning to look back, abandoning brothers, children, wives, parents, numerous kin, dear companions, the fatherlands in which they were born and reared, since the familiar has a great power of attraction and is the most powerful of baits. They do not emigrate to another city like unfortunate or worthless slaves who demand to be sold by their owners, thus obtaining for themselves a change of masters but not freedom. For every city, even the best governed, teems with tumult and indescribable disturbances that no one could abide after having been once guided by wisdom. Instead they spend their time outside the walls pursuing solitude in gardens or solitary places, not from having cultivated a cruel hatred of men, but because they know that intercourse with persons of dissimilar character is unprofitable and injurious.

IX. MYSTICISM
The Limit of Happiness Is the Presence of God

But it is something great that Abraham asks, namely that God shall not pass by nor remove to a distance and leave his soul desolate and empty (Gen. 18:3). For the limit of happiness is the presence of God, which completely fills the whole soul with his whole incorporeal and eternal light. And (the limit) of misery is (his) passing on the way, for immediately thereafter comes heavy and profound darkness, which possesses (the soul). Wherefore also the fratricide Cain says, "Great is the guilt of my punishment that you leave me" (Gen. 4:13), indicating that there is no greater punishment for the soul than to be abandoned by God. Moreover, in another place Moses says, "Lest the Lord be removed from them," showing that for the soul to be separated from the contemplation of the Existent One is the most complete of evils. For these reasons he attempts to lead the people toward God, not (any men), for this is not possible, but god-loving souls that can (be led), when a heavenly love and desire have come on them and seized them. (QG 4.4)

Make Your Soul a Shrine of God, For the Beginning and End of Happiness Is to Be Able to See God

For the Savior is beneficent and kind, and he wishes to except the rational race from all living creatures. He therefore honors them with an even ampler gift, a great benefaction in which all kinds of good things are found, and he graciously grants his appearance, if only there be a suitable place, purified with holiness and every (kind of) purity. For if, O mind, you do not prepare yourself of yourself, excising desires, pleasures, griefs, fears, follies, injustices, and related evils, and do (not) change and adapt yourself to the vision of holiness, you will end your life in blindness, unable to see the intelligible sun. If, however, you are worthily initiated and can be consecrated to God and in a certain sense become an animate shrine of the Father, (then) instead of having closed eyes, you will see the First (Cause) and in wakefulness you will cease from the deep sleep in which you have been held. Then will appear to you that manifest One who causes incorporeal rays to shine for you, and grants visions of the unambiguous and indescribable things of nature and the abundant sources of other good things. For the beginning and end of happiness is to be able to see God. But this cannot happen to him who has not made his soul, as I said before, a sanctuary and altogether a shrine of God. (Q' 2.51)

....

The Quest for God Is Never Fruitless

The quest for God, best of all existing things, the Incomparable, the Cause of all, gladdens us the moment we embark on our search, and is never without issue, since by reason of his gracious nature he advances to meet us with his virgin graces, and shows himself to those who long to see him, not as he is, for this is impossible, since even Moses "turned away his face, for he was afraid to look upon God" (Exod. 3:6) but so far as it was allowable that created nature should approach the inconceivable Power. (Fug. 141)

The Mind Possessed by Divine Love

When the mind is possessed by divine love, when it exerts itself to reach the innermost shrine when it moves forward with all effort and zeal, under the impact of the divine inspiration it forgets everything else, forgets itself, and retains memory and attachment for him alone whose attendant and servant it is, to whom it dedicates the incense offering of hallowed and intelligible virtues. But when the inspiration is stilled and the intense longing subsides, it races back from the divine and becomes man and encounters the human interests that lay in wait for it in the outer court to snatch it away should it but venture forth from within. (Somn. 2.232)

The Wise Man's Insatiable Longing for the Divine

But (Scripture) shows that the character of the wise man is not quickly satisfied but is constant and hard to efface and hard to remove from the idea of that which is above the good and above the wise man and above the very best. And various conversations come together, one after the other, so that he never departs from the conversation of speech because of his insatiable and incessant desire and longing, by which the sovereign (mind) is drawn and seized; and it is led by the attractive force of sovereign existences. (QG 4.140)

....

Recognition of Man's Nothingness

Among these is Abraham who gained much progress and improvement toward the acquisition of the highest knowledge: for when above all he knew himself, then above all did he despair of himself, in order that he might arrive at a precise knowledge of the truly Existent. And this is how it is: He who has profoundly

195

comprehended himself, profoundly despairs of himself, having perceived in advance the absolute nothingness of creating being. And the man who has despaired of himself knows the Existent. (Somn. 1.60)

Departure from Self

Who then shall be the heir? Not the sort of reasoning that voluntarily abides in the prison of the body, but that which loosed from its bonds and liberated has come forth outside the walls, and if we may say so, abandoned its own self. For "he who shall come out of you," it says, "shall be your heir" (Gen. 15:4).

If then, my soul, a yearning comes upon you to inherit the divine goods, abandon not only your land, that is, the body; your kinsfolk, that is, the senses; your father's house (Gen. 12:1), that is, speech, but escape also your own self and stand aside from yourself, like persons possessed and corybants seized by Bacchic frenzy and carried away by some kind of prophetic inspiration. For it is the mind that is filled with the Deity and no longer in itself, but is agitated and maddened by a heavenly passion, drawn by the truly Existent and attracted upward to it, preceded by truth, which removes all obstacles in its path so that it may advance on a level highway—such a mind has the inheritance. (Her. 68–70)

Attachment to God

"The tribe of Levi," he says, "shall have no lot or portion among the children of Israel, for the Lord himself is their portion" (Deut. 10:9); and there is an utterance intoned by the oracles in the name of God that runs as follows: "I am your portion and inheritance" (Num. 18:20). For in truth the mind that has been utterly purified, and that renounces all things belonging to creation, knows and recognizes but One alone, the Uncreated, to whom it has drawn nigh, and by whom it has been taken as a partner. For who is able to say "God himself is alone to me," save one who clings to nothing that comes after him? And this is the

Levite temper of mind, for the word means "He is to me (i.e., mine)," since different things are honored by different people, but by him alone is honor rendered to the highest and most excellent Cause of all things. (Plant. 63–64)

Referring All Things to God

There are two minds, that of the universe, which is God, and the individual mind. He who flees from his own mind takes refuge with the Mind of all things. For he that abandons his own mind grants that that which pertains to the human mind is nothing, and attributes all things to God. On the other hand, he that flees from God affirms that He is the cause of nothing, but that he himself is the cause of all things that come into being. Many indeed say that all things in the world are borne along spontaneously, without anyone to guide them, and that the human mind by itself established arts, professions, laws, customs, rules of conduct within the state, individual and communal, regarding both men and irrational animals. But note, my soul, the difference between the two views; for the one abandons the particular, created, and mortal mind, and verily chooses as its patron the universal Mind, uncreated and imperishable; the other view, on the contrary, rejects God, and mistakenly calls in as its ally the mind, which is insufficient even to help itself. (LA 3.29–31)

The Soul That Rests in God

The clearest evidence for the soul beloved of God is the psalm in which are contained the words "the barren has borne seven, but she that is multiple has languished in her offspring" (1 Sam. 2:5). And yet it is the mother of one child—Samuel— who is speaking. How then can she say that she has borne seven, unless, in full accord with reality, she believes the Monad to be identical with the hebdomad, not only in arithmetical lore, but also in the harmony of the universe and in the thoughts of the virtuous soul? For Samuel who is appointed to God alone and associates with no one else at all possesses a nature in conformity with the One and the Monad, the truly Existent. But this state is that of the Seven, when a soul rests in God and toils no longer at any mortal task, and has abandoned the Six, which God has apportioned to those incapable of obtaining the first prize, but must necessarily lay claim to the second. (Deus 10–12)

Contemplation of God without Audible Speech

For in this way only could that which is best in ourselves become inclined to serve the Best of all Existents: if first the man were resolved into soul, his brother body and its endless lusts being severed and cut in two; if next the soul cast off, as I have said, that neighbor of our rational element, the irrational, which, like a torrent divided five ways through the channels of the senses, excites the onrush of the passions; if immediately thereafter reasoning sever and disperse that which seems to be closest to it, the uttered word, so that the thought within the mind may be left behind alone, bereft of body, bereft of sense perception, bereft of the utterance of resonant speech. For thus left behind, it will live a life in accord with such solitude, and will cleave in purity and without distraction to the Alone Existent. (Fug. 91–92)
....

The Mind Enjoys Timeless Contact with the Entire Universe

For the mind, alone of all our endowments, being swiftest of all things, outstrips and outdistances the time in which it seems to be found, and by virtue of invisible faculties enjoys timeless contact with both the whole and its parts, and with their respective causes. And having already come not only as far as the ends of earth and sea but of air and sky also, not even there did it come to a halt, holding the world to constitute a narrow boundary for its continuous and unceasing course, and eager to advance beyond, and apprehend if possible the nature of God, which except for its bare existence is inapprehensible. For how was it likely that the human mind being so tiny, hemmed in by such puny masses as brain or heart, should be able to contain such an immense magnitude of sky and universe, had it not been an inseparable portion of that divine and blessed soul? For nothing is severed or detached from the divine, but only extended. When the mind, therefore, that has received its share in the perfection of the whole conceives of the universe, it stretches out as widely as the bounds of the whole, for its force is susceptible of attraction. (Det. 89–90)

Meeting with the Logos Sudden and Unexpected

It is extraordinarily apt that he [Abraham] does not say that he came to the place, but that he met with a place (Gen. 18:33); for coming is a matter of choice, but meeting is often without one's volition, and this is so in order that the divine Logos, manifesting itself suddenly as a fellow-traveler to a desolate soul, might tender it an unexpected joy, greater than hope. "For Moses too leads the people forth to meet God" (Exod. 19:17), knowing full well that he comes invisibly to the souls that long to converse with him. (Somn. 1.71)

....

The Soul That Sees God Enjoys Equipoise and Tranquillity

Note what is said about wise Abraham, that he was "standing in front of God" (Gen. 18:22), for when is it likely that a mind should stand and no longer sway as on a balance except when it is opposite God, seeing and being seen? For its equilibrium derives from two sources; from seeing the Incomparable, because it is not then drawn in a contrary direction by things similar to itself; from being seen, because the mind that the Ruler judges worthy to come within his sight he assigns for the best alone, namely for himself.

199

To Moses, too, the following oracle was delivered: "But as for you, stand here with me" (Deut. 5:31), from which one may adduce both points mentioned above, the unwavering character of the man of virtue and the absolute firmness of the Existent. For he who draws near to God is made akin to the Existent, and in accordance with his immutability becomes self-standing. Moreover, the mind that has found rest has clearly recognized how great a good tranquillity is, and astounded at its beauty has grasped that it is either God's portion alone or of that nature which lies midway between mortal and immortal kind. (Somn. 2.226–228)

The Early Kabbalah

One of the fundamental questions addressed by Jewish mysticism is how and why the world was created. How did the singular, intangible God, inaccessible to the senses and intellect, created a universe that is Its opposite: multifarious, tangible, accessible to the senses and intellect? And what was God's purpose in creating *humans*? Such questions are central to a tradition that asserts the goal and the possibility of interface with the innermost recesses of God, offering the hope of answering them.

Jewish mysticism offers the issue of creation as a starting point for its literature: the *Book of Formation* (*Sefer Yetzirah*), ascribed, by tradition, to Rabbi Akiva, offers a description of creation based on the ten numbers and the twenty-two Hebrew letters.

While such abstract concepts are one starting point, another is the Torah. There is an inherent logic in this, since the Torah is traditionally understood to contain, in every syllable, the word of God, and since the opening passages of the Torah lay out a systematic narrative of creation. Alas, that narrative is rather opaque: what does it really mean when it refers to pre-creation reality as *"tohu vavohu*[1]*"*? What does it mean when it asserts that "God said: 'let there be light'"—how precisely does God *say* anything?

Mainstream Jewish thought acknowledges this opacity with the early rabbinic commentaries known as *midrash*. That term, from a Hebrew root meaning "to dig beneath the surface," refers to an enormous text that seeks to understand the Torah and other biblical books by pulling up from beneath the obvious, literal surface of their words the real meaning buried underneath.

The Jewish mystical tradition is inherently midrashic. Like mainstream *midrash*, it often connects elements of the passage

---

1 There is a variety of spellings for this term, including *tohu va-bohu.*

201

under discussion to passages in other parts of the Hebrew Bible to extract hidden meanings. But it digs still further: it deconstructs words, pulling them apart to find embedded metaphors and meanings in syllables and letters—even in the very shapes and sounds of letters.

The heart and soul of this process is found in Kabbalah. That term, meaning "what has been received," refers to an extended phase (ca. 1100–1750) within the Jewish mystical tradition that defines itself *not* as outside the mainstream, but deeply within it. For it seeks answers to the ultimate questions in every nook and cranny of Jewish thought. Moreover, whereas earlier *Merkavah* mysticism tended to emphasize God's awesome, transcendent distance from us, Kabbalah tends to emphasize God's immanent, loving closeness.

Among the fathers of early Provencal Kabbalah was Rabbi Isaac "the Blind" (ca. 1160–1235). His epithet, "*sagi nehor*," meaning "of much light," plays on the idea that his physical blindness was balanced by piercing spiritual insight. Among his writings is an extended discussion of the creation of the world, which he defines as a process of *emanation*: God extends Its essence out of Itself in order to form the universe that is therefore an extension of the limitless God.

The form that Rabbi Isaac's discussion takes is a commentary, a word-and-phrase-by-word-and-phrase interpretation of the opening passages of Genesis, connecting them to *spherot*—ten "countings," outgrowths of the ten numbers that express God's emanation into reality. His opening observation focuses on the first Hebrew letter in the narrative, "*bet*," which is referred to as a crown (*keter*, which is also the first *spherah*), because it precedes—rests on—the word for "head" (*rosh*, heart of the word *reshit*, meaning "[the] beginning"). The word "beginning" he equates with wisdom (*hokhmah*, the second *spherah*) by way of a connection to a phrase from Psalm 111:10.

The pre-reality of *tohu vavohu* he explains by taking the words of that phrase apart. And he pursues the idea of wisdom phrase by phrase from the first to the second to the third verse of the narrative by the same processes of deconstruction and turning to verses elsewhere in the Torah or the Hebrew Bible at large.

In the last phrase in his discussion, Rabbi Isaac equates the "four streams" flowing out of the Garden of Eden with the Divine Presence—*shekhinah*—that is found throughout the world in each dimension and direction. Thus the impossibly distant Creator fills the universe with Itself in a manner intimate with the creation—which includes ourselves.

Rabbi Isaac's pupil, Rabbi Azriel, adds to the early kabbalistic engagement of the question of creation through not only an interpretive discussion of the *sephirot*. He introduces the idea of what is even beyond *keter*—the *Eyn Sof*: the "endless"—as both a deeper connective to and a more profound distance from God's innermost recess.

Rabbi Azriel's method combines the midrashic penchant for connecting diverse biblical passages with features favored by a number of medieval Jewish and Christian thinkers: presenting content through questions and answers (a method based on Plato's dialogue style) and an interest in Aristotle (reflected, for example, in contrasting potential and actualized *sephirot* within *Eyn Sof*).

Ori Z. Soltes

RABBI ISAAC

The Process of Emanation

IN THE BEGINNING (*Be-re'shit*): The letter bet is the most elevated Crown (*keter*), and therefore this bet is larger than all other bets.' The word "beginning" (*re'shit*) is in fact Wisdom (*bokhmah*). In truth, then, two sefirot are encompassed in one word.

From whence do we know that Wisdom is called "beginning"? It states: "The beginning of wisdom is the fear of the Lord" (Psalms 111:10). With both Crown and Wisdom He created THE HEAVENS AND THE EARTH—that is: Beauty (*tferet*) and Diadem ('*atarab*). He also created the [two] 'ets, and these are the supernal powers which are Lovingkindness (*besed*) and Fear (*pahad*). All of creation is summarized in this. Afterward, he explained the entire matter, beginning with the result of creation, Diadem, through which the entire Structure is made complete. And it states:

AND THE EARTH WAS UNFORMED AND VOID (*tohu va-bohu*): Earth is Diadem. Before it was emanated from the Cause of causes, it was *tobu*, something that is astounding (*mathe'*), for it has nothing substantial within it, nor does it possess any form. But when it was emanated it then became a substance more ethereal than Spirit.

VOID (*bohu*): This means "in it" (*bo*)—when it was emanated, something substantial was made in it. And our Rabbis, may their memories be blessed, explained that these [two] are called collectively "the foundation stone."

AND DARKNESS OVER THE SURFACE OF THE DEEP: This is the depth of above and the depth of below.

AND A WIND FROM GOD SWEEPING OVER THE WATER: Wisdom envelops everything, as in "sweeping over her young" (Deuteronomy 32:11).

OVER THE WATER: Everything was called water, for Loving-kindness—the summit of five sefirot—is water. More precisely, [Wisdom] is the power of water, for water pours forth from its overflow.

GOD (Elohim) SAID, "LET THERE BE LIGHT." GOD—This is Repentance (*teshuvah*). And thus he, may his memory be blessed, said: "To wrap oneself—to wrap oneself in a prayer shawl, and this means to wrap oneself in Wisdom." And it states:

LET THERE BE LIGHT: This means Beauty, for the Torah came forth from Wisdom. From Nothing (*me-ayin*) spread forth the thirty-two paths which stem from Wisdom. These [paths] are the source and the derivatives of the Torah and all other sciences.

And He wraps Himself [with the Torah] and peers into it and builds worlds and destroys worlds. He saw that all things were hidden and He said, "Let all these things expand from potentiality to actuality, that they be actuated and uncovered," "they" being the now actualized Beauty and Diadem.

AND THERE WAS LIGHT: It does not say "and it was so" as in the case with all other created things, because in the rest of creation essences were emanated which themselves formed essences but not forms. But here forms were developed. For this reason the light of Beauty and Diadem is incomparable to the supernal light, because when it states LET THERE BE LIGHT it refers to Beauty and Diadem. And from this particular light spread forth all essences and entities. Also, [God] utilized the light of Beauty and Diadem until the fourth day, but He foresaw that the world could not endure this light, due to [the light's] abundant merit. He therefore set it aside for the righteous people of the future. This light is sevenfold more intense than all the other luminaries of light, and thus it states: "And the light of the moon shall become like the light of the sun; and the light of the sun shall become sevenfold, like the light of the seven days" (Isaiah 30:26).

AND GOD SAW THE LIGHT THAT IT WAS GOOD (tov): This is derived from "when he tends (*be-hetivo*) the lamps" (Exodus 30:7). The matter is ignited as if one lights a candle one from the other. Thereby He grants a power to the essences to expand and draw forth.

AND GOD SEPARATED THE LIGHT FROM THE DARK-NESS: He delimited to each one the extent of their expansion and extension. And thus:

GOD CALLED THE LIGHT DAY: He likened the masculine power—which is Beauty—to the day; and so Diadem—which is feminine—to the night. Furthermore, neither became manifest until their effects came forth and the world was created.

LET THERE BE A FIRMAMENT IN THE MIDST OF THE WATER: This is Lovingkindness. Now we have already said that the water is from the overflow of Lovingkindness and from the FIRMAMENT. Likewise, Beauty in the midst of the water contains water which is Lovingkindness, part above and part below. Thus the order of all things can be likened to the skins of onions. For our Sages, may their memories be blessed, said that just as there is the divine Presence above, so too is the divine Presence below; and all things are like the skins of onions." What they mean is this: Each attribute emanates [downward] and accepts from that which stands above it. Therefore Solomon said, "For one high official is protected by a higher one, and both of them by still higher ones" (Ecclesiastes 5:7). Therefore I have written that each attribute mutually lends to the other, as is written: "A good man lends with a good grace" (Psalms 112:5). And it is at this moment that the endeavor [of creation] began.

AND GOD MADE FROM THE FIRMAMENT: He began to sketch within Beauty the form of space and limit, but He did not make material space like a man who would clear away an area in order to construct a building. And Scripture does not say regarding [the firmament] "for it was good" because Thought (mahshavab) had not finished [its work] until it had cleared away space for Diadem, which is the nun.

On the third day [of creation], He said the verse LET THE DRY LAND BE SEEN. This is feminine, as it states: "It is not good for man to be by himself" (Genesis 2:18), and "man" is none other than Beauty.

AND GOD CALLED THE DRY LAND EARTH: The Will (*rason*), which is the furthest extension of Thought the Supernal Crown that no one can comprehend was drawn to the dry land, which is feminine. For the meaning of "dry land" is something which cannot bear fruit. It could not bear fruit until "man" was created so that he could draw the furthest reaches of Thought to [the land]. And this is the rule for all things. It is akin to what the Sages, may their memories be blessed, said: "The depth of the beginning and the depth of the end," meaning the beginning of Wisdom and its depth.

Put another way—highest Crown is above it. The "end" is feminine and thus our Rabbis, may their memories be blessed, said: "The entire world was created exclusively for the sake of Israel," and this means "due to the merit of Israel"—because of the unique qualities inherent in Israel. For [Israel] receives the divine overflow from the very root, core, and trunk of the Tree—from the middle pillar which draws from the branches.

AND THE GATHERING OF WATER HE CALLED SEAS: The middle pillar draws from the Source to Beauty like the spinal cord draws from the brain. This is similar to "All the streams flow to the sea" (Ecclesiastes 1:7). All the channels are drawn forth from Beauty to Diadem by way of the Foundation of the world (*yesod 'olam*), which is the Righteous One (*saddiq*), as in "For there shall be the seed of peace; [the vine shall give her fruit, and the ground shall yield its increase, and the heavens shall give their dew, and I will cause the remnant of this people to possess all things]" (Zachariah 8:12).

LET THE EARTH BEAR GRASS: As it says—the setting aside of space for Diadem so it could shower abundance on all generations.

LET THERE BE LIGHTS: These are shapeless entities without form, and the overflow of the activities of Beauty and Diadem became visible. Therefore they are called "great [lights]" (Genesis 1:15), for they are the first [things] in history. Beauty is called the greater light and Diadem the smaller light. Now they were the first in history—this means they were the first of five material sefirot, and in the fifth—

LET THE WATERS SWARM: It is the seed of the world; that is to say, "Let the supernal waters emanate by way of Beauty and Diadem."

SWARMS OF LIVING CREATURES: These are all the supernal forms derived from Beauty and Diadem and therefore He blessed them. And this is akin to the blessing that accepts from above and then descends to the lower realms.

AND LET THE FOWL FLY ABOVE THE EARTH: This is the commissioning of Lovingkindness and Fear for Beauty and Diadem. This is the meaning of AND LET FOWL FLY ABOVE THE EARTH—let each one emanate from its respective power to Beauty and Diadem.

AND GOD CREATED THE GREAT SEA-MONSTERS: These are the four hosts of the divine Presence—Michael, Gabriel, Rafael, and Uriel. Until this [verse] the term "creation" had not been used. But from this point onward the world of separate entities begins. [The world of separate entities] is the separate intellects—the angels—and the living soul within the angels which is the everascending Spirit.

WHEREWITH THE WATERS SWARMED, EACH TO ITS KIND: This is Lovingkindness. For we have already stated that water comes from the overflow of Lovingkindness. Those powers that receive from [Lovingkindness] must receive this overflow in accordance with each of their respective activities.

AND FILL THE EARTH: This is feminine, as it is stated: "in a stomach that is filled" (Ecclesiastes 11:5). All the channels are drawn to her and from her they are actualized.

AND LET THE FOWL MULTIPLY UPON THE EARTH: Included are all the powers which are drawn forth from Diadem. On the sixth day the Structure was completed in perfection, as it is stated, "In our form and in our image" (Genesis 1:26). This symbolizes the completion of the Structure so that it may bear fruit. This is what is meant by

"Which God had created so it may do" (Genesis 2:3). Up to this point throughout the six days of creation the name YHVH had not been mentioned, for the ten sefirot are implicit in it. The letter yod (') alludes to Wisdom and the coronet alludes to Crown. The first H alludes to Understanding (binab). The V alludes to Beauty along with the six extremities, while the final H is a sign for Diadem. Now how could the Tetragrammaton be mentioned before the completion of the Structure? Therefore the Sages, may their memories be blessed, said: "From IN THE BEGINNING to THEY WERE COMPLETED—'It is the glory of God to conceal a thing' (Proverbs 25:2); but henceforth—'Search out a matter' (ibid)." These are Beauty and Diadem. Thus it is stated: "And on the seventh day He rested, and was refreshed" (Exodus 31:17). The soul extended into the body and the powers were formed and finalized. Then history began, as we already explained. And Scripture then continues THESE ARE THE GENERATIONS OF THE HEAVEN AND THE EARTH—instead of "heaven and earth" read Beauty and Diadem.

AND BEHOLD, IT WAS VERY GOOD: On all the other days Scripture states that "it was good" (Genesis 10:4, 10, 12, 18, 21, 25), because on all the other days the illumination of Beauty and Diadem and their drawing forth continued to shine, for they are the furthest reaches of Thought. Finally, on the sixth day IT WAS VERY GOOD. The start of the matter is implicit in its end, for [the word] "very" (*me'od*) is Wisdom.

AND THE HEAVENS WERE COMPLETED (*va-yakhullu ha-shamayyim*) is derived from the word "bride" (*kallab*) and ornaments (*qishshurim*).

A RIVER WENT OUT OF EDEN: Beauty comes forth from between Lovingkindness and Fear; from even higher, from supernal Wisdom.

TO WATER THE GARDEN: The garden is Diadem.

AND FROM THENCE IT WAS PARTED: The sefirot continue until Diadem. Diadem is to be counted among them, unique but inseparable. But from then on the world of separate entities branches off.

AND THEY BRANCHED INTO FOUR STREAMS: These are the four hosts of the divine Presence which we have already mentioned. Here they are mentioned as they become actualized. Corresponding to them are the four dimensions: the dimension of the East, the dimension of the West, the dimension of the North, and the dimension of the South.

....

RABBI AZRIEL

Explanation of the Ten Sefirot

1. If a questioner asks: Who can compel me to believe that the world has a Ruler?

Answer: Just as it is inconceivable that a ship be without a captain, so too is it impossible that the world be without a ruler. This Ruler is infinite (*eyn sof*) in both His Glory and Word, as in the matter that is written: "I have seen an end to every purpose, but Your commandment is exceedingly immense" (Psalms 119:96), and it is written: "For God shall bring every act into judgment—every *hidden* thing whether good or bad" (Ecclesiastes 12:14). That which is *hidden* is without end and limit; it is unfathomable and nothing exists outside it.

The philosophers admit to this fact that the Cause of all causes and the Origin of origins is infinite, unfathomable, and without limit. According to the way of the Ruler we see that the end of every act is hidden from the probing of an investigator, as in the matter that is written: "So that no man can find out the work which God has made from the beginning to the end" (ibid. 3:11). And it is further recorded: "Should the wise man can say that he knows, even he will not be able to find it" (ibid. 8:17)...

2. If a questioner asks: Who can compel me to believe in Eyn-Sof?

Answer: Know that everything visible and perceivable to human contemplation is limited, and that everything that is limited is finite, and that everything that is finite is insignificant.

Conversely, that which is not limited is called Eyn-Sof and is absolutely undifferentiated in a complete and changeless unity. And if He is [truly] without limit, than nothing exists outside Him. And since He is both exalted and hidden, He is the essence of all that is concealed and revealed. But since He is hidden, He is both the root of faith and the root of rebelliousness. Regarding this it is written: "In his faith a righteous man shall live" (Habakkuk 2:4). Furthermore, the philosophers are in agreement with these statements that our perception of Him cannot be except by way of negative attribution. And that which radiates forth from Eyn-Sof are the ten *sefirot*. [And this is sufficient for the enlightened.]

3. If the questioner persists: By what necessity do you arrive at the assertion that the *sefirot* exist? I rather say that they do not exist and that there is only Eyn-Sof!

Answer: Eyn-Sof is perfection without any inperfection. If you propose that He has unlimited power and does not have finite power, then you ascribe imperfection to His perfection. And if you claim that the first limited being that is brought into existence from Him is this world lacking in perfection then you ascribe imperfection to the force which stems from Him.

Since we should never ascribe imperfection to His perfection, we are compelled to say that He has a finite power which is unlimited. The limitation first existentiated from Him is the *sefirot*, for they are both a perfect power and an imperfect power. When they partake of the abundant flow stemming from His perfection they are perfected power, and when the abundant flow is withdrawn they possess imperfect power. Thus, they are able to function in both perfection and imperfection, and perfection and imperfection differentiate one thing from another.

Now if you were to claim that He alone willed the creation of the world without [recourse to] the *sefirot*, the response to this [assertion] is that the intention indicates an imperfection in the intender. Alternatively, if you claim He did not intend His creation if such were the case, then creation was a random accident.

211

All things which are the outcome of a random accident have no order. Yet we witness that creation is ordered, with the sun during the day and the moon and stars at night. They exist by an order and by order they are generated and pass away. This order by which they exist and pass away is called the *sefirot*, for they are the force behind every existent being in the realm of plurality. Since the existentiation of created beings is brought about by means of the sefirot, each one differs one from the other: some are elevated, some are lowly, while others are intermediate. This is the case despite the fact that they are all derived from one principle. Every being is from Eyn-Sof, and nothing exists outside of Him.

4. If the questioner persists and asks: Agreed, you have demonstrated the necessity of *sefirot*; but by what [argument] do you establish that they are ten and yet one power?

Answer: I have already informed you that the *sefirot* are the beginning and commencement of all that is subject to limitation. Everything subject to limitation is bounded by substance and place, for there is no substance without place and there is no place except by means of substance. There is at least a third force in substance, and this third force is manifest in length, width, and depth: Thus there are nine. Since substance cannot exist without place and since there is no space except by means of substance, the number is not complete regarding substance and place with anything less than ten. Thus it states: "ten and not nine." And since we cannot complete the number without taking into account substance—itself bounded by substance and place—it states: "ten and not eleven." Just as the three produce nine; the fourth—which is place—when added to the three, produces sixteen. But it is sufficient for us to use ten in order to hint to the fact that place is derived from substance, and substance is but one power.

5. If the inquirer continues to ask: How can you say that the *sefirot* are emanated? I say they were created like all the other created beings!

Answer: I have already informed you that Eyn-Sof is perfect without any imperfection, and that the agent which initially is

212

brought forth from Him must also be perfect. Thus, the dynamic of emanation is fittingly the beginning of all creation, for the potency of emanation is the essence of the creation of all things. Had there been no emanative potency extracted from Eyn-Sof—lacking in nothing—how would we recognize the abundant perfection stemming from Eyn-Sof? How would the dynamic of the *sefirot* properly receive and subsequently circulate [the abundant flow] to all the needy beings without being diminished? For, when one draws from something in creation it is decreased and diminished. Since the *sefirot* are the first act existentiated from Eyn-Sof, it is appropriate that He be their dynamic, perfect without imperfection. Yet they are the ones who flow upon the impoverished, receiving from Eyn-Sof.

6. About this the inquirer persists: How can we possibly say that He is One and the multiplicity of ten unites within Him? By this we may preserve the truth in our hearts but certainly not in our statements.

Answer: I have already informed you that the One is the foundation of the many and that in the many no power is innovated only in Him. He is more than them and each of them is superior to its antecedent, and the potency of one is in the other. Nevertheless, the first is the dynamic of all the others. Though this first is the dynamic of the other, it is not so specifically but only generally. The metaphor for this is the fire, the flame, the sparks, and the aura: They are all of one essence even though they are different one from the other and divisible into separate components.

If the inquirer persists after you have established that there are *sefirot* and that they are ten and they were emanated and not created and their multiplicity is derived from unity and asks: Now answer me, why should I [not] ascribe to them measure, limit, and corporeality?

Answer: I have already informed you that Eyn-Sof is perfection without imperfection, and that He has a finite power which is unlimited and that the limitation emanating from Him which delimits all existent beings is the *sefirot*, having the power to act in

213

perfection and imperfection. Had He not existentiated for them limits, we would be unable to recognize that He has the power to existentiate limitation. As a testimony to the fact that nothing exists outside of Him, He brought into existence limitation, so that the confined beings could recognize their own boundaries. And though there are no limits above, the musings stemming from Eyn-Sof suggest that He is above and beyond extension in boundaries.

All that is limited, whether apprehended by the pondering of the heart or hinted at in thought extending below, can be found in speech and vision. Further, anything subject to limitation has magnitude and corporeality, because anything existent that is grasped by contemplation of the heart is called "body," not only spiritual things but even the *sefirot*. For they are [part of] the rule of all limited entities: They are the root of limitation. This limitation which is unlimited is emanated, and thus it states: "Their measure is ten without end." Finally, the philosophers stated that man's intellect is finite, and that from the way of the Ruler we see that everything has limitation, magnitude, and measure.

8. If the inquirer continues: Now you must answer me— these *sefirot*, when did they come into existence? If you now answer me that they were almost contemporaneous with the creation of the world, then it may be countered: Why did He intend their emanation at that precise moment and not at some earlier point would this not be a change of mind in Perfection? And if you answer that they are His eternality, then they would subsist in His undifferentiatedness; and if such were the case, what would be the difference between God and the *sefirot*?

Answer: Some of the *sefirot* existed in potentia within Eyn-Sof before they became actualized, like the first *sefirah* which is equal to all the others. There were some that were intelligible that were then emanated, like the second *sefirah* from which the preexistent Torah came forth. There were some that were perceived and some that were innate, such as those *sefirot* which were needed for this world and which were emanated almost contemporaneously with the creation of the world.

And since in the existentiation of the first two *sefirot* the hidden and intelligible powers [of the two] were totally intermingled, their reality nourished the other [*sefirot*]. As the Sages, may their memories be blessed, said, "Could not [the world] have been created with one statement?"

As to your other question, "that they would subsist in His undifferentiatedness?"

Answer: Even though we should avoid coining metaphors regarding Eyn-Sof, in order to help you understand let us compare the matter to a candle. The candle lights a myriad of other candles. Each lit candle shines more, yet they are all equal in comparison to the first candle and they all derive from one principle. But one must not liken the latter to the former. Their phylogenesis should not be compared to His ontogenesis, for He is greater than them and their energy is brought forth from Him, because of His supra-preeminence. Furthermore, no change takes place in Him. Rather, the dynamic of emanation becomes revealed through the division of their existence. Thus, one cannot say that there was a change of mind in Him, even though nothing exists outside of Him.

9. If the questioner continues: What is the nature of [the *sefirot*]?

Answer: The nature of *sefirah* is the synthesis of every thing and its opposite. For, if they did not possess the power of synthesis, there would be no energy in anything. For that which is light is not darkness and that which is darkness is not light.

Therefore, we should liken their nature to the will of the soul, for it is the synthesis of all the desires and thoughts stemming from it. Even though they be multifarious, their source is one, either in thesis or antithesis. This is the case with every function of the soul: intellect, esthetics, love, and mercy—even though they are all [created] ex nihilo, their existence is not absolute.

But, by embellishing substance with imagination, we can liken the first power to the concealed light. The second power [can be likened] to the light which contains every color. This light is like *tekbelet*, the essence (*takhlit*) of all colors in which there is no known hue. The third power [can be compared] to green light. The fourth power can be likened to white light. The fifth power can be likened to red light. The sixth power is composed of whiteness and scarlet. The seventh power is the power of scarlet tending toward whiteness. The eighth power is the power of whiteness tending toward scarlet. The ninth power is composed of whiteness and scarlet and scarlet tending toward whiteness and whiteness tending toward scarlet. The tenth power is composed of every color.

10. If the inquirer persists and asks: What are their names, their order, and their rank?

Answer: The name of the first power is Elevated Height (*rom-ma'alah*), for it is elevated above the probing of an investigator. The second is called Wisdom (*hokmah*), for it is the beginning of conceptualization. The third is called Understanding (binah). Up to this point is the world of intelligence (*'olam ha-sekhel*).

The fourth is called Lovingkindness (*hesed*). The fifth is called Fear (*pahad*). The sixth is called Beauty (*tferet*). Up to this point is the world of the soul (*'olam ha-nefesh*).

The seventh is called Victory (*nesah*). The eighth is called Majesty (*hod*). The ninth is called the Righteous One, Foundation of the world (*saddiq yesod 'olam*). The tenth is call justice (*sedeq*). Up to this point is the world of the body (*'olam ba-guf*).

Following is the order of their activity. The first is the divine power. The second is for angelic power. The third is for prophetic power. The fourth extends lovingkindness to the heights. The fifth passes judgment with the fear of His strength. The sixth has compassion in fear upon the lower worlds. The seventh nurtures and strengthens the vegetative soul. The eighth weakens and infirms it. The ninth draws together all their powers, sometimes for one purpose, sometimes for another. The tenth is the lower attribute of severity. It is composed of the power of all the others in order to judge the lower worlds.

The energy of the human soul is drawn from them and their powers in the following way:

Elevated Height exists as the power of that soul which is called "only one" (*yehidah*); Wisdom exists in the soul as the animative soul; Understanding exists in the power of spirit; Fear in the power called "animus" (*neshamah*); Beauty in the power of blood; Victory in the power of bone; Majesty in the flower of flesh; Foundation of the World in the power of the sinew; and justice in the power of the skin.

And their placement above is as follows:

Elevated Height encompasses and encircles Wisdom and Understanding, which in turn surround all that is beneath them. Lovingkindness is drawn to Eternity, which is on the right side. Fear is drawn to Majesty, which are in the middle, and justice is opposite them.

11. Should the questioner persist: You have now informed me as to their names, rank, and order. You have further informed me as to the position of justice, which receives from all their power. Now tell me whether there is bestowing and receiving in each one.

Answer: Know that no emanation is radiated forth except to proclaim the unity within Eyn-Sof. If the receptor did not unite with the bestower into one power, then it would not be possible to recognize that the two are really one. In their unity one knows that power of union. Upon seeing the uniting force made manifest, how much more so one should not ruminate upon it in secret. Thus, everything is both receptor and bestower....

Zohar

The central phase of Jewish mysticism is Kabbalah, which itself evolves in three phases and various places: early (ca. 1100–1250, mainly in Germany, Provence, and northeastern Spain), middle (ca. 1250–1500, mainly in northern Spain), and late (ca. 1500–1750, mainly in Palestine, Italy, and Central Europe). Kabbalah may be distinguished from the earlier *Merkavah* period and the later Hasidic period.

The middle, classical phase of Kabbalah is marked by a number of texts by various authors, but the most renowned of these is the *Zohar*. The *Zohar*—the word, drawn from Daniel 12:3, means "splendor"—was first published in 1305 after the death of Moses de Leon. Presumably it was used during the last third or so of the thirteenth century within his circle of students, and he is believed by most modern scholars to be its author, or at least its redactor and the compiler of its far-flung contents.

In effect an extended mystical midrash, the six-volume work is written in an awkward Aramaic intended to emulate that language in common Jewish use in Judaea-Palestine in the first few centuries of the Common Era. Indeed, the claim made by Moses de Leon's widow (and presumably by him while he was alive) was that he was merely the recorder in writing of a text that had been authored by no less a luminary than Shimeon Bar Yohai, who, together with his teacher, Rabbi Akiva, was preeminent in the early second century both as a mainstream rabbi and as a mystic.

As Moses, traditionally understood to be the conduit through which God speaks the Torah, is nonetheless a character within it, so Shimeon, as author of the *Zohar*, is nonetheless the preeminent character within it: its interpretive tales are the tales he tells within its pages.

Thus in the selection before us, instruction is offered as coming from Rabbi Shimeon in response to a query regarding a Torah passage. The primary imagery, paradoxically enough—given that God is by definition invisible—is visual. Rabbi Shimeon refers to colors that can be seen and those that cannot be seen: he distinguishes outer from inner vision, describing how one may physically enhance one's ability to move from the one to the other.

But that methodological discussion, tied to his analysis of the Torah passage, is a metaphor for the distinction between the limited knowledge of God's name accorded to the three Hebrew Patriarchs and the fuller knowledge accorded to Moses. It all hinges on the idea of *ineffability*: the idea that God's true Name—the Name conveying God's innermost essence—cannot be articulated in the here and now any more than invisible colors may be seen with the outer eye.

The entire narrative of Rabbi Shimeon's commentary is framed and designed to illuminate the issue that resides at the heart of the *Zohar*, of Kabbalah at large, and of the entire Jewish mystical tradition. How can the mystic come to merge with and know the impossibly inaccessible God—inaccessible to the senses and the intellect, to the instruments with which we typically access the world around us—whose hiddenmost essence is yet somehow deemed accessible?

One answer is that if we could know God's true, essence-bearing Name—the Ineffable Name—then we could know God. For to know the essence-bearing name of something is to know its essence and thus to know it. Of course, to say "Odysseus" or "Abraham," while it may in some sense conjure them, does not bring them before us in the same way as if they walked into the room. And God is in any case not a *something*. Moreover, God's essence cannot truly be "captured" in *any* name, the way the essence of Odysseus or Abraham might.

So at the outset of the *Zohar* passage, not only does the primordial light from Genesis 1:2 flash from "within the Concealed of the Concealed from the mystery of the Infinite," so that the

Creator of that light is inconceivably distant and ineffably hidden from the first act of creation. But—deconstructing the syntax of the opening phrase, as Hebrew allows, turning subject into object: "In the beginning God created..." (Gen 1:1) becomes "In the beginning [He] created 'God'"—not God, but God's common, everyday Name (*Elohim*) becomes the first thing that God creates.

God's Name is the palace that connects earth to the hidden-most recesses of heaven. Among prophets, only Moses entered the innermost chambers of the palace to which the Jewish mystic seeks access—through meditating on just such a text.

Ori Z. Soltes

The Ten Sefirot

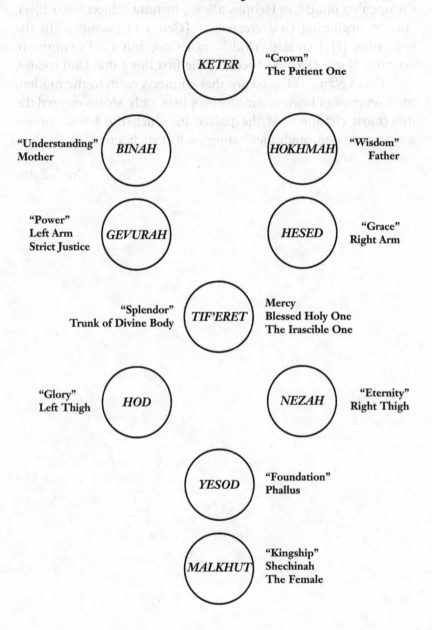

KETER
"Crown"
The Patient One

"Understanding"
Mother
BINAH

HOKHMAH
"Wisdom"
Father

"Power"
Left Arm
Strict Justice
GEVURAH

HESED
"Grace"
Right Arm

"Splendor"
Trunk of Divine Body
TIF'ERET
Mercy
Blessed Holy One
The Irascible One

"Glory"
Left Thigh
HOD

NEZAH
"Eternity"
Right Thigh

YESOD
"Foundation"
Phallus

MALKHUT
"Kingship"
Shechinah
The Female

222

The Creation of Elohim

In the Beginning

When the King conceived ordaining He engraved engravings in the luster on high. A blinding spark flashed within the Concealed of the Concealed from the mystery of the Infinite, a cluster of vapor in formlessness, set in a ring, not white, not black, not red, not green, no color at all. When a band spanned, it yielded radiant colors. Deep within the spark gushed a flow imbuing colors below, concealed within the concealed of the mystery of the Infinite. The flow broke through and did not break through its aura. It was not known at all until, under the impact of breaking through, one high and hidden point shone. Beyond that point, nothing is known. So it is called Beginning, the first command of all.

"The enlightened will shine like the zohar of the sky, and those who make the masses righteous will shine like the stars forever and ever" (Daniel 12:3).

Zohar, Concealed of the Concealed, struck its aura. The aura touched and did not touch this point. Then this Beginning emanated and made itself a palace for its glory and its praise. There it sowed the seed of holiness to give birth for the benefit of the universe. The secret is: "Her stock is a holy seed" (Isaiah 6:13).

Zohar, sowing a seed for its glory like the seed of fine purple silk. The silkworm wraps itself within and makes itself a palace. This palace is its praise and a benefit to all.

With the Beginning the Concealed One who is not known created the palace. This palace is called Elohim. The secret is:

"With Beginning, (Genesis 1:1) created Elohim."

Colors and Enlightenment

One day Rabbi Shim'on was sitting. Rabbi El'azar, his son, and Rabbi Abba were with him. Rabbi El'azar said "The verse writ-

ten here: I have appeared to Abraham, to Isaac, and to Jacob...
Why appeared? The word should be spoken."

He answered "El'azar, my son, it is a high mystery! Come
and see: Certain colors can be seen; certain colors cannot. These
and those are the high mystery of faith. But human beings do not
know; they do not reflect.

The colors that can be seen no one was pure enough to see
them until the Patriarchs came and mastered them. Therefore the
word appeared, for they saw the colors which are revealed. Which
are revealed? Colors of El Shaddai, colors in a cosmic prism.
These can be seen.

But the colors above, hidden and invisible, no human has
mastered them except for Moses. Therefore the verse concludes:
'But by My name YHVH, I was not known to them.' I was not
revealed to them in high colors. Do you think that the Patriarchs
were not aware of those colors at all? They were aware, through
those that are revealed.

It is written: 'The enlightened will shine like the zohar of the
sky, and those who make the masses righteous will shine like the
stars forever and ever' (Daniel 12:3).

'The enlightened will shine.' Who is enlightened? The wise
one who contemplates by himself, from himself, words that
human beings cannot mouth.

'Will shine like the zohar of the sky.' Which sky? The sky of
Moses which stands in the center; this zohar of his is concealed
and not revealed. It stands above the sky that does not shine, in
which colors can be seen. There those colors can be seen, but they
do not glow with the brilliance of the hidden colors.

Come and see: There are four lights. Three are concealed and
one is revealed. A shining light. A glowing light; it shines like the
clear brilliance of heaven. A purple light that absorbs all lights. A
light that does not shine but gazes toward the others and draws
them in. Those lights are seen in her as in a crystal facing the sun.
The first three are concealed, overseeing this one, which is
revealed.

The secret is: the eye. Come and see: Three colors appear in the eye, but none of them glow, for they are overshadowed by a light that does not shine. These are images of the colors that are hidden, which oversee them.

These were shown to the Patriarchs, so they would know those hidden ones that glow through these that do not glow. The ones that glow and the ones that are hidden were revealed to Moses in that sky of his. These oversee those colors that are seen in the eye.

The secret is: close your eye and roll your eyeball. Those colors that shine and glow will be revealed. Permission to see is granted only with eyes concealed, for they are high and concealed, overseeing those colors that can be seen but do not glow.

And so we read: 'Moses attained the mirror that shines,' which oversees the one that does not shine. The rest of humanity, that mirror that does not shine. The Patriarchs saw, through these colors that are revealed, those hidden ones, which oversee the ones that do not shine. Therefore it is written: 'I appeared to Abraham, to Isaac, and to Jacob through El Shaddai,' through the colors that can be seen. 'But by My name YHVH, I was not known to them.' These are high colors, hidden and glowing. Moses was so pure that he gazed into them!

The secret is: the eye, closed and open. Closed, it sees the mirror that shines. Opened, it sees the mirror that does not shine. So, 'I appeared' in the mirror that does not shine, which is open and revealed. This is described as seeing. But the mirror that shines, which is concealed, this is described as knowing, as it is written: 'I was not known.'"

Rabbi El'azar and Rabbi Abba came and kissed his hands. Rabbi Abba cried, and said "Woe when you disappear from the world!

The world will be an orphan without you! Who will be able to illumine the words of Torah?"

Abraham Isaac Kook

Rabbi Abraham Isaac Kook (1865–1935) was one of the most influential rabbis of the twentieth century. He was born in Latvia of a mother who came from a mystical—Hasidic—background and a father from a legalistic, anti-mystical background, and arrived in Ottoman Palestine in 1904 as a rabbi in the port city of Jaffa. After waiting out World War I in Europe he returned to British Mandatory Palestine in 1921 as the first Ashkenazi Chief Rabbi, founded a renowned Yeshiva in Jerusalem three years later, and remained at both posts until his death in 1935.

Rabbi Kook wrote extensively—although most of his work was published posthumously—on a range of topics, from mainstream legalistic Jewish thinking (*halachah*) and midrashic engagement of the Torah and other Jewish texts (*aggada*) to mysticism and the spiritual role of the nascent Zionist movement in Jewish spirituality.

In the selection before us, Rabbi Kook does a number of things. He furthers the focus on wisdom (*hokhmah*) that is part of the mystical tradition, distinguishing divinely sourced from humanly sourced wisdom. He offers a summary statement of what mysticism is all about: ferreting out the hidden meanings within the Torah that can provide secret knowledge regarding God. He observes that such a process of inquiry draws every generation to engage in it in its own ways.

Rabbi Kook offers a panhenotheistic (recognizing the one God in all of creation) perspective of the world drawn from the Hasidic tradition (ca. 1750–present): the Creator is found in every detail, however minute, of the creation and thus, for the mystic, no gesture, no sound, no moment, however apparently tiny and insignificant, is without potential importance with regard to coming to understand and merge with God. Thus mysticism is esoteric and rarified yet all-encompassing and accessible.

This apparent paradox—mysticism looks outward and inward, seeks beyond the transcendent yet within the most immanent; God is farther than the most distant star but closer than my own breath—means that, far from being disconnected from the world, mysticism has the potential to order it, sublimely. Rabbi Kook's assertion is that the tendency to think in narrow-minded terms—to see the world only from within one's own discipline or tradition, which generates chaos and conflict among perspectives—is not the only way of being in the world. He contends that a truly spiritual perspective unifies points of view, synthesizes and orders the *elementa* of reality—and that this is both a statement of future possibility and hope and one articulated by spirituality and mysticism.

Within the specifics of the Jewish tradition Rabbi Kook applies this perspective to the two primary modes of rabbinic thought: *halachah* (essentially, legalistic thinking) and *aggada* (essentially, legend-bound, phantasmagorical thinking). He notes not only that these two modes of thought are historically interwoven in rabbinic literature but that the future is contained within a more broadly shared recognition of that interweave.

The future is contained within the intermixing of the realities of what is hidden—beneath both the surface of the Torah and the surface of the world—and what is already revealed along those surfaces. Thus the esoteric and the practical, the empirical and the mystical, he forecasts with hope, will together shape the Jewish messianic future within the universal future.

One can infer from his words the sort of role he played in the Zionist movement of his era. As a synthesizer, he saw the viability and indeed the importance of the Zionist idea. He championed it against Jewish religious traditionalists who saw the movement as abrogating God's messianic intentions—because humans were taking matters into their own hands with regard to "ingathering the exiles"—observing that, given the vagueness of those intentions as Judaism has understood them throughout history, we cannot be sure that we are not intended by God to *be* the instrument for effecting the exilic ingathering and the messianic era. At the same time he criticized those who so thoroughly secularized the movement that God disappeared from it. His discussion of mystical thought suggests how Jewish spirituality can and should be understood to be a unifying, world-repairing mechanism.

Ori Z. Soltes

The Wisdom of the Holy as an Influence on Life

The wisdom of the holy ranks higher than all other aspects of wisdom in this respect, that it transforms the will and personal disposition of those who pursue it, drawing them toward those lofty heights on which its concern is focused. All branches of worldly wisdom, though they describe important and noble subjects, lack this impact, to draw the nature of the person who explores them to their own level of value. Indeed, they do not relate to the other aspects of the person's nature, only to his scientific dimension.

The reason for this is that all aspects of the holy emanate from the ultimate source of life, and the content of what is hallowed has the power to engender new being, "to stretch out the heavens and lay the foundations of the earth" (Isa. 51:16), and certainly to stamp a dramatic new image on the person probing it. The secular sciences lack this potency; they do not, in themselves, engender anything new. They only portray to the mind what is found in existence. Thus they cannot turn the one who studies them into a new being, to sever him from an evil inclination in his basic self and change him into a new type of person, pure and vibrant with the light of what is the true and abiding life. (Vol. 1, p. 1)

The Summons to the Mystical

When an individual, and similarly a generation, has reached a state where its spiritual propensities are summoned to expression, then it will no longer satisfy its pressing thirst with any fragmentary knowledge unless this very knowledge leads to a content that is broad and free, that will engender great ecstasy in the root disposition of the soul, deriving from the source of its being. Thus the mystical elements of the world, the hidden meanings of the

Torah, the secret knowledge about God, are called forth from each generation.

The stubbornness of seeking spiritual satisfaction in the outer aspect of things enfeebles one's powers, fragments the human spirit, and leads the stormy quest in a direction where it will find emptiness and disappointment. In disillusionment the quest will continue in another direction.

This is the mission of the strong, those for whom the light of God is the whole meaning of their lives. Even if they have been hurt by great disappointment, even if they have grown faint because of insufficient faith in themselves, even if they have become wearied by their battle against a great multitude that follows confidently its own opinion, let them not cease their beneficent labors, let them not allow their strength to give way. In their hands is the banner of the hidden meanings of the Torah, riches of knowledge, a comprehensible and inner-directed faith, abiding deliverance for the Jewish people and for man, for body and soul, for this world and for all worlds, for great and small, for old and young.

If we say something and turn speechless, if we commence an utterance and the concept is lost in silence, if we lack the strength to liberate the word, to find the expression, we will not, for this reason, become dismayed and retreat from our fixed goal. The difficulty of speech will not serve as a restraint on the stream of the lofty desire in which the word of God is revealed, which bids us speak, to gird the stumbling with strength, to proclaim peace to the adversaries of the world. "I will cause a new utterance to be heard in the land: Peace, peace to the far and near, said the Lord; and I will heal him" (Isa. 57:19). (Vol. I, pp. 5–6.)

The Mystical Dimension That Embraces Everything

Philosophy embraces only a given part of the spiritual world. By nature it is detached from whatever is outside its sphere. By this itself it is fragmented in its being. The grace of perceiving how all feelings and tendencies, from the small to the large, are interdependent, how they act on each other, how separate worlds are organically related—this it cannot portray. For this reason it must always remain an aristocratic discipline, set apart for special individuals.

Greater than this is the mystical quest, which by its nature penetrates to the depths of all thought, all feelings, all tendencies, all aspirations, and all worlds, from beginning to end. It recognizes the inner unity of all existence, the physical and the spiritual, the great and the small, and for this reason there is, from its perspective, no bigness or smallness. Everything is important, and everything is invested with marked value. There is no lost gesture, there is no vain imagining.

Corresponding to this there is no limit to the possibility of ascending toward the heights. There is no wisdom or perception concerning which one may say that it is enough, and that it cannot be linked to a higher illumination, in comparison with which it seems in a state of dimness. Even the supernal crown, which is a dazzling light, a pure light, is darkness in comparison with the Cause of causes, before whom all lights are turned into darkness.

Because of this advantage, mystical vision, in being able to embrace within itself all thoughts and all sparks of the spiritual, is alone fit to chart for us the way to go.

Therefore, the mystical dimension is the soul of religion, the soul of the Torah. From its substance derives all that is revealed, all that is circumscribed, all that can be conceived by logic, and all that can be carried out in actions. The far-reaching unity of the mystical dimension embraces all creatures, all conditions of thought and feeling, all forms of poetry and exposition, all expressions of life, all aspirations and hopes, all objectives and ideals, from the lowest depths to the loftiest heights. The source of life deriving from the highest realm of the divine, which only the light of prophecy, the clear illumination, the light seen by Adam, the supernal lights can disclose, streams into and passes through all stirrings of thought, all movements of the spirit.

Only the mysterious mind of the Supreme One fixes the particular formations, what shall be regarded as first and what as last, which phenomenon shall obscure the unity because of its lowly state, and which is above it because of its greatness. "And before the One what can you count?" (Sefer Yezirah, ch. 1, Mishnah 7). (Vol. I, pp. 9–10.)

The Spiritual Unification of the Future

One of the great afflictions of man's spiritual world is that every discipline of knowledge, every feeling, impedes the emergence of the other. The result is that most people remain limited and one-sided, and their shortcomings are continually on the increase.

The cloud that each discipline casts on the other also leads the devotee of a particular discipline to feel a sharp antagonism toward the discipline that is remote to him, whose values are outside his concerns.

This defect cannot continue permanently. Man's nobler future is destined to come, when he will develop to a sound spiritual state so that instead of each discipline negating the other, all knowledge, all feeling will be envisioned from any branch of it.

This is precisely the true nature of reality. No spiritual phenomenon can stand independently. Each is interpenetrated by all. Only the limitations of our mental capacities impede us from glimpsing those aspects of the spiritual domain that are immanent in every part of it. When man rises in his spiritual development his eyes will open to see properly. "Then the blind will see and the deaf will hear, and the earth will be full of the knowledge of the Lord as the waters cover the sea" (Isa. 35:5, 11:9). (Vol. I, p. 22.)

The Unification of *Halakha* and *Aggadah*

The *halakha* and the *aggadah* must be united. The necessity that moves us to concern ourselves with both must also lead to their spiritual unification. The fact that one who concerns himself with *halakha* feels he has entered a different world when he enters the realm of *aggadah* and vice versa destroys much of the spiritual stimulation that is inspired by the peace of mind that comes from inner unity.

We are summoned to chart paths in the methods of study through which the *halakha* and the *aggadah* will be merged in a substantive unity.

The concept of bringing together distant realms—this is the basis of building and perfecting the spiritual world. This is a basic tendency that runs like a distinctive thread through all manifestations of life, in all its dimensions, and it must emerge in ever broader form. After the analytical disposition has done its work of analysis in order to clarify each discipline according to its category, it must make room for the synthesizing disposition to be activated in the soul, which has been illuminated by the concept of unification. Thereby will all knowledge, all the spiritual disciplines in their respective categories, be revealed as different organs in one enduring, multifaceted body that is illumined by one enduring, multifaceted living soul.

As we commence the process of unifying *halakha* and *aggadah*, many other unifications and harmonies will be stimulated in its wake. The heavenly and the earthy realms, our physical and intellectual selves, with all the hidden riches in each of them, will join to activate in each the process needed for its full growth and development.

This will release new light on the particular subject to which we have set our eyes and our hearts in our study of the Torah, the unification of *halakha* and *aggadah*.

This unification is only the disclosure of the unity that has always existed below the surface. Whoever has failed to taste the flavor of *halakha* has not tasted the flavor of the fear of sin. The pursuit of Torah and the fear of sin must always be blended. The labor of study must be seen as dedicated, in a systematic manner, to this principle of unification, whose consequences will be of immense importance.

In truth there is always a halakhic element in the *aggadah*, and similarly an inner aggadic content in the *halakha*. For the most part the aggadic content is present in the qualitative aspect of the *halakha*, and the halakhic content in the theory behind the quantitative proliferation of the *aggadah*. Without any searching or special sensitivity we are influenced, while studying *halakha*, by the aggadic dimension hidden therein; and while studying *aggadah*, by the particular halakhic formulations, which are merged in the aggadic content.

However, not everyone can see with a proper perspective these trends, each of which is at all times present in the domain of the other. The alienation from each other of these worlds that are so closely linked and substantively related has resulted in a sickly separation in the method of our study and its development, and confines in narrow circles both these domains, the halakhic domain as well as the aggadic domain.

We must stress the joining of these two forces in a proper form, so that each will give added strength to the content of the other, help clarify its particulars and shed more light on its general concepts, on the depth of its logic and its far-reaching significance. The *halakha* must be made more appealing through association with the *aggadah*, in an appropriate manner, and the *aggadah* likewise needs to be assessed in its relation to the clearly defined, fixed laws and the particularized delimiting logic represented in the established structure of the *halakha*. Thereby will the vitality and fruitfulness of both be doubled.

The necessity that moved the masters of Talmudic dialectics in former generations to attempt at times to link the *aggadah* and the *halakha* derives in truth from this claim for unification of these two forces that act with such congruence.

We have already been called upon to bring together many talents and branches of knowledge for the clarification of our studies, of our whole way of life. The very nature of halakhic study demands that it include many approaches, the views of the early and later masters, who were so numerous in the course of the generations. Deep probing and wide horizons are especially a must for us. It is therefore necessary that we reach out as well with references to unifying the contents of the *halakha* and the *aggadah*, in which are included all the contributing factors of logic and history, morals and faith, sentiment and custom, and, above all, pure inspiration, which is pervaded with the dew of life embodied in the general light of the Torah. This should grace everyone pursuing the study of the Torah for its own sake, to give him special delight and blessing as he rejoices in the Torah, which strengthens the heart. (Vol. I, pp. 25–28.)

The Masters of the Concealed and the Revealed

The arrangement that separates the revealed from the concealed, in the Torah and in all wisdom generally, has its basis in the different dispositions among the enlightened ones.

The person inclined to the revealed does not need any mystical vision for the perfection of his individuality. His inner refinement and his moral sense are satisfied through the assimilation of the spiritual elements immanent in every perception of the revealed. As far as the Jew, a disciple of the Torah, is concerned, his Jewish soul is well perfected with an inner dimension through the accumulation of perceptions that emerge within it, and he fashions out of them a rich spiritual content.

Fundamentally we are compelled to say that there is a certain richness of the mystical among the devotees of the revealed, which makes it unnecessary for them to labor over refined, spiritual subject matter. They already possess satisfactory substantive matter from the realm of the spiritual. This sufficiency leads them occasionally to feel impatient with all mystical concerns. On the contrary, they themselves feel a lack in the knowledge of particulars related to the practical, and their way of life is filled with impediments, to the degree that they lack such knowledge. It is this that prods them to profuse arguments and discussions related to action.

The devotees of the mystical are the very opposite. They find enough within themselves to satisfy them with reference to the outer level of existence. The practical way seems straight to them. They resolve doubts as they occur, without weariness. But the modest possession embodying the mystical spirit presents them with endless claims to complete it. They feel a kind of fierce hunger and mighty thirst for concepts relating to the hidden, the concealed. Questions about lofty matters, which touch on the highest mysteries, give them no peace. They press on them to continue the endeavor to find answers, at least for some of their details and the ways we may envision them.

It is rare to find a person who responds fully to the claims of the revealed and the concealed at the same time. There is always some opposition from one to the other. It is only when a person is sensitive to his surroundings and realizes the precious elements that each of the two sides have accumulated by their labors that he is seized as it were by a strong kind of the "envy among scholars" and he then seeks to nourish himself by both methods. For the most part he finds roadblocks on his way, but he tries to overcome them.

Such people are always oppressed by a heavy burden, by a troubled mind, but they bring much good to the world. It is they, after all, who by their spirit create a new world, in which the heavenly and the earthly embrace each other.

After they bring out this composite vision from potentiality to actuality, others can then come and accept what has been readied and there comes into being in the course of the centuries a regular spiritual disposition to embrace these separate and opposite disciplines together. Then there is indeed revealed a creative force of double potency. "Wisdom cries aloud in the street" (Prov. 1:20); "sound wisdom is double 6 for effecting deliverance" (adapted from Job 11:6); "write the vision clearly upon the tablets" (Hab. 2:2). (Vol. I, pp. 36–37.)

FIVE

CHRISTIANITY

The Gospel of John

The Gospel of John, which gives internal evidence of being that of John "the disciple whom Jesus loved" (21:20), recounts the life of Jesus Christ from the baptism to the resurrection. Early Christian tradition identifies John as one of the twelve apostles whom Jesus gathered around him as he entered into his public life and ministry. Additional internal evidence—John the apostle is regularly omitted—and a lack of any definitive challenge as to his authorship in the first three centuries of the Church, tend to solidify the belief in John's authorship of this Gospel. Even so, some modern scholarship argues that John was illiterate and could not have written the Gospel. It is generally agreed, however, that the text dates to about 85–90 CE, roughly a half-century after the death of Jesus, although some scholars date it as late as the year 100. It is also thought to have been written at Ephesus, which theory would coordinate with the belief that Mary, the mother of Jesus and Mary Magdalene, witness to the resurrection and known as the "apostle to the apostles," fled there after the crucifixion. (There is a longstanding tradition at Ephesus that Mary the mother of Jesus died there.)

The Gospel is generally divided into four sections: the Prologue, the Book of Signs, the Passion narrative, and the Epilogue. Each of the three latter sections is both presaged and completed in the Prologue. The Book of Signs, which differs in some details from the other three Gospels, gives an account of Jesus' ministry, including some of his teachings. In these central chapters, Jesus speaks of himself in the first person as "the bread of life" (6:35), "the light of the world" (8:12), "the gate for the sheep" (10:7), "the good shepherd" (10:11), "the resurrection and the life" (11:25), "the way, the truth, and the life" (14:6), and "the true vine" (15:1). The Passion narrative begins with John's account of the Last Supper, at which the Eucharist was instituted, through Jesus' arrest, crucifixion, death, burial, and resurrection. In John, Mary Magdalene sees the risen Jesus and runs to tell the apostles. The Epilogue tells of Jesus' postresurrection appearances, including to the gathered apostles in the upper room twice, the second time in the presence of the apostle Thomas, and at the Sea of Tiberias, where he ate with them.

The Prologue to the Fourth Gospel delimits the fact and the place of Jesus Christ in Christian belief and mysticism, or Christology. In contrast to the Synoptic Gospels (Matthew, Mark, and Luke), the Gospel of John is less historical and more theological. We need not enter into textual criticism here in order to recognize the impact and import of this Prologue, which was for centuries recited in part (verses 1–14) at every celebration of the Eucharist. While the following passage—and the entire Gospel it precedes— is not "mystical" in that it does not describe contemplative union with God, it encapsulates the philosophical and theological understanding of the place of Christ in Christian belief. Hence, it forms the basis for the Christo-mysticism so central to the understanding of Christian mysticism. The Prologue, together with the entire Gospel, forms a pure statement and demonstration that Jesus was (and is) the Christ.

Earlier selections in this anthology show a type of mystical writing that can be analogous to Christo-mysticism. The mysticism that recognizes a mediator between the human and the Godhead appears in a different manner in the bhakti-mysticism of the *Bhagavad Gita* and is somewhat akin to the Bodhisattva ideal in Mahāyāna Buddhism. John's Prologue calls Jesus the Eternal Word—the Logos—of God, superior to all other mediators.

The Prologue also presents the solution to the distinctions known in pure God-mysticism: between spirit and matter, between time and eternity, between the unknowable and the known, each resolved in the person of Jesus Christ. It does so by combining the divine nature with the physical, asserting that Jesus was indeed both fully God and fully man.

The Prologue to the Gospel of John is not a mystical treatise of the sort that follow in this section of the anthology; it was not written for those wishing to follow the contemplative life. Neither is it a spiritual roadmap for the interior or the exterior life. Rather, it is the explication of the Christian doctrine of the incarnation—God become human—in theological and philosophical terms, apparently designed to be both root and underpinnings of the spiritual lives of all Christian believers.

Phyllis Zagano

GOSPEL OF JOHN

1 In the beginning was the Word, and the Word was with God, and the Word was God.

2 He was in the beginning with God;

3 all things were made through him, and without him was not anything made that was made.

4 In him was life, and the life was the light of men.

5 The light shines in the darkness, and the darkness has not overcome it.

6 There was a man sent from God, whose name was John.

7 He came for testimony, to bear witness to the light, that all might believe through him.

8 He was not the light, but came to bear witness to the light.

9 The true light that enlightens every man was coming into the world.

10 He was in the world, and the world was made through him, yet the world knew him not.

11 He came to his own home, and his own people received him not.

12 But to all who received him, who believed in his name, he gave power to become children of God;

13 who were born, not of blood nor of the will of the flesh nor of the will of man, but of God.

14 And the Word became flesh and dwelt among us, full of grace and truth; we have beheld his glory, glory as of the only Son from the Father.

15 (John bore witness to him, and cried, "This was he of whom I said, 'He who comes after me ranks before me, for he was before me.'")

16 And from his fulness have we all received, grace upon grace.

17 For the law was given through Moses; grace and truth came through Jesus Christ.

18 No one has ever seen God; the only Son, who is in the bosom of the Father, he has made him known.

19 And this is the testimony of John, when the Jews sent priests and Levites from Jerusalem to ask him, "Who are you?"

20 He confessed, he did not deny, but confessed, "I am not the Christ."

21 And they asked him, "What then? Are you Elijah?" He said, "I am not." "Are you the prophet?" And he answered, "No."

22 They said to him then, "Who are you? Let us have an answer for those who sent us. What do you say about yourself?"

23 He said, "I am the voice of one crying in the wilderness, 'Make straight the way of the Lord,' as the prophet Isaiah said."

24 Now they had been sent from the Pharisees.

25 They asked him, "Then why are you baptizing, if you are neither the Christ, nor Elijah, nor the prophet?"

26 John answered them, "I baptize with water; but among you stands one whom you do not know,

27 even he who comes after me, the thong of whose sandal I am not worthy to untie."

28 This took place in Bethany beyond the Jordan, where John was baptizing.

29 The next day he saw Jesus coming toward him, and said, "Behold, the Lamb of God, who takes away the sin of the world!

30 This is he of whom I said, 'After me comes a man who ranks before me, for he was before me.'

31 I myself did not know him; but for this I came baptizing with water, that he might be revealed to Israel."

32 And John bore witness, "I saw the Spirit descend as a dove from heaven, and it remained on him.

33 I myself did not know him; but he who sent me to baptize with water said to me, 'He on whom you see the Spirit descend and remain, this is he who baptizes with the Holy Spirit.'

34 And I have seen and have borne witness that this is the Son of God."

35 The next day again John was standing with two of his disciples;

36 and he looked at Jesus as he walked, and said, "Behold, the Lamb of God!"

37 The two disciples heard him say this, and they followed Jesus.

38 Jesus turned, and saw them following, and said to them, "What do you seek?" And they said to him, "Rabbi" (which means Teacher), "where are you staying?"

39 He said to them, "Come and see." They came and saw where he was staying; and they stayed with him that day, for it was about the tenth hour.

40 One of the two who heard John speak, and followed him, was Andrew, Simon Peter's brother.

41 He first found his brother Simon, and said to him, "We have found the Messiah" (which means Christ).

42 He brought him to Jesus. Jesus looked at him, and said, "So you are Simon the son of John? You shall be called Cephas" (which means Peter).

43 The next day Jesus decided to go to Galilee. And he found Philip and said to him, "Follow me."

44 Now Philip was from Beth-sa'ida, the city of Andrew and Peter.

45 Philip found Nathan'a-el, and said to him, "We have found him of whom Moses in the law and also the prophets wrote, Jesus of Nazareth, the son of Joseph."

46 Nathan'a-el said to him, "Can anything good come out of Nazareth?" Philip said to him, "Come and see."

47 Jesus saw Nathan'a-el coming to him, and said of him, "Behold, an Israelite indeed, in whom is no guile!"

48 Nathan'a-el said to him, "How do you know me?" Jesus answered him, "Before Philip called you, when you were under the fig tree, I saw you."

49 Nathan'a-el answered him, "Rabbi, you are the Son of God! You are the King of Israel!"

50 Jesus answered him, "Because I said to you, I saw you under the fig tree, do you believe? You shall see greater things than these."

51 And he said to him, "Truly, truly, I say to you, you will see heaven opened, and the angels of God ascending and descending upon the Son of man."

St. Paul's First Letter to the Corinthians

Unlike the Gospel of John, which is credited to an eyewitness to the life, death, and resurrection of Jesus, the letters of Paul of Tarsus are from an early Christian who never saw Jesus in the flesh, but who depended on the testimony of others and the growing belief of his followers.

About five years before the birth of Christ, Saul was born in the important trading city of Tarsus, which is located about twenty kilometers from the Mediterranean Sea in south central Turkey. A Jew and a Roman citizen, for a time he persecuted Christians until, as he recounts it, he had a profound experience of Christ on the road to Damascus. The center of his conversion (around 33–36 CE) is his belief that Jesus was actually the Lord and Messiah foretold by the Prophets and promised to the Jews.

Following his conversion, Paul became the "apostle to the Gentiles," planting churches throughout the Mediterranean during three missionary journeys. The first, with the apostle Barnabas, left Antioch for Cyprus, thence to southern Asia Minor, and back to Antioch (Acts 13—14). The second, with Silas, took him by land through Syria toward Turkey, but he was diverted to Macedonia to Philippi, Athens, and other Greek towns, including Corinth, where he established a church (Acts 15:36—18:22). Around the year 53CE, Paul set out on his third preaching journey throughout the Mediterranean. Various events (including at least one shipwreck) brought him to Jerusalem, then Rome and Malta, and back to Corinth (Acts 18:23—20:38). In about 56 CE, Paul wrote his first letter to the Corinthians from Ephesus, on the west coast of present-day Turkey about 180 nautical miles from Corinth. A year later, he sent Titus with his second letter to them.

Some years later, while imprisoned in Rome (61–63 CE), Paul wrote many of his letters to the nascent churches of his journeys, including those at Colossae, Philippi, and Ephesus, as well as a personal letter to Philemon.

Originally written in Greek, Paul's First Letter to the Corinthians is perhaps the oldest document that gives witness to the resurrection, which he reports occurred about twenty years earlier. Counted as the seventh book of the New Testament, it is explicitly christological. In contrast to the dense philosophy of John, however, Paul's letter includes a clearer disquisition on the fact and place of Jesus, in addition to providing practical admonitions for the quarreling factions among the people of Corinth. The letter provides specific advice to the Christians of Corinth on how to manage the spiritual and temporal welfare of the Church. Its central teaching, however, is of the doctrine of the resurrection, and the first eleven verses are the earliest written account of the resurrection of Jesus in the New Testament. The remaining verses explain the centrality of the resurrection in Christianity.

Specific portions of this central chapter are dated to within a decade of the immediate events surrounding the death and resurrection of Jesus. First Corinthians 15:3–7 is a statement of belief (a creed) that pre-dates Paul and is located by many scholars as that of the apostolic community at Jerusalem. The central elements of the passage, however, are found in later Christian creeds, and indeed do frame the central beliefs of Christianity. Paul states that he is handing on or handing over what he had received (from the Jerusalem apostolic community?), specifically, the knowledge that Christ died for the sins of humanity as foretold in the scripture, that he was buried, and raised on the third day, also in accordance with the scriptures, that he appeared to Peter and later to the Twelve, and sometime later to five hundred disciples, and then to James, and then to all the apostles. These words are echoed in the two prevalent creeds used today, one known as the "Apostles' Creed" and the other the "Nicene Creed."

Following this central creedal statement, Paul presents the

doctrine of resurrection for all believers, responding to doubts within the Corinthian assembly (1 Cor 15:12–19), after which Paul promises that Christ will return again with all things subject to him (1 Cor 15:20–28). He then makes reference to an unusual practice—baptism of the dead—it appears in order to prepare them for the second coming of Christ (1 Cor 15:29). He warns against charlatans (1 Cor 15:33–34) and concludes this chapter with an explanation of resurrection, particularly focusing on the resurrection of the body as available to all who are baptized and believe in Christ.

Paul famously concludes with the passage (referencing Hosea) "O death, where is your sting? O grave, where is your victory?"

Phyllis Zagano

1 CORINTHIANS 15

1 Now I would remind you, brethren, in what terms I preached to you the gospel, which you received, in which you stand,

2 by which you are saved, if you hold it fast—unless you believed in vain.

3 For I delivered to you as of first importance what I also received, that Christ died for our sins in accordance with the scriptures,

4 that he was buried, that he was raised on the third day in accordance with the scriptures,

5 and that he appeared to Cephas, then to the twelve.

6 Then he appeared to more than five hundred brethren at one time, most of whom are still alive, though some have fallen asleep.

7 Then he appeared to James, then to all the apostles.

8 Last of all, as to one untimely born, he appeared also to me.

9 For I am the least of the apostles, unfit to be called an apostle, because I persecuted the church of God.

10 But by the grace of God I am what I am, and his grace toward me was not in vain. On the contrary, I worked harder than any of them, though it was not I, but the grace of God which is with me.

11 Whether then it was I or they, so we preach and so you believed.

12 Now if Christ is preached as raised from the dead, how can some of you say that there is no resurrection of the dead?

13 But if there is no resurrection of the dead, then Christ has not been raised;

14 if Christ has not been raised, then our preaching is in vain and your faith is in vain.

15 We are even found to be misrepresenting God, because we testified of God that he raised Christ, whom he did not raise if it is true that the dead are not raised.

16 For if the dead are not raised, then Christ has not been raised.

17 If Christ has not been raised, your faith is futile and you are still in your sins.

18 Then those also who have fallen asleep in Christ have perished.

19 If for this life only we have hoped in Christ, we are of all men most to be pitied.

20 But in fact Christ has been raised from the dead, the first fruits of those who have fallen asleep.

21 For as by a man came death, by a man has come also the resurrection of the dead.

22 For as in Adam all die, so also in Christ shall all be made alive.

23 But each in his own order: Christ the first fruits, then at his coming those who belong to Christ.

24 Then comes the end, when he delivers the kingdom to God the Father after destroying every rule and every authority and power.

25 For he must reign until he has put all his enemies under his feet.

26 The last enemy to be destroyed is death.

27 "For God has put all things in subjection under his feet." But when it says, "All things are put in subjection under him," it is plain that he is excepted who put all things under him.

28 When all things are subjected to him, then the Son himself will also be subjected to him who put all things under him, that God may be everything to every one.

29 Otherwise, what do people mean by being baptized on behalf of the dead? If the dead are not raised at all, why are people baptized on their behalf?

30 Why am I in peril every hour?

31 I protest, brethren, by my pride in you which I have in Christ Jesus our Lord, I die every day!

32 What do I gain if, humanly speaking, I fought with beasts at Ephesus? If the dead are not raised, "Let us eat and drink, for tomorrow we die."

33 Do not be deceived: "Bad company ruins good morals."

34 Come to your right mind, and sin no more. For some have no knowledge of God. I say this to your shame.

35 But some one will ask, "How are the dead raised? With what kind of body do they come?"

36 You foolish man! What you sow does not come to life unless it dies.

37 And what you sow is not the body which is to be, but a bare kernel, perhaps of wheat or of some other grain.

38 But God gives it a body as he has chosen, and to each kind of seed its own body.

39 For not all flesh is alike, but there is one kind for men, another for animals, another for birds, and another for fish.

40 There are celestial bodies and there are terrestrial bodies; but the glory of the celestial is one, and the glory of the terrestrial is another.

41 There is one glory of the sun, and another glory of the moon, and another glory of the stars; for star differs from star in glory.

42 So is it with the resurrection of the dead. What is sown is perishable, what is raised is imperishable.

43 It is sown in dishonor, it is raised in glory. It is sown in weakness, it is raised in power.

44 It is sown a physical body, it is raised a spiritual body. If there is a physical body, there is also a spiritual body.

45 Thus it is written, "The first man Adam became a living being"; the last Adam became a life-giving spirit.

46 But it is not the spiritual which is first but the physical, and then the spiritual.

47 The first man was from the earth, a man of dust; the second man is from heaven.

48 As was the man of dust, so are those who are of the dust; and as is the man of heaven, so are those who are of heaven.

49 Just as we have borne the image of the man of dust, we shall also bear the image of the man of heaven.

50 I tell you this, brethren: flesh and blood cannot inherit the kingdom of God, nor does the perishable inherit the imperishable.

51 Lo! I tell you a mystery. We shall not all sleep, but we shall all be changed,

52 in a moment, in the twinkling of an eye, at the last trumpet. For the trumpet will sound, and the dead will be raised imperishable, and we shall be changed.

53 For this perishable nature must put on the imperishable, and this mortal nature must put on immortality.

54 When the perishable puts on the imperishable, and the mortal puts on immortality, then shall come to pass the saying that is written: "Death is swallowed up in victory."

55 "O death, where is thy victory? O death, where is thy sting?"

56 The sting of death is sin, and the power of sin is the law.

57 But thanks be to God, who gives us the victory through our Lord Jesus Christ.

58 Therefore, my beloved brethren, be steadfast, immovable, always abounding in the work of the Lord, knowing that in the Lord your labor is not in vain.

Augustine of Hippo

Augustine (354–430), inarguably the most influential Christian writer after St. Paul, was born in the small town of Thagaste in Northern Africa. He was not baptized as a child because there was no post-baptismal remedy for sin at the time. He was educated at Thagaste and nearby Madaura, and received professional training as a rhetorician in Carthage. In 383 he traveled to Rome, and after a year moved farther north to Milan.

In Milan, he came to know the bishop (and, later, doctor of the Church) Ambrose (ca. 340–397), who baptized Augustine in 387. Soon after, Augustine set off for Africa with his mother and friends, but at the Roman port of Ostia she fell ill and died. On reaching Thagaste, he founded a monastic community, where he lived quietly until Bishop Valerius of Hippo Regius convinced him to be ordained priest in 391, and in 395 to become his coadjutor. Augustine became the bishop of the territory when Valerius died soon after. Augustine suffered his final illness and died on August 28, 430, as the Vandals (an East Germanic Tribe) overran North Africa.

Augustine's voluminous writings form a compendium of Christian theology and of the interior life. His work is recognizable as neo-Platonist, but whenever religion and philosophy collide, Augustine moves toward religion. Perhaps his most famous book is the *Confessions*, from which the following selections come. In it, he examines and explains his early life and conversion to Christianity in the form of a long "letter" to the Christian God he has come to believe in.

The selections here conclude with the well-known section on his finding God:

> Late have I loved you, O Beauty, so ancient and so new,
> late have I loved you! And behold, you were within me

and I was outside, and there I sought for you, and in my deformity I rushed headlong into the well-formed things that you have made. You were with me, and I was not with you.

Augustine's *Confessions* detail his growing up and growing away from profligate ways as he increasingly understood the fact of God in the world and in his life, and was written coincidentally with his conversion and baptism. The work, comprising thirteen books, is regarded as the first autobiography in the West. Succeeding books, or chapters, describe Augustine's boyhood and education, his understanding of God, his rejection of Manachaeism ("the error of two substances") and of the God of Neo-Platonism ("a God to fill the infinite distances of all space"), and the inner turmoil of his conversion to Christianity. Augustine further reflects on the meaning of the Hebrew Bible's Book of Genesis, on the meaning of time, and on the Christian doctrine of the Trinity.

In the selections that follow, Augustine speaks of the workings of the five senses (sight, hearing, smell, taste, touch) and of how he eventually came to understand the world as reflective of God's limitless power and beauty. His logic eventually brings him to the understanding that God's creation is all-encompassing and good.

I saw and clearly realized that all things you have made are good, and there are certainly no substances which you have not made.

If all creation is good, he writes, then it is impossible to reject any of creation, for only the insane person would reject what is good in favor of what is not good. Such would not be a rational choice, and man for Augustine is clearly a rational being, able to freely choose among goods and against evil.

Still, even though he knows he loves the good, and therefore God, he does not know who (or what) is God. He takes us through the process of his moving from a rational understanding to a more intuitive understanding of God.

"But what do I love when I love you?" Augustine asks. It is not the sensations coming from the world of nature—it is not the beauty of the earth or of light, it is not the sweet sounds of songs, it is not the fragrance of flowers, it is not the taste of honey, nor is it the tenderness of embraces. Yet, he says, he does love a kind of light, and sound, and fragrance, and taste, and tenderness, but he experiences only such sensations that are limitless, known, and able to be understood only by analogy to what the human experiences in life.

Augustine knows this love, and understands that he loves God, but as he describes his ongoing search in the following passages he relates the ways in which he came to know the God to whom he has addressed his entire book. Augustine says he thought perhaps the entire earth (and, by extension, all creation) was God, but he learned it was not. He asked (with his five senses) all about him, and within himself, but he could only find the answer that whatever he examined was not God, but was made by God. So what does he learn from all around him? He recognizes that his senses give him information and in essence establish his very being, for he lives as the sum of his experiences and can recall these sense experiences at will from the storehouse of his memory. As he lists his various experiences and understandings, he marvels that:

> Certainly these things are not brought into our memory
> but only their images are captured with marvelous swift-
> ness and stored up in wonderful secret places and are
> marvelously brought forth by the act of remembering.

How can that be, we might wonder with him. How can all these things known through the senses be stored within yet not be present within and still be available to him at will? He marvels as well at the fact that if he stops for a moment recalling something, it slips back into his memory, only to be available to his recollection at will. And so he remembers what is true as well as arguments against what is true, and so, he addresses God: "Where

259

then did I find you so that I might learn of you? For you were not already in my memory before I learned of you."

He concludes that God was all around, both in the present and as recalled in his memory, but for him to recognize, and laments that it took him so long to bring into his interior senses:

Late have I loved you, O Beauty, so ancient and so new, late have I loved you! And behold, you were within me and I was outside, and there I sought for you, and in my deformity I rushed headlong into the well-formed things that you have made. You were with me, and I was not with you. Those outer beauties held me far from you, yet if they had not been in you, they would not have existed at all. You called, and cried out to me and broke open my deafness; you shone forth upon me and you scattered my blindness: You breathed fragrance, and I drew in my breath and I now pant for you: I tasted and I hunger and thirst; you touched me, and I burned for Your peace.

Phyllis Zagano

CONFESSIONS, BOOK 10

And being admonished by all this to return to myself, I entered into my inmost part, with you as leader, and I was able to do so because you were my helper. I entered within and saw, with my soul's eye (such as it was), an unchangeable light. It was shining above the eye of my soul and above my mind, not that ordinary light visible to all flesh nor something of the same kind, only greater as though it might be our ordinary light shining more brightly and with its greatness filling all things. Your light was not that kind but another kind, utterly different from all these.

Nor was it above my mind as oil is above the water it floats on, nor as the sky is above earth; it was higher than my soul because it made me, and I was below because I was made by it. Whoever knows truth knows that Light, and whoever knows it, knows eternity. Charity knows it. O eternal Truth and true Love and beloved Eternity! You are my God, to you I sigh day and night. And when I first knew you, you lifted me up so that I might see that there was something to see but that I was not yet the man to see it. And you beat back the weakness of my gaze, shining on me too strongly, and I trembled with love and dread. And I knew myself to be far from you in the region of unlikeness, as if I heard your voice from on high: "I am the food of strong men; grow and you will feed on me; nor will you change me like ordinary food into your flesh, but you will be changed into me." And I learned that "for iniquity you have rebuked man, you made my soul to waste away like a moth" (Ps 39:11), and I said "Is truth therefore nothing at all, since it is neither diffused through infinite spaces nor through finite ones?" And you cried from afar: "I am who am" (Ex. 3) and I heard, as one hears in the heart, and from that moment there was no reason for me to doubt. I would more easily doubt that I lived than doubt that there truth existed: which is "clearly seen, being understood by the things that are made" (Rom 1:20).

And I reflected upon the other things which are inferior to you, and perceived that they neither have being wholly nor are they wholly nonbeing. They have being certainly because they are from you, and yet they have nonbeing because they are not what you are. For that truly is which remains unchangeable. "It is good then for me to hold fast to God" (Ps 73:28) because, if I do not abide in Him, neither can I abide in myself. But He remaining in Himself renews all things; and "you are my God, since you need none of my goods" (Ps 16:2).

And it became clear to me that those things which are subject to corruption are good. They would not be subject to corruption if they were the highest good or not good at all. For, if they were the highest good, they would be incorruptible, but if they were not good at all, there would not be anything in them to be corrupted. For corruption harms, and unless goodness in a thing were diminished, corruption would not harm. Either, therefore, corruption does no harm at all, which cannot be the case, or, which is quite certain, all things which are corrupted are deprived of something good in them. But if things are deprived of all goodness, they will have no being at all. For if they continue to exist and can no longer be corrupted, they will be better than before, because they will be permanently beyond the reach of corruption. And what is more monstrous than to say that those things which have lost all goodness have become better? If they were deprived of all goodness, they would be altogether nothing. Therefore, as long as they are, they are good. Therefore, all things which exist are good, and that evil the origin of which I sought is not a substance because, if it were a substance, it would be good. For either it would be an incorruptible substance, that is, the highest good, or it would be a corruptible substance which, unless it were good, would not be corruptible. Therefore I saw and clearly realized that all things you have made are good, and there are certainly no substances which you have not made. And since all things which you have made are not equal, they have an individual existence and also exist as part of a whole. They are good individually and likewise are altogether very good since God "made all things very good" (Gn 1:31).

To you, then, nothing at all is evil. This is true not only of you but of your whole creation, because there is nothing outside it to break in and corrupt the order which you have imposed on things. But in parts of creation because things clash with one another, they are thought evil; but those same things agree with other things and are good, and in themselves they are good. All these things which do not harmonize with one another are suitable to the lower part of reality which we call earth, which has the cloudy and windy sky suitable for it. And God forbid that I should ever say, "These things ought not to be," because if I saw only these things, certainly I would desire better, but even for these alone I ought to praise you: Since these things of earth show that you ought to be praised; "dragons and all abysses, fire, hail, snow, ice and stormy wind which fulfill your word; mountains and all hills, fruitful trees, and all cedars; beasts and all cattle; creeping things and flying fowls; kings of the earth and all people; princes and all judges of the land; young men and maidens; old men and children, let them praise your name" (Ps 148:1–12). Since even in heaven they praise you, praise you, our God, in the heights all your angels, all your hosts, sun and moon, all the stars and light, the heaven of heavens and the waters above the heavens, praise your name: I did not now desire better because I was thinking of them all, and I embraced the better judgment that certainly the higher things are better than the lower things, but all things together are better than the higher ones by themselves.

There is no sanity in those to whom any one of your creatures is displeasing just as there was no sanity in me when many things which you have made displeased me. And because my soul did not dare to be displeased by my God, I was unwilling to admit that whatever did displease it was yours. Thus, my soul moved to the error of two substances, and was restless and speaking perversely. And next it went back again and fashioned for itself a God to fill the infinite distances of all space, and it imagined this God to be you and had placed it in its own heart so that once again it became the temple of its own idol, a temple abominable to you. But you, unknown to me, laid your kindly hand upon my head and covered up my eyes lest they see vanity, and then I relaxed a little from myself, and sleep fell upon my madness. And I awakened in you and saw that you were infinite in a different way, and this sight was not derived from the eyes of flesh.

....

For "you, Lord, judge me," because, although "no man knoweth the things of a man, but the spirit of man which is in him" (1 Cor 2:11), yet there is still something of man which even the spirit of man that is in him does not know, but you, O Lord, who made him, know everything about him. As for me, though in your sight I despise myself and esteem myself but dust and ashes, yet I know something of you which I know not of myself. And certainly we see "now through a glass darkly, not yet face to face" (1 Cor 13:12), and therefore, as long as I wander away from you, I am more present to myself than to you; yet I know that you are in no way subject to violence, whereas in my case I do not know what temptations I can and cannot resist. Yet there is still hope, because "you are faithful, who will not suffer us to be tempted above that we are able: but will with the temptation also make a way to escape, that we may be able to bear it" (1 Cor 10:13). Therefore, I shall confess what I know of myself, I shall confess also what I do not know of myself, since what I know of myself I know by means of your light shining upon me, and what I do not know remains unknown to me until in your countenance "my darkness be made as the noonday" (Is 58:10).

It is not with doubtful but with assured awareness, O Lord, that I love you. You pierced my heart with your Word and I loved you. But also heaven and earth and all within them, behold, they bid me on every side to love you, nor do they cease telling this to all, "that they may be without excuse" (Rom 1:20). But more deeply "will you have mercy or whom you will have mercy, and will show compassion to whom you will show compassion"

(Rom 9:15); otherwise, heaven and earth proclaim your praises to deaf ears. But what do I love when I love you? Not the beauty of body nor the gracefulness of temporal rhythm, not the brightness of light so friendly to the eyes, not the sweet and various melodies of songs, not the fragrance of flowers and ointments and spices, not manna and honey; not limbs receptive to fleshly embraces: I love not these when I love my God. And yet I do love a kind of light, melody, fragrance, food, embracement when I love my God; for He is the light, the melody, the fragrance, the food, the embracement of my inner self: Where that light shines into my soul which no place can contain, and where that voice sounds which time does not take away, and where that fragrance smells which no wind scatters, and where there is that flavor which eating does not diminish, and where there is that clinging that no satiety will separate. This is what I love when I love my God.

And what is this? I asked the earth and it said: "I am not He," and all things in it made the same confession. I asked the sea and the deeps and the creeping things and they answered: "We are not your god; seek above us." I asked the blowing breezes, and the entire air with its inhabitants said: "Anaximenes was deceived; I am not god." I questioned the sky, the sun, the moon, the stars: "Nor are we the god whom you seek," they said. And I said to all these which surround the doors of my flesh: "Tell me about my God, since you are not he, tell me something about Him." And they exclaimed in a loud voice: "He made us." My question was in my contemplation of them; and their answer was in their beauty. And I turned my attention upon myself and said: "Who are you?" and I answered: "A man." Now I find in myself a soul and body, one exterior, the other interior. Which of these should I have used in seeking for my God? I had already searched for Him by means of the body, searching from earth to sky, as far as I could direct the beams of my eyes as messengers. But the interior part of me is the better. To this part all my bodily messengers gave in their reports and this inner reality sat in judgment weighing the replies of heaven and earth and all things within them when they said: "We are not God," and when they said: "He made us." The inner man knew these things through the ministry of the outer man; I, the inner man, knew all this; I, the soul, through my bodily senses; I asked the whole mass of the world about my God, and it answered me: "I am not He, but He made me."

Is not the face of the earth clearly seen by all who have sound senses? Why then does it not speak the same things to all? Animals great and small see it well enough but they cannot ask questions of it. Reason does not preside over their senses to judge on what they report. Men can ask so that they may clearly understand "the invisible things of God, which are understood by the things which are made" (Rom 1:20), but by loving these things, they become subject to them, and subjects cannot judge. Nor will these creatures answer those questioning unless the questioners are capable of judging. Not that they alter their speech, that is, their beautiful appearance. If one man merely looks at them while another not only looks but questions, they do not appear one thing to one man, and a different thing to the other. They look identically the same to both, but to one man they say nothing and to the other they speak. It would be truer to say that they speak to all but are understood only by those who compare the voice which comes to them from outside with the truth within. For truth says to me: "Your God is not sky or earth, or any body." Their own nature declares this. They recognize that there is less bulk in a part than in a whole. Now, my soul, I tell you that you are my better part, since you animate the whole bulk of the body, giving life to it, which no body confers on a body. But God, however, is even for you the Life of your life.

What then do I love when I love my God? Who is He above the summit of my soul? Through this very soul of mine I shall ascend to Him. I shall go beyond my life-force by which I cling to the body and fill its frame with life. Not by that force do I find my God: If so, "the horses and mules which lack understanding" (Ps 32:9) could find him since their bodies also live by that same force. But there is another force, not only that by which I not only

266

give life, but give sensation to my flesh which the Lord fashioned for me, commanding the eye not to hear, and the ear not to see, but giving me the eye to see by and the ear to hear by, assigning to each of the other senses its own particular duty and function. Through these senses, with all their different functions, I act as one soul. I shall also go beyond this force, for this also the horse and the mule have: They also sense through the body.

I shall therefore also go beyond this power of my nature, ascending by degrees to Him who made me. And I come to the fields and spacious palaces of memory where lie the treasures of innumerable images of all kinds of things brought into it by the senses. There is stored up whatever we think, if by thought we have enlarged or diminished or in any way altered those things which the sense has touched, and there also is everything else that has been brought in and deposited and has not yet been swallowed up and buried in forgetfulness. When I am in this treasure house, I ask for whatever I like to be brought forth to me; whereupon, some things are produced at once, some things take longer and have, so to speak, to be fetched from a more remote part of the store, and some things come pouring out all together and, when indeed we want and are searching for something quite different, they thrust themselves forward as though saying: "Perhaps you are looking for us?" These I drive away with the hand of my heart from the face of my remembrance until I discover at last what I desire, emerging from its hidden place into my sight. Some things are produced easily and in perfect order just as they are desired: What comes first gives place to what comes next, and, as it gives place, it is stored up ready to be brought forth when I need it again. This all takes place when I repeat anything by heart.

There all sensations are preserved distinctly and in categories according to how they enter, such as light and all colors and bodily shapes brought in by the eyes; all sorts of sounds through the ears, and all odors through the nostrils; all tastes through the mouth; and by the sensation of the whole body we derive our impression of what is hard or soft, of whatever is hot or cold, or whatever is smooth or rugged, heavy or light, whether from outside or inside the body itself. All these sensations are received into the great harbor of memory with its many secret and indefinable recesses, to be produced when need requires, each coming in by its own entry and there stored up. Yet the things themselves do not enter, but the images of things perceived are there ready at hand for thought to recall.

Who can say how these things are formed? Yet it is clear by which senses they entered and were stored up. For even while I remain in darkness and silence I can, if I wish, call forth colors in my memory and note the difference between black and white and any other colors I like, and when I reflect on the images drawn in by my eyes, sounds do not come running in to disturb them, though they also are in my memory, stored up, as it were, in a separate compartment. For I can summon forth sounds also, if I wish, and they are immediately present; with no movement of tongue or vocal chords I sing as much as I please, nor do those images of color, although present in the memory, intrude and interrupt when I summon something from that other storehouse containing impressions brought in by the ear. And so I call forth as I like all other things brought in and stored up by the other senses. I can discern the difference between the smell of lilies and violets though I am actually smelling nothing at the time, and I prefer honey to sweet wine, something smooth to something rough merely by memory, using neither the sense of taste nor that of touch.

This I do within, in that huge court of my memory. There I have available to me the sky, the earth, the sea, and all those things in them which I have been able to perceive—apart from what I have forgotten. There also I encounter myself; I recall myself, what, when, and where I have done something; and how I felt at the time. There are all things I remember to have experienced myself or to have heard from others. From the same storehouse also I can summon forth pictures of things which have either happened to me or are believed on the basis of experience. I can myself weave them into the context of the past; and from these I infer future actions and events and hopes, and on these again I contemplate as if they were present. "I shall do this and that," I say to myself in this deep recess of my mind, full of the images of so many and such great things, "and this or that follows." "Oh, if only this or that could happen!" or "May God prevent this or that!" So I say to myself, and while I am speaking, the images of all the things that I am saying are present to my mind, all from this same treasury of my memory: in fact, if the images were not there, I would not be able to speak of these things at all.

How great is the power of memory, how exceedingly great, O God; a vast and unlimited interior; who has plumbed its depths? Yet this is a power of my mind and belongs to my nature; I myself do not grasp all that I am. Is then the mind too narrow to hold itself so that the questions arise: Where is this which belongs to it, and it cannot grasp? Is it outside itself and not inside? How then does it not grasp itself? Faced with all this, great wonder arises in me, astonishment seizes me. And men go abroad marveling at the heights of mountains, at the huge waves of the sea, at the broad courses of the rivers, the vastness of the ocean, the circular motions of the stars, and yet do not notice themselves and see nothing marvelous in the fact that when I was mentioning all these things I was not observing them with my eyes. Yet I could not have spoken of them unless these mountains and caves and rivers and stars, which I have seen, and the ocean of which I have heard, had been visible to me inside, in my memory, and with precisely the same great intervals and proportions as if I were really seeing them outside myself. Yet by the act of seeing I did not draw them into myself; not they themselves but only their images are within me, and I know by what bodily sense each impression came to me.

But this immense capacity of my memory contains far more than this. Here also are all those things I have learned of the liberal sciences, and have not yet forgotten, removed, somehow, to an inner place which is not really a place. Nor do I have with me the images of these but the sciences themselves. For what literature is, what the art of disputation is, or how many kinds of ques-

269

tions there are, everything of this kind which I know is in my memory in a special way. In this case I do not retain the image and leave the thing outside me. It is not a matter of the sound of words which has ceased sounding, like a voice, having left a definite impression upon the ear through a vestigial image by which it can be recalled as though it were sounding, when in fact it is not sounding; nor like an odor which, while passing and vanishing into air affects the sense of smell and so brings into the memory an image of itself which can be recalled by an act of recollection; nor like food, which surely has no taste when already in the stomach but yet has a kind of taste when in our memory; nor like something perceived by the sense of bodily touch which can still be imagined in our memory when we are no longer in contact with it. Certainly these things are not brought into our memory but only their images are captured with marvelous swiftness and stored up in wonderful secret places and are marvelously brought forth by the act of remembering.

But when I hear that there are three kinds of questions—"Does the thing exist? What is it? What kind is it?"—I do indeed hold in mind the images of the sounds of which these words are composed, and I know that they have noisily passed through the air and have now ceased to be. But as to the things themselves signified by these sounds, I never attained them by any bodily sense nor discerned them anywhere else than in my mind; yet in my memory I have stored up not their images, but the things themselves. How they got into me, let them say if they can. For as I examine all the gateways of my body, I cannot find by which one they entered. The eyes say: "If these images were colored, we announced them." The ears say: "If they made a sound, we reported them." The nostrils say: "If they had an odor, they entered through us." And the sense of taste says: "Unless there is a taste to them, do not ask me." Touch says: "If the thing is not a body, I did not handle it, and if I did not handle it, I gave no information about it."

From where then and how did they enter into my memory? I do not know. For when I learned them, I was not accepting them because of trust in another; I was recognizing them in my own mind; I approved them as true and committed them to my own mind, so storing them that I might recall them when I wished. So they were in my mind even before I learned them but they were not in my memory. Then where were they? Or why was it that, when I heard them spoken, I recognized them and said: "That is right; that is true" unless indeed they were already in my memory, but so remote and so buried, as it were, in the deepest recesses that if they had not been drawn forth by the encouragement of someone else I should perhaps not have been able to conceive of them?

We find, consequently, that to learn those things which we do not draw into us as images through our senses, but which we discern inside ourselves as they actually are without the help of images, means merely this: By thinking we are, so to speak, collecting together things which the memory did contain, though in a disorganized and dispersed way, and by attending carefully to them we arrange for them to be, so to speak, stored up ready at hand in that same memory where previously they lay hidden, disregarded and dispersed; so that now they will readily come forward to the mind which becomes familiar with them. My memory included many things like this which have been discovered, and, as I said, placed ready at hand. These are the things which we are said to have learned and to know. Yet if I stop, even for a brief span of time, bringing them up into my mind, they are submerged again and slip back into some kind of distant hiding place, so that I have to think them out anew from that same place—for they have no other place—and once again collect them so that they may be known. They must be collected as from their scattered sites: so one speaks of "cogitating." For *cogo* [collect] and *cogito* [recollect] are related to each other as *ago* [do] is to *agito* [do constantly], *asfacio* [make] is to *factito* [make frequently]. But the mind has appropriated to itself this word ("cogitation") so that we correctly use that word only of things "collected" in the mind, not of things gathered together elsewhere.

Likewise, the memory contains the innumerable principles

271

and laws of numbers and dimensions which no bodily sense impressed on it because they have neither color, nor sound, nor taste, nor smell, nor feeling. I have heard the sounds of the words by which these principles are signified when we speak of them, but sounds differ from principles. The sounds will vary according to whether the words used are Greek or Latin but the principles are neither Greek nor Latin nor any other language. I have seen the lines drawn by architects, lines as small as the thread of a spider's web. But the principles involved are something different; they are not images of those things reported to me by my bodily eye, and whoever knows these principles recognizes them within himself without any conception of any kind of body. I have also perceived with all my bodily senses the numbers we use in counting; but the numbers by which we count are not the same as these, nor are they images of these, and therefore they really exist. Anyone who does not see them may laugh at me for speaking thus of them, and while he laughs at me, I shall pity him.

All these things I hold in my memory and how I learned them I also hold in my memory. I have also heard and hold in memory false arguments against these things. Although they are false, it is not false to say that I remember them, and I also remember that I have distinguished between the truths and the false objections made to these truths. Therefore, I often remember that I have previously understood these things, and what I now discern and understand I record in my memory so that later I may remember what I have understood now. So I remember that I have understood these things, and if later I recall that I have now been able to remember these things, I shall recall this through the force of memory.

....

Where then did I find you so that I might learn of you? For you were not already in my memory before I learned of you. Where, then, did I find you so that I might learn of you unless in yourself above me? There is no place; we go "backward and forward" (Jb 23:8) yet there is no place. Everywhere, O Truth, you preside over all asking counsel of you and you simultaneously respond to all the diverse requests for counsel. You respond clearly, but not all hear clearly. All ask what they wish, but they do not always hear what they wish. He is your best servant who is not so eager to hear from you what he himself wills as to will what he hears from you.

Late have I loved you, O Beauty, so ancient and so new, late have I loved you! And behold, you were within me and I was outside, and there I sought for you, and in my deformity I rushed headlong into the well-formed things that you have made. You were with me, and I was not with you. Those outer beauties held me far from you, yet if they had not been in you, they would not have existed at all. You called, and cried out to me and broke open my deafness; you shone forth upon me and you scattered my blindness: You breathed fragrance, and I drew in my breath and I now pant for you: I tasted and I hunger and thirst; you touched me, and I burned for Your peace.

Bernard of Clairvaux

Bernard (1090–1153), the third of seven children (six sons), was born to Burgundy nobility near Dijon, France as the eleventh century was closing. Well educated in literature and scripture, at the age of twenty-three he led twenty-nine young Burgundy noblemen, including four of his brothers, to the reform monastery of Citeaux, approximately twelve miles from Dijon.

Citeaux was founded in 1098 by reformers who sought to follow the Rule of Benedict more closely; thus it stood in opposition to the laxity of Cluny, which was founded in 910. Approximately three years after joining Citeaux and what came to be known as the Cistercian order, Bernard was sent to found a new monastery in a place he named Claire Vallée, hence, "Clairvaux." His father and all his brothers soon joined him at Clairvaux, and his reputation for austerity and erudition drew many others. Under Bernard's direction the monastery flourished, so much so that it soon sent out bands of monks to found new monasteries in France.

Throughout his tenure at Clairvaux, Bernard was immersed in the political affairs of the Church. He attended the Council of Troyes, accompanied Pope Innocent II into Italy, and defeated Abelard in a public debate on the doctrine of the Trinity in 1140. In the mid-twelfth century, at the request of the pope, Bernard preached a new crusade, which eventually failed.

The twelfth-century Renaissance in Europe also saw the reformation of many monasteries and a deep concern with the problem of love at every level. As the concept of romantic love evolved, it was echoed by the concept of mystical love, key to Bernard's mystical insight and spirituality. For Bernard, all life is about learning how to love.

The following selection is from Bernard's famous treatise *De amore Dei*—On Loving God—in which he demonstrates that the proper manner of loving God is to love wholeheartedly and without measure. Bernard characteristically details the different degrees of this love and teaches how the love of the creature for the Creator should be as measureless as the love of the Creator for the creature. Definitively rooted in Christian belief, Bernard freely refers to Gospel passages and the writings of St. Paul in support of his argument. In many respects, his tone is like that of Augustine in his *Confessions*, as Bernard directly addresses God:

> "I will love you, Lord, my strength, my fortress, my refuge, my deliverer" (Ps 17:2–3), you who are everything I can desire and love. My God, my Helper, I shall love you in proportion to your gift and my capacity, less indeed than is just, but to do that is beyond me. Even though I cannot love you as much as I ought, still I cannot love you more than I am able.

For Bernard, loving God is the reason for existence, yet loving God is not for God's benefit, but rather for ours. He teaches briefly in this selection that we perceive him dimly, but we can still perceive him. That perception brings with it deeper belief.

In VI. 22 Bernard picks up a philosophical argument for the existence of God—God as both the efficient and final cause, or God as the primary cause as well as the end of his being, and of all being. Hence, Bernard says, all love for God is repaid. Bernard demonstrates this concept with support for Christian belief taken from scripture:

> His love both prepares and rewards ours (cf. 1 Jn 4:19). Kindly, he leads the way. He repays us justly. He is our sweet hope. He is riches to all who call upon him (Rom 10:12). There is nothing better than himself. He gave himself in merit. He keeps himself to be our reward. He gives himself as food for holy souls (Wis 3:13). He sold himself to redeem the captives (Lam 3:25).

Bernard then details the four degrees of love:

1. When man loves himself for his own sake;
2. When man loves God for his own good;
3. When man loves God for God's sake;
4. When man loves himself for the sake of God.

Each degree moves the individual closer to the mystical marriage, which theme had become prominent in the twelfth century as the concept of romantic love intertwined with that of the mystical love of God.

Phyllis Zagano

HOW GOD SHOULD BE LOVED

VI. 16. First see in what measure God deserves to be loved by us, and how he deserves to be loved without measure. For (to repeat briefly what I have said) "he first loved us" (1 Jn 4:10). He loved—with such love, and so much and so generously—us who are so insignificant and who are what we are. I remember that I said at the beginning that the way to love God was to love without measure. Now since the love which is directed to God is directed to something immense, something infinite (for God is both immense and infinite)—who, I ask, ought to draw a line to our love or measure it out? And what about the fact that our love itself is not freely given but given in payment for a debt? So immensity loves; eternity loves; the love which passes knowledge gives itself (Eph 3:19); God loves, whose greatness knows no bounds (Ps 114:3), whose wisdom cannot be counted (Ps 146:5), whose peace passes all understanding (Phil 4:7), and do we measure out our response?

"I will love you, Lord, my strength, my fortress, my refuge, my deliverer" (Ps 17:2-3), you who are everything I can desire and love. My God, my Helper, I shall love you in proportion to your gift and my capacity, less indeed than is just, but to do that is beyond me. Even though I cannot love you as much as I ought, still I cannot love you more than I am able. I shall be able to love you more only when you deign to give me more; and even then you can never find my love worthy. "Your eyes have seen my imperfection," and "all shall be written down in your book" (Ps 138:16), all who do what they can, even if they cannot do all that they should. It is clear, I think, how much God ought to be loved, and for what merit in him. For his own merit, I say, but to whom is it really clear how great that is? Who can say? Who can feel it?

VII. 17. Now let us see how he is to be loved for our benefit. How far does our perception of him fall short of what he is? We

278

must not keep silent about what we can see clearly, even if all is not clear to us. Above, when we proposed to seek why and how God is to be loved, I said that there were two meanings of the question with which we began. We asked why he should be loved, meaning by what merit of his or for what benefit of ours. Both questions can, it seems, be asked. After speaking of God's merit, not as he deserves, but as well as I am able, it remains for me to say something about the reward, as far as it will be given to me to do.

....

VI. 22. I said before that God is the cause of loving God. I spoke the truth, for he is both the efficient and the final cause. He himself provides the occasion. He himself creates the longing. He himself fulfills the desire. He himself causes himself to be (or rather, to be made) such that he should be loved. He hopes to be so happily loved that no one will love him in vain. His love both prepares and rewards ours (cf. 1 Jn 4:19). Kindly, he leads the way. He repays us justly. He is our sweet hope. He is riches to all who call upon him (Rom 10:12). There is nothing better than himself. He gave himself in merit. He keeps himself to be our reward. He gives himself as food for holy souls (Wis 3:13). He sold himself to redeem the captives (Lam 3:25).

Lord, you are good to the soul which seeks you. What are you then to the soul which finds? But this is the most wonderful thing, that no one can seek you who has not already found you. You therefore seek to be found so that you may be sought for, sought so that you may be found. You can be sought, and found, but not forestalled. For even if we say "In the morning my prayer will forestall you" (Ps 87:14), it is certain that every prayer which is not inspired is half-hearted.

Now let us see where our love begins, for we have seen where it finds its end.

VIII. 23 Love is one of the four natural passions. 24 They are well enough known; there is no need to name them. It is clearly right that what is natural should be at the service of the Lord of nature. That is why the first and great commandment is, "You shall love the Lord your God" (Mt 22:37).

The First Degree of Love: When Man Loves Himself for His Own Sake

But because nature has become rather frail and weak, man is driven by necessity to serve nature first. This results in bodily love, by which man loves himself for his own sake. He does not yet know anything but himself, as it is written, "First came what is animal, then what is spiritual" (1 Cor 15:46). This love is not imposed by rule but is innate in nature. For who hates his own flesh (Eph 5:29)? But if that same love begins to get out of proportion and headstrong, as often happens, and it ceases to be satisfied to run in the narrow channel of its needs, but floods out on all sides into the fields of pleasure, then the overflow can be stopped at once by the commandment "You shall love your neighbor as yourself" (Mt 22:39).

It is wholly right that he who is your fellow in nature (2 Pt 1:4) should not be cut off from you in grace, especially in that grace which is innate in nature. If a man feels it a heavy burden to help his brothers in their need and to share in their pleasures, let him keep his desires in check all by himself if he does not want to fall into sin. He can indulge himself as much as he likes as long as he remembers to show an equal tolerance to his neighbor. O man, the law of life and discipline impose restraint (Sir 45:6) to prevent you chasing after your desires until you perish (Sir 18:30), and to save you from making of nature's good things a way to serve the soul's enemy through lust.

Is it not much more right and honest to share nature's goods with your fellow man, that is, your neighbor, than with an enemy? If you take the advice of Wisdom and turn away from your pleasures (Sir 18:30) and make yourself content with food and clothing as the Apostle teaches (1 Tm 6:8), soon you will find that your love is not impeded by carnal desires which fight against the soul (1 Pt 2:11). I think you will not find it a burden to share with your fellow man what you withhold from the enemy of your soul. Then will your love be sober and just, when you do not deny your brother what he needs from the pleasures you have denied yourself. It is in this way that bodily love is shared, when it is extended to the community.

VIII. 24. But what are you to do if when you share with your neighbor you yourself are left without something you need? What but ask in full faith (Acts 4:29, 28:31) from him who gives generously to everyone and does not grudge (Jas 1:5), who opens his hand and pours blessing on every creature (Ps 144:16). There is no doubt that he will come to your aid generously when you are in need, since he is so generous in time of plenty. Scripture says, "First seek the Kingdom of God and his justice and all these things will be added to you" (Mt 6:33; Lk 12:31). He promises without being asked to give what is needed to whoever is not greedy for himself and loves his neighbor. This is to seek the kingdom of God and to implore his help against the tyranny of sin, to take on the yoke of chastity and sobriety rather than to let sin rule in your mortal body (Rom 6:12). More: This is righteousness, to share what is common to your nature with him who has the same gift of nature.

VIII. 25. But to love one's neighbor with perfect justice it is necessary to be prompted by God. How can you love your neighbor with purity if you do not love him in God? But he who does not love God cannot love in God. You must first love God, so that in him you can love your neighbor too (Mk 12:30–31).

God therefore brings about your love for him, just as he causes other goods. This is how he does it: He who made nature also protects it. For it was so created that it needs its Creator as its Protector, so that what could not have come into existence without him cannot continue in existence without him. So that no rational creature might be in ignorance of this fact and (dreadful thought) claim for himself the gifts of the Creator, that same Creator willed by a high and saving counsel that man should endure tribulation; then when man fails and God comes to his aid and sets him free, man will honor God as he deserves. For this is what he says, "Call upon me in the day of tribulation. I will deliver you, and you shall honor me" (Ps 49:15). And so in that way it comes about that man who is a bodily animal (1 Cor 2:14), and does not know how to love anything but himself, begins to love God for his own benefit, because he learns from frequent experience that in God he can do everything which is good for him (Phil 4:13), and that without him he can do nothing (Jn 15:5).

The Second Degree of Love, When Man Loves God for His Own Good

IX. 26. Man therefore loves God, but as yet he loves him for his own sake, not God's. Nevertheless the wise man ought to know what he can do by himself and what he can do only with God's help; then you will avoid hurting him who keeps you from harm. If a man has a great many tribulations and as a result he frequently turns to God and frequently experiences God's liberation, surely even if he had a breast of iron or a heart of stone (Ez 11:19; 36:26), he must soften toward the generosity of the Redeemer and love God not only for his own benefit, but for himself?

The Third Degree of Love: When Man Loves God for God's Sake

Man's frequent needs make it necessary for him to call upon God often, and to taste by frequent contact, and to discover by tasting how sweet the Lord is (Ps 33:9). It is in this way that the taste of his own sweetness leads us to love God in purity more than our need alone would prompt us to do. The Samaritans set us an example when they said to the woman who told them the Lord was there, "Now we believe, not because of your words, but because we have heard him for ourselves and we know that truly he is the Savior of the world" (Jn 4:42). In the same way, I urge, let us follow their example and rightly say to our flesh, "Now we love God not because he meets your needs; but we have tasted and we know how sweet the Lord is" (Ps 33:9).

There is a need of the flesh which speaks out, and the body tells by its actions of the kindnesses it has experienced. And so it will not be difficult for the man who has had that experience to keep the commandment to love his neighbor (Mk 12:31). He truly loves God, and therefore he loves what is God's. He loves chastely, and to the chaste it is no burden to keep the commandments; the heart grows purer in the obedience of love, as it is written (1 Pt 1:22). Such a man loves justly and willingly keeps the just law.

This love is acceptable because it is given freely. It is chaste because it is not made up of words or talk, but of truth and action (1 Jn 3:18). It is just because it gives back what it has received. For he who loves in this way loves as he is loved. He loves, seeking in return not what is his own (1 Cor 13:5), but what is Jesus Christ's, just as he has sought not his own but our good, or rather, our very selves (2 Cor 12:14). He who says, "We trust in the Lord for he is good" (Ps 117:1) loves in this way. He who trusts in the Lord not because he is good to him but simply because he is good truly loves God for God's sake and not for his own. He of whom it is said, "He will praise you when you do him favors" (Ps 48:19) does not love in this way.

That is the third degree of love, in which God is already loved for his own sake.

The Fourth Degree of Love: When Man Loves Himself for the Sake of God

X. 27. Happy is he who has been found worthy to attain to the fourth degree, where man loves himself only for God's sake. "O God, your justice is like the mountains of God" (Ps 35:7). That love is a mountain, and a high mountain of God. Truly, "a rich and fertile mountain" (Ps 67:16). "Who will climb the mountain of the Lord?" (Ps 24:3). "Who will give me wings like a dove, and I shall fly there and rest" (Ps 54:7). That place was made a place of peace and it has its dwelling—place in Sion (Ps 75:3). "Alas for me, my exile has been prolonged!" (Ps 119:5). When will flesh and blood (Mt 16:17), this vessel of clay (2 Cor 4:7), this earthly dwelling (Wis

9:15), grasp this? When will it experience this kind of love, so that the mind, drunk with divine love and forgetting itself, making itself like a broken vessel (Ps 30:13), throw itself wholly on God and, clinging to God (1 Cor 6:17), become one with him in spirit and say, "My body and my heart have fainted, O God of my heart; God, my part in eternity" (Ps 72:26)? 1 should call him blessed and holy to whom it is given to experience even for a single instant something which is rare indeed in this life. To lose yourself as though you did not exist and to have no sense of yourself, to be emptied out of yourself (Phil 2:7) and almost annihilated, belongs to heavenly not to human love.

And if indeed any mortal is rapt for a moment or is, so to speak, admitted for a moment to this union, at once the world presses itself on him (Gal 1:4), the day's wickedness troubles him, the mortal body weighs him down, bodily needs distract him, he fails because of the weakness of his corruption and—more powerfully than these—brotherly love calls him back. Alas, he is forced to come back to himself, to fall again into his affairs, and to cry out wretchedly, "Lord, I endure violence; fight back for me" (Is 38:14), and, "Unhappy man that I am, who will free me from the body of this death?" (Rom 7:24).

IX. 28. But since Scripture says that God made everything for himself (Prv 16:4; Rv 4:11) there will be a time when he will cause everything to conform to its Maker and be in harmony with him. In the meantime, we must make this our desire: that as God himself willed that everything should be for himself, so we, too, will that nothing, not even ourselves, may be or have been except for him, that is according to his will, not ours. The satisfaction of our needs will not bring us happiness, not chance delights, as does the sight of his will being fulfilled in us and in everything which concerns us. This is what we ask every day in prayer when we say, "Your will be done, on earth as it is in heaven" (Mt 6:10). O holy and chaste love! O sweet and tender affection! O pure and sinless intention of the will—the more pure and sinless in that there is no mixture of self—will in it, the more sweet and tender in that everything it feels is divine.

To love in this way is to become like God." As a drop of water seems to disappear completely in a quantity of wine, taking the wine's flavor and color; as red-hot iron becomes indistinguishable from the glow of fire and its own original form disappears; as air suffused with the light of the sun seems transformed into the brightness of the light, as if it were itself light rather than merely lit up; so, in those who are holy, it is necessary for human affection to dissolve in some ineffable way, and be poured into the will of God. How will God be all in all (1 Cor 15:26) if anything of man remains in man? The substance remains, but in another form, with another glory, another power.

When will this be? Who will see this? Who will possess it? "When shall I come and when shall I appear in God's presence" (Ps 41:3)? O Lord my God, "My heart said to you, 'My face has sought you. Lord, I will seek your face' "(Ps 26:8). Shall I see your holy temple (Ps 26:4)?

IX. 29. I think that cannot be until I do as I am bid. "Love the Lord your God with all your heart and with all your soul and with all your strength" (Mk 12:30). Then the mind will not have to think of the body. The soul will no longer have to give the body life and feeling, and its power will be set free of these ties and strengthened by the power of God. For it is impossible to draw together all that is in you and turn toward the face of God as long as the care of the weak and miserable body demands one's attention. So it is in a spiritual and immortal body, a perfect body, beautiful and at peace and subject to the spirit in all things, that the soul hopes to attain the fourth degree of love, or rather, to be caught up to it; for it lies in God's power to give to whom he will. It is not to be obtained by human effort. That, I say, is when a man will easily reach the fourth degree: when no entanglements of the flesh hold him back and no troubles will disturb him, as he hurries with great speed and eagerness to the joy of the Lord (Mt 25:21; 25).

But do we not think that the holy martyrs received this grace while they were still in their victorious bodies—at least in part? They were so moved within by the great force of their love that they were able to expose their bodies to outward torments and think nothing of them. The sensation of outward pain could do no more than whisper across the surface of their tranquillity; it could not disturb it.

XI. 30. But what of those who are already free of the body? We believe that they are wholly immersed in that sea of eternal light and bright eternity.

Francis of Assisi and Clare of Assisi

Francis (1182–1226), perhaps the most popular of Christian saints, made the story of Jesus real to the people of Assisi and, ultimately, the world. First, however, he made it real to himself. Born to relative wealth as Giovanni Francesco di Bernardone, son of a cloth merchant, Francis lived in the high style of the times before going off to war in 1204 to fight for Assisi against neighboring Perugia. A vision directed him back to Assisi, and soon he left on pilgrimage to Rome, where he begged along with real beggars at St. Peter's Basilica. Francis returned to Assisi a changed man, ready to answer the God who asked him to "repair my house." Determined to live in poverty, he preached freely in the streets and soon attracted a band of followers. His trip to Egypt in 1221 to speak to the Islamic leaders controlling the Nile ended with him in the presence of the Sultan Malik al-Kamil, where they dialogued about the God of Abraham. His order, which had been approved by Pope Innocent III in 1210, grew exponentially, and by 1248 there were over nine thousand Franciscan houses.

Clare (1194–1253), born Chiara Offreduccio in Assisi, was of higher social status than Francis and twelve years his junior. The eldest daughter of the Count of Sasso-Rosso, she was asked by her parents to marry at the age of fifteen, but she asked to wait until she was eighteen. Even before she met Francis, Clare had divested herself of her inheritance and made a vow of virginity. However, by that time she had heard the preachings of Francis, who told her she was a chosen soul of God. She ran away that Palm Sunday (with the blessing of the local bishop) to follow Francis. He met her and her companion and, since he had been made a deacon, he could tonsure her and receive her to his order. She went to live with the Benedictine nuns, but soon moved, with her sister Catherine, known as Agnes, to the Church of San Damiano, which Francis himself had rebuilt. Because of the radically poor lifestyle she and her eventual followers adopted, they became known as the "Poor Ladies," and were formally called the Order of St. Clare just ten years after her death. Her order, now Second Order Franciscans, is colloquially known as the "Poor Clares."

The Franciscan Order has three parts: The First Order (priests and brothers), the Second Order (cloistered nuns—Poor Clares), and the Third Order, which has two branches: those who live alone or with their families as Secular Franciscans under a rule approved by Pope Paul VI in 1978, and Third Order Regular Franciscans, whose rule was approved by Pope John Paul II in 1982.

The Franciscan spirit—Franciscan spirituality—is captured in Francis' "The Canticle of Brother Sun": "Praised be You, my Lord, with all your creatures." The simplicity of Franciscan poverty, coupled with Francis' gentle awe at all creation, are demonstrated in the few lines of perhaps his most famous poem. In it, Francis speaks to and thanks them for their very nature: "Brother Sun," "Sister Moon," "Brother Wind," "Sister Water," "Brother Fire," "Sister Mother Earth," "Sister Bodily Death," all of which praise God.

Francis' "The Canticle of Exhortation to Saint Clare and Her Sisters" is a small poem of encouragement and direction, which echoes the advice of the writer of the *Ancrene Riwle*: "Do not look at the life outside, for that of the Spirit is better."

The final selection from Francis, his brief "The Prayer Before the Crucifix," demonstrates Francis' commitment to the three theological virtues of Christianity—faith, hope, and charity, as he asks the Lord God to support in him "a correct faith, a certain hope, a perfect charity."

Clare's known writings are relatively sparse and predominantly directed at living the enclosed life of a nun of the order. For many years Clare and her sisters had difficulty in creating the contemplative life for women they envisioned with the spirit of Francis. Following the Fourth Lateran Council (1215), their actual status was in jeopardy and their Cardinal protector gave them Constitutions affiliated to the Benedictine order, including a monastery enclosure with property modeled on a medieval walled city. Clare, however, envisioned a life for herself and her sisters not wholly separated from the realities and needs of those nearby. Not until Clare was on her deathbed in 1253 was her desire for genuine poverty for her communities realized. Clare was the first woman to write a rule of life that received papal approval.

Clare's known writings are four letters to Blessed Agnes of Prague, a Testament and Blessing, and her Form of Life.

Clare's four letters to Blessed Agnes of Prague, a princess of Bohemia, are regarded as arguments for and explanations of the total self-donation to God required of the nun. Clare's fourth and final (as far as is known) letter to Agnes describes the crucified Christ as the center of her own spiritual life, and includes Clare's famous image of the "mirror." Clare advises Agnes to "look upon that mirror each day, O queen and spouse of Jesus Christ, and continually study your face within it, so that you may adorn yourself within and without with beautiful robes and cover yourself with the flowers and garments of all the virtues, as becomes the daughter and most chaste bride of the Most High King."

As in other traditions, the Franciscan spirituality demonstrated by the writings of Francis and Clare advise total self-donation to God, who alone grants life. The particular understandings of Christianity through the life of Jesus bring another dimension to the spiritual life, one that gives example (here for Franciscans) of how to live the evangelical counsels of poverty, chastity, and obedience.

Phyllis Zagano

FRANCIS OF ASSISI

"The Canticle of Brother Sun"

Most High, all—powerful, good Lord,
Yours are the praises, the glory, the honor, and all blessing.
To You alone, Most High, do they belong,
and no man is worthy to mention Your name.
Praised be You, my Lord, with all your creatures,
especially Sir Brother Sun,
Who is the day and through whom You give us light.
And he is beautiful and radiant with great splendor;
and bears a likeness of You, Most High One.
Praised be You, my Lord, through Sister Moon and the
    stars,
in heaven You formed them clear and precious and
    beautiful.
Praised be You, my Lord, through Brother Wind,
and through the air, cloudy and serene, and every
    kind of weather
through which You give sustenance to Your creatures.
Praised be You, my Lord, through Sister Water,
which is very useful and humble and precious and chaste.
Praised be You, my Lord, through Brother Fire,
through whom You light the night
and he is beautiful and playful and robust and strong.
Praised be You, my Lord, through our Sister Mother Earth,
who sustains and governs us,
and who produces varied fruits with colored flowers
    and herbs.
Praised be You, my Lord, through those who give pardon
    for Your love
and bear infirmity and tribulation.

Blessed are those who endure in peace
for by You, Most High, they shall be crowned.
Praised be You, my Lord, through our Sister Bodily Death,
from whom no living man can escape.
Woe to those who die in mortal sin.
Blessed are those whom death will find in Your most
    holy will,
for the second death shall do them no harm.
Praise and bless my Lord and give Him thanks
and serve Him with great humility.

"The Canticle of Exhortation to Saint Clare and Her Sisters"

Listen, little poor ones called by the Lord,
who have come together from many parts and provinces:
Live always in truth, that you may die in obedience.
Do not look at the life outside, for that of the Spirit
    is better.
I beg you through great love, to use with discretion the
    alms which the Lord gives you.
Those who are weighed down by sickness
and the others who are wearied because of them,
all of you: bear it in peace.
For you will sell this fatigue at a very high price
and each one [of you] will be crowned queen in heaven
    with the Virgin Mary.

"The Prayer Before the Crucifix"

Most high, glorious God, enlighten the darkness of my heart
and give me, Lord, a correct faith, a certain hope, a perfect charity,
sense and knowledge, so that I may carry out Your holy and true
command.

CLARE OF ASSISI

"The Fourth Letter to Blessed Agnes of Prague"

To her who is the half of her soul and the special shrine of her heart's deepest love, to the illustrious Queen and Bride of the Lamb, the eternal King: to the Lady Agnes, her most dear mother, and, of all the others, her favorite daughter: Clare, an unworthy servant of Christ and a useless handmaid (Lk 17:10) of His hand-maids in the monastery of San Damiano of Assisi: health and [a prayer] that she may sing a new song with the other most holy vir-gins before the throne of God and of the Lamb and follow the Lamb wherever He may go (cf. Rev 14:34).

O mother and daughter, spouse of the King of all ages, if I have not written to you as often as your soul and mine as well desire and long for, do not wonder or think that the fire of love for you glows less sweetly in the heart of your mother. No, this is the difficulty: the lack of messengers and the obvious dangers of the roads. Now, however, as I write to your love, I rejoice and exult with you in the joy of the Spirit (1 Thes 1:6), O bride of Christ, because, since you have totally abandoned the vanities of this world, like another most holy virgin, Saint Agnes, you have been marvelously espoused to the spotless Lamb Who takes away the sins of the world (1 Pt 1:19; Jn 1:29).

Happy, indeed, is she to whom it is given to share this
    sacred banquet,
to cling with all her heart to Him
    Whose beauty all the heavenly hosts admire unceasingly,
    Whose love inflames our love,
    Whose contemplation is our refreshment,
    Whose graciousness is our joy,

Whose gentleness fills us to overflowing,
Whose remembrance brings a gentle light,
Whose fragrance will revive the dead,
Whose glorious vision will be the happiness of all the
    citizens of the heavenly Jerusalem;

Inasmuch as this vision is the splendor of eternal glory (Heb 1:3), the brilliance of eternal light and the mirror without blemish (Wis 7:26), look upon that mirror each day, O queen and spouse of Jesus Christ, and continually study your face within it, so that you may adorn yourself within and without with beautiful robes and cover yourself with the flowers and garments of all the virtues, as becomes the daughter and most chaste bride of the Most High King. Indeed, blessed poverty, holy humility, and ineffable charity are reflected in that mirror, as, with the grace of God, you can contemplate them throughout the entire mirror.

Look at the parameters of this mirror, that is, the poverty of Him Who was placed in a manger and wrapped in swaddling clothes. O marvelous humility, O astonishing poverty! The King of the angels, the Lord of heaven and earth, is laid in a manger! Then, at the surface of the mirror, dwell on the holy humility, the blessed poverty, the untold labors and burdens which He endured for the redemption of all mankind. Then, in the depths of this same mirror, contemplate the ineffable charity which led Him to suffer on the wood of the Cross and die thereon the most shameful kind of death. Therefore, that Mirror, suspended on the wood of the Cross, urged those who passed by to consider, saying: "All you who pass by the way, look and see if there is any suffering like My suffering!" (Lam 1:12). Let us answer Him with one voice and spirit, as He said: Remembering this over and over leaves my soul downcast within me (Lam 3:20)! From this moment, then, O queen of our heavenly King, let yourself be inflamed more strongly with the fervor of charity!

[As you] contemplate further His ineffable delights, eternal riches and honors, and sigh for them in the great desire and love of your heart, may you cry out:

Draw me after You!
We will run in the fragrance of Your perfumes,
   O heavenly Spouse!
I will run and not tire,
      until You bring me into the wine—cellar,
      until Your left hand is under my head
      and Your right band will embrace me happily
      [and] You will kiss me with the happiest kiss of Your
         mouth.

In this contemplation, may you remember your poor little mother, knowing that I have inscribed the happy memory of you indelibly on the tablets of my heart, holding you dearer than all the others.

What more can I say? Let the tongue of the flesh be silent when I seek to express my love for you; and let the tongue of the Spirit speak, because the love that I have for you, O blessed daughter, can never be fully expressed by the tongue of the flesh, and even what I have written is an inadequate expression.

I beg you to receive my words with kindness and devotion, seeing in them at least the motherly affection which in the fire of charity I feel daily toward you and your daughters, to whom I warmly commend myself and my daughters in Christ. On their part, these very daughters of mine, especially the most prudent virgin Agnes, our sister, recommend themselves in the Lord to you and your daughters.

Farewell, my dearest daughter, to you and to your daughters until we meet at the throne of the glory of the great God (Tit 2:13), and desire [this] for us.

Inasmuch as I can, I recommend to your charity the bearers of this letter, our dearly beloved Brother Amatus, beloved of God and men (Sir 45:1), and Brother Bonagura. Amen.

294

Anchorite Spirituality

The *Ancrene Wisse*, or *Ancrene Riwle*, was written in the thirteenth century by an unknown author for the use of the many recluses or anchoresses who, especially during the high Middle Ages, walled themselves up in anchorholds—typically, small additions to churches—for life. Their solitary life, complemented by anchorites (men who took up the same vocation), was dedicated to prayer and penance. Some anchoresses/anchorites had their anchorholds inside churches or monasteries. All depended upon others to bring them food and water as well as, it would seem, empty their chamber pots. They would view the celebration of Mass through a small window, or "squint," and spoke to others only through a window grill, which was often covered with a cloth.

The word *anchoress* or *anchorite* comes from *anachorein*—the Greek word meaning "to go apart." Anchoresses are recorded as early as the fourth century in Great Britain and Ireland, and throughout northern Europe in succeeding centuries. While never a vocation for large numbers of persons—between the twelfth and thirteenth centuries there were ninety-two known anchoresses and twenty known anchorites in Engand alone—the concept of being walled up forever with God has remained attractive throughout the centuries. One of history's best known anchoresses is Julian of Norwich (ca. 1342–ca. 1416), whose fourteenth–fifteenth-century anchorhold still exists at All Saints' Church in King's Lynn, Norfolk, England. In contemporary times, U.S.-born Julia Crotta (1907–1990) lived as an anchorite within the monastery of Camaldolese Benedictine nuns in Rome from 1945 until her death at eighty-two as Sister Nazarena of Jesus, OSB Cam.

Among the best-known guidebooks for anchoresses is *The Ancrene Riwle*, presumed to have been written by a priest for three natural sisters who wished to undertake anchoretic life. Probably written in Britain's West Midlands, the work's eight chapters address the anchoress's exterior life through the "Outer Rule" (parts 1 and 8) and interior life through the "Inner Rule" (parts 2–7). The selection that follows is representative of the type of beginning instructions women would receive on adopting the vocation of anchoress, or recluse. The entire work is representative of one approach to contemplative spirituality of the Middle Ages, particularly in England, where substantial numbers of women adopted this way of life.

The personal choice of contemplative life, particularly eremitic or reclusive life, has long been revered in many religious traditions. To choose a life seeking God, solely and simply, implies a radical renunciation of the world, its pleasures and allures. While today's Christian contemplatives mostly live in community in convents or monasteries, the women for whom the selection that follows was intended faced different challenges—spiritual, intellectual, emotional, and physical—from others. The principal trap of such a life is the reduction to solipsism—only one's own mind and one's own thoughts are real—and the temptation of total self-involvement.

The "defense of the heart"—to keep it from being either troubled or captured by anyone or anything other than God—is here defined and explained by means of the ways of the sense of sight, which is later complemented by explanations of the ways of the senses of hearing, smell, taste, and touch. As the writer says, "whoever protects these well does as Solomon commands: protects well their heart and their soul's health."

The distractions of the world, whether the view of passersby, the temptation to chat with those bringing alms or food, or the simple desire to daydream are all to be guarded against. The writer advises, "love your windows as little as you possibly can," saying they should be small and kept covered, preferably with black cloth. Writing in lovely metaphor, the author tells the reader to ensure that the "cloth is fastened on every side and well-attached, and guard your eyes there in case your heart flies out and goes away."

Later, he writes in answer to the presumed assertion that the world, while tempting, is beautiful. He responds to the notion that "The apple that I look on is forbidden me to eat, not to look at!"—indirectly referring to men—by observing that the sin of Eve is easily repeated and would condemn the anchoress to hell. The problem, he later states, is not so much that the anchoress would look at men, but that men would look at the anchoress: "all came about not because the women looked foolishly on men, but because they uncovered themselves in the sight of men, and did things through which they had to fall into sin." He goes on to warn against men, giving vent to the notion that women must be protected against both men and themselves, clearly indicating the seriousness of sins of the flesh as they were so considered in the Middle Ages, and before and since in many quarters.

Other writers in this text do not so directly address fleshly desires, but every tradition teaches a spirituality of chastity—reservation of the sexual appetites to marriage—and in their contemplative traditions teach the notion that the higher form of a life of prayer requires continent celibacy.

Phyllis Zagano

PART II: THE OUTER SENSES

Here begins the second part, of the defense of the heart by the five senses.

Omnia custodia serva tuum quia ex ipso vita procedit (Proverbs 4:2–3). "Protect your heart well with every kind of defense, daughter," says Solomon, "for if she is well locked away, the soul's life is in her." The heart's guardians are the five senses, sight and hearing, tasting and smelling, and the feeling in every part. And we must speak of all of them, for whoever protects these well does as Solomon commands: protects well their heart and their soul's health. The heart is a most wild beast and makes many a light leap out. As St. Gregory says, *Nihil cordefugiatus*, "nothing flies out of a person sooner than their own heart." David, God's prophet, at one time mourned that she had escaped him: *Cor meum dereliquit me* (Psalm 39:1–3), that is, "My heart has fled from me." And another time he rejoices and says that she has come home: *Invenit servus tuus suum* (2 Samuel 7:27). "Lord," he says, "my heart has come back again; I have found her." When so holy a man and so wise and so wary lets her escape, anyone else may anxiously dread her flight. And where did she break out of David, the holy king, God's prophet? Where? God knows, at the window of his eye, because of one sight that he saw while looking out just once, as you will hear after.

Therefore my dear sisters, love your windows as little as you possibly can. Let them all be little, the parlor's smallest and narrowest. Let the cloth in them be of two kinds: the cloth black, the cross white, both inside and outside. The black cloth symbolizes to the world outside that you are black and unworthy, and that the true sun has burned you outwardly, and so made you as outwardly unlovely as you are, with the gleams of his grace (Sg 1:5). The white cross is proper to you. For there are three crosses, red and black and white. The red is proper to those who are ruddied

298

and reddened as the martyrs were through the shedding of their blood for God's love. The black cross is proper to those who are doing their penance in the world for terrible sins. The white cross is rightly proper to white maidenhood and to purity, which it is very hard to keep well. By a cross, hardship is always to be understood—so the white cross symbolizes the defense of white chastity, which it is very hard to protect well. The black cloth, apart from its symbolism, does less harm to the eyes and is thicker against the wind and harder to see through, and keeps its color better against the wind and other things. Look that your parlor cloth is fastened on every side and well-attached, and guard your eyes there in case your heart flies out and goes away as it did from David, and your soul sickens as soon as she is gone.

I write much for others that in no way touches you, my dear sisters. For you do not have a name—nor ever will have through the grace of God—for being peeping anchoresses, or using enticing looks and behavior, as some, alas, sometimes unnaturally do. For it is against nature and an immoderately strange thing that the dead should dote on those living in the world, and go mad with them through sin.

"But dear sir," says someone, "Is it then so mightily evil to peep out?" Yes it is, dear sister, because of the evil which comes of it. It is evil and mightily evil to every anchoress, especially to the young—and to the old because they set a bad example to the younger, and give them a shield to guard themselves with. For if anyone blames them, then they say right away, "But sir, she does it too, who is better than I am, and knows better than I what she ought to do!" Dear young anchoress, often a most skillful smith forges a most puny knife. Follow the wise in their wisdom and not in their folly. An old anchoress may do something good that would be bad if you did it. But to peep out without harm neither of you can do. Take note now what harm has come of peeping: not one harm or two, but all the woe that now is and ever was and ever will be—all comes from sight. See here the proof that this is true.

Lucifer, because he saw himself and gazed at his own fairness, leaped into pride, and from an angel became a hideous devil. Of Eve our first mother it is written that sin found its very first entry into her through her sight: *Vidit igitur mulier quod bonum esset lignum ad vescendum, et pulcrum oculis, aspectuque delectabile, et tulit de fructu eius et comedit, deditque viro suo* (Genesis 3:6): that is, "Eve looked on the forbidden apple and saw it was fair; and she began to delight in looking at it, and set her desire on it, and took and ate of it, and gave it to her husband." See how Holy Writ speaks, and how profoundly it tells the way sin began, thus: sight went before and made a way for harmful desire—and the act that all humanity feels came after it.

This apple, dear sister, symbolizes all the things that desire and the delight of sin turn to. When you look at a man, you are in Eve's situation: you look at the apple. If someone had said to Eve when she first cast her eye on it, "Ah, Eve, go away, you are looking at your death," what would she have answered? "My dear sir, you are wrong, why are you challenging me?"

The apple that I look on is forbidden me to eat, not to look at! Thus would Eve readily enough have answered. O my dear sisters, Eve has many daughters who follow their mother, who answer in this way: "But do you think," someone says, "that I will leap on him just because I look at him?" God knows, dear sister, stranger things have happened. Eve your mother leapt after her eyes, from the eye to the apple, from the apple in paradise down to the earth, from the earth to hell, where she lay in prison four thousand years and more, she and her husband both, and condemned all her offspring to leap after her to death without end. The beginning and the root of all this sorrow was one light look; just so, as it is often said, much comes from little. So let every weak woman fear greatly—seeing that she who had just then been wrought by the hands of God was betrayed through a single look, and brought into deep sin which spread over all the world.

Egressa est Dyna filia Jacob ut videret mulieres alien igenas, et cetera (Genesis 34:1): "A maiden, Jacob's daughter, called Dinah," as it tells in Genesis, "went out to look at strange women" yet it does not say that she looked at men. And what do you think came of that looking? She lost her maidenhood and was made a whore. Thereafter, because of that same act, the pledges of high patriarchs were broken and a great city was burned, and the king, his son and the citizens were slain, the women led away. Her father and her brothers were made outlaws, noble princes though they were. This is what came of her looking. The Holy Spirit caused all such things to be written in the book to warn women of their foolish eyes. And take note of this: that this evil caused by Dinah did not come from the fact that she saw Hamor's son, whom she sinned with, but came from her letting him lay eyes on her—for what he did to her was very much against her will at first.

In the same way Bathsheba, by uncovering herself in David's sight, caused him to sin with her, a holy king though he was, and God's prophet (2 Samuel 11:2-5). Now, here comes a weak man—though he holds himself estimable if he has a wide hood and a closed cloak—and he wants to see some young anchoresses. And he just has to see whether her looks please him, she whose face has not been burnt by the sun—as if he was a stone! And he says she may confidently look upon holy men—yes, someone like him, with his wide sleeves. But, arrogant sir, have you not heard about David, God's own darling? —Of whom God himself said *Inveni virum secundum cor meum* (Acts 13:22): "I have found," he said, "a man after my own heart." This man, whom God himself in this precious saying declared a king and a prophet chosen above all, this man, because of one look cast on a woman as she washed herself, let out his heart and forgot himself, so that he did three immeasurably serious and mortal sins: with Bathsheba, the lady he looked at, adultery; on his faithful knight, Uriah her lord, treachery and murder (2 Samuel 11). And you, a sinful man, are so brazen as to cast foolish eyes upon a young woman! Yes, my dear sisters, if anyone is eager to see you, never believe good of it, but trust him the less. I would not have it that anyone see you unless he has special leave from your director. For all the three

301

sins I have just spoken about, and all the evil caused by Dinah that I spoke about before, all came about not because the women looked foolishly on men, but because they uncovered themselves in the sight of men, and did things through which they had to fall into sin.

For this reason it was commanded in God's law that a pit should always be covered, and if anyone uncovered a pit and a beast fell in, the one who had uncovered the pit had to pay for it (Exodus 21:33–34). This is a most fearsome saying for a woman who shows herself to the eyes of men. She is symbolized by the one who uncovers the pit; the pit is her fair face and her white neck and her light eyes, and her hand, if she holds it out in his sight. And also her words are a pit, unless they are well-chosen. Everything to do with her, whatever it may be, which might readily awaken sinful love, our Lord calls all of it a pit. This pit he commanded to be covered, lest any beast fall in, and drown in sin. The beast is the animal man who thinks nothing about God, and does not use his senses as one ought to do, but seeks to fall into this pit that I speak of, if he finds it open. But the judgment is very severe on whomever uncovers the pit, for she must pay for the animal that has fallen in. She is guilty of that animal's death before our Lord, and must answer for his soul on Doomsday, and pay for the loss of the animal, and have no other coin but herself. This is a most heavy payment! And God's judgment and his commandment is that she pay without fail, because she uncovered the pit in which it drowned. You who uncover this pit, you who do anything by which a man is carnally tempted through you, even if you do not know it, fear this judgment greatly. And if he is tempted so that he sins mortally in any way, even if it is not with you but with desire toward you, or if he tries to fulfill with someone else the temptation which has been awakened through you, because of your deed, be quite sure of the judgment. For opening the pit you must pay for the animal, unless you are absolved of it. [You must, as they say, suffer the rod, that is,] suffer for his sin. A dog will happily enter wherever he finds an opening.

Inpudicus oculus inpudici cordis est nuncius—Augustine: "What the mouth cannot say for shame, the wanton eye speaks, and is like a messenger for the wanton heart." But now, here is some woman who would not for anything desire uncleanness with a man—and yet she does not care if he thinks about her, and is tempted by her. Yet St. Augustine puts these two both in one pairing: to want, and to wish to be wanted: *Non solum appetere sed et appeti velle criminosum*—"To desire a man, or be willing to be desired by a man, both are deadly sins." *Oculi prima tela sunt adultere* "The eyes are the arrows [and the first weapons] of lechery's pricking." And just as men war with three kinds of weapons—with arrow's shooting, and with spear's point, and with sword's edge—with just the same weapons—that is with arrows from the eyes, with the spear of wounding words, with the sword of deadly handling—this stinking whore lechery wars with the lady's chastity, who is God's spouse. First she shoots arrows from wanton eyes, which fly lightly forth like a feathered shaft and stick in the heart. Next she shakes a spear and advances on her, and with stirring words gives the spear's wound. The sword's blow—that is, handling—is final, for a sword strikes from near at hand and gives the death-blow. And, alas, it is as good as over for those who come so close together that they handle one another or in any way touch one another. Whoever is wise and innocent should guard herself from the arrows, that is, guard her eyes; for all the evil that follows comes from the arrows of the eyes. And is she not most reckless and foolhardy, who holds her head out boldly over an exposed battlement, when someone is attacking the castle with bolts from outside? Truly our enemy, the warrior from hell, shoots more bolts at one anchoress, so I believe, than at seven and fifty ladies in the world. The battlements of the castle are her house's windows [and she does not lean out of them lest she have the devil's bolts in her eyes when she least expects it, for he is always attacking. She keeps her eyes in, for once she is blinded she is easily felled; blind the heart and she is easily overcome, and with sin soon brought to the ground].

Bernardus: Sicut mors per peccatum inorbem, ita per has fenestras in mentem—"Just as death came into the world through sin," says St. Bernard, "so through the window of the eye death has her entrance into the soul." Lord Christ! People would shut fast every window of the house if they could shut death out of it, [the death of the body]—and an anchoress will not enclose her eye-windows against the death of the soul? And they might quite as properly be called "ill-windows", for they have done much ill to many an anchoress.

[All Holy Writ is full of warnings about the eye.] David says *Averte oculos meos ne videant vanitatem* (Psalm 118:37)—"Lord," says David, "Turn away my eyes from the world's wrongness." Job says, *Pepigifedus cum oculis meis ne cogitarem de virgine* (Job 31:1), "I have made an agreement with my eyes," says Job, "so that I may not misthink." What is he saying? Do we think with our eyes? God knows it, he speaks well. For after the eye comes the thought and after that the deed. Jeremiah knew this well, who lamented in this way: [*Oculus meus depraedatus est animam meam*] (Lamentations 3:51): "Alas," he says, "my eyes have robbed all my soul." When God's prophet made such a lament over his eyes, what lamentation and sorrow on account of their eyes do you think comes to many men [and to many women]? The Wise Man asks in his book whether anything harms women more than their eyes: *Oculo quid nequius? Totam faciem lacrimare faciet quem vidit* (Ecclesiasticus 31:15): "The whole face must flow with tears," he says, "just because of what the eye sees."

So for the reasons I have given, in the same way as all the openings of all your windows have been kept closed from the view of everyone, so let them remain closed from now on—and the more tightly they can be closed, the more tightly they should be. In general, the rule is: God will guard well all those who close them; and all those who leave them open, God will punish and allow to fall into sin...either with their foolish eyes, or their mouth, or their hands....These and many other such things, unbecoming and unnatural in an anchoress more than in anyone else, would never have happened if she had kept her window tightly shut. And if anyone contradicts me, I call her conscience to witness fiercely against her, that if she lingers at her window with an eye or a mouth, or ever receives a hand or a foolish word, she is all adorned and falsely tricked out in a spurious sanctity. Ah, treacherous traitor! "God, I would not do something evil or dirty to you," says he or she—but these very people soil themselves and anger God, who sees what treason is inside the foolish heart. Not only every fleshly touching but even every foolish word is a hateful villainy and worthy of God's anger, though it grow no further between a man and an anchoress. Yet through the just vengeance of God it goes further and further, and often—and when one least expects it—turns into that foul sin. Alas, we have heard of it plenty of times! Let no one trust in the anchoress who lets in a man's eye and shows herself. Above everything that you have written in your rule about outward things, I would have this point, this article about being well-enclosed, best kept.

Julian of Norwich

Of the many anchoresses remembered in history, Julian of Norwich (ca. 1342–ca. 1416) is perhaps the best known, mainly due to her mystical writings. In "The Short Text" she records mystical vistions of Christ she experienced at the age of thirty-one, and which she analyzed theologically later in "The Long Text." These form the basis of her book, *The Sixteen Revelations of Divine Love*, or *The Showings* (ca. 1393), believed to be the first book written in English by a woman. (The first biography written in English by a woman was written by Margery Kempe, who mentions in it her going to seek counsel from Julian.)

The Revelations, or *The Showings*, from which the following selections are taken, display a theological optimism perhaps unwarranted in Julian's time, as England and all of Europe reeled from the devastations of the plague. Among her most comforting, and better-known, visions is of God showing her in her interior vision the protection God shows for the world: "...he showed me something small, no bigger than a hazelnut, lying in the palm of my hand, as it seemed to me, and it was as round as a ball. I looked at it with the eye of my understanding and thought: What can this be? I was amazed that it could last, for I thought that because of its littleness it would suddenly have fallen into nothing. And I was answered in my understanding: It lasts and always will, because God loves it; and thus everything has being through the love of God."

Such recognition, that the smallest created living thing, which God made, God loves, and God preserves convinced her of her union with God, and that therefore no created thing could separate them.

In the seventh chapter of *The Revelations* Julian discloses her understandings of the place of Mary, the Mother of Jesus ("our

Lady St. Mary"), whom she presents as an exemplar of humility before God, and filled with grace because of the acceptance of her lowliness. One of the best remembered images of Julian's writing follows, as she describes the droplets of blood coming from the head of the wounded Christ, a "bodily vision of the copious bleeding of the head" caused immediately prior ot the crucifixion of Jesus Christ by a "crown" made from thorns being forced into his head. The bleeding, says Julian, was actually beautiful. She writes that the drops she saw were "round like a herring's scales" or "like raindrops off a house's eaves"; that the vision was both fearful and sweet, and that to her "our good Lord" while to be revered and feared is also both familiar and courteous, this last understanding delighting her and creating a certainty of her belief.

In the thirty-second chapter Julian reiterates her famous understanding that "all shall be well," the assurance she has from God (as in the first passage) that God controls and cares for all the world and specifically for each individual.

In the fifty-ninth chapter she describes her understanding of the motherhood of God. Her presentation of the concept is wholly within Christian teaching, but is often misunderstood by those who find God-as-mother threatening to their theological systems. For Julian, God is feminine in that she "is the foundation of our nature's creation" that Jesus coming into history as a human and taking on human nature did so "where the motherhood of grace begins" and, thirdly, that the motherhood of God operates through, actually penetrates, all nature in a single love.

Unlike Augustine, whose spiritual lens was eventually that of a bishop, or Bernard of Clairvaux, who was a monastic, or Francis, whose apostolic spirituality was rooted in absolute poverty, Julian (and one might presume, other anchoresses) was a woman who posessed a rare combination of means and education to live her life of solitude. We can assume, especially from the writings of Margery Kempe, that Julian did indeed entertain conversation at the window of her anchorhold, but we can also assume that her position in the community was one of spiritual acumen, so that people would seek out her spiritual advice and perhaps ask for her prayers for their concerns.

Although she has not been canonized as a saint by the Catholic Church, Julian is called St. Julian in the Anglican tradition. She is revered as a mystic teacher in the Catholic, Anglican, and Lutheran traditions, and her anchorhold still exists at All Saints' Church in King's Lynn, Norfolk, England.

Phyllis Zagano

SHOWINGS (LONG TEXT)

At the same time as I saw this sight of the head bleeding, our good Lord showed a spiritual sight of his familiar love. I saw that he is to us everything which is good and comforting for our help. He is our clothing, who wraps and enfolds us for love, embraces us and shelters us, surrounds us for his love, which is so tender that he may never desert us. And so in this sight I saw that he is everything which is good, as I understand.

And in this he showed me something small, no bigger than a hazelnut, lying in the palm of my hand, as it seemed to me, and it was as round as a ball. I looked at it with the eye of my understanding and thought: What can this be? I was amazed that it could last, for I thought that because of its littleness it would suddenly have fallen into nothing. And I was answered in my understanding: It lasts and always will, because God loves it; and thus everything has being through the love of God.

In this little thing I saw three properties. The first is that God made it, the second is that God loves it, the third is that God preserves it. But what did I see in it? It is that God is the Creator and the protector and the lover. For until I am substantially united to him, I can never have perfect rest or true happiness, until, that is, I am so attached to him that there can be no created thing between my God and me.

This little thing which is created seemed to me as if it could have fallen into nothing because of its littleness. We need to have knowledge of this, so that we may delight in despising as nothing everything created, so as to love and have uncreated God. For this is the reason why our hearts and souls are not in perfect ease, because here we seek rest in this thing which is so little, in which there is no rest, and we do not know our God who is almighty, all wise and all good, for he is true rest. God wishes to be known, and it pleases him that we should rest in him; for everything

310

which is beneath him is not sufficient for us. And this is the reason why no soul is at rest until it has despised as nothing all things which are created. When it by its will has become nothing for love, to have him who is everything, then is it able to receive spiritual rest.

And also our good Lord revealed that it is very greatly pleasing to him that a simple soul should come naked, openly and familiarly. For this is the loving yearning of the soul through the touch of the Holy Spirit, from the understanding which I have in this revelation: God, of your goodness give me yourself, for you are enough for me, and I can ask for nothing which is less which can pay you full worship. And if I ask anything which is less, always I am in want; but only in you do I have everything.

And these words of the goodness of God are very dear to the soul, and very close to touching our Lord's will, for his goodness fills all his creatures and all his blessed works full, and endlessly overflows in them. For he is everlastingness, and he made us only for himself, and restored us by his precious Passion and always preserves us in his blessed love; and all this is of his goodness.

The Seventh Chapter

And to teach us this, as I understand, our good Lord showed our Lady St. Mary at the same time, that is to signify the exalted wisdom and truth which were hers as she contemplated her Creator. This wisdom and truth showed her in contemplation how great, how exalted, how mighty and how good was her God. The greatness and nobility of her contemplation of God filled her full of reverent fear; and with this she saw herself so small and so humble, so simple and so poor in comparison with her God that this reverent fear filled her with humility. And founded on this, she was filled with grace and with every kind of virtue, and she surpasses all creatures.

And during all the time that our Lord showed me this spiritual vision which I have now described, I saw the bodily vision of the copious bleeding of the head persist. The great drops of blood fell from beneath the crown like pellets, looking as if they came from the veins, and as they issued they were a brownish red, for the blood was very thick, and as they spread they turned bright red. And as they reached the brows they vanished; and even so the bleeding continued until I had seen and understood many things. Nevertheless, the beauty and the vivacity persisted, beautiful and vivid without diminution.

The copiousness resembles the drops of water which fall from the eaves of a house after a great shower of rain, falling so thick that no human ingenuity can count them. And in their roundness as they spread over the forehead they were like a herring's scales.

At the time three things occurred to me: The drops were round like pellets as the blood issued, they were round like a herring's scales as they spread, they were like raindrops off a house's eaves, so many that they could not be counted. This vision was living and vivid and hideous and fearful and sweet and lovely; and in all this vision which I saw, what gave me most strength was that our good Lord, who is so to be revered and feared, is so familiar and so courteous, and most of all this filled me full of delight and certainty in my soul.

And so that I might understand this, he showed me this plain example. It is the greatest honour which a majestic king or a great lord can do for a poor servant, to be familiar with him; and especially if he makes this known himself, privately and publicly, with great sincerity and happy mien, this poor creature will think: See, what greater honour and joy could this noble lord give me than to demonstrate to me, who am so little, this wonderful familiarity? Truly, this is a greater joy and delight to me than if he were to give me great gifts, and himself always to remain distant in his manner. This bodily example was shown, so exalted that this man's heart could be ravished and he could almost forget his own existence in the joy of this great familiarity.

So it is with our Lord Jesus and us, for truly it is the greatest possible joy, as I see it, that he who is highest and mightiest, noblest and most honourable, is lowest and humblest, most familiar and courteous. And verily and truly he will manifest to us all this marvelous joy when we shall see him. And our good Lord wants us to believe this and trust, rejoice and delight, strengthen and console ourselves, as we can with his grace and with his help, until the time that we see it in reality. For the greatest abundance of joy which we shall have, as I see it, is this wonderful courtesy and familiarity of our Father, who is our Creator, in our Lord Jesus Christ, who is our brother and our saviour. But no man can know this wonderful familiarity in this life, unless by a special revelation from our Lord, or from a great abundance of grace, given within by the Holy Spirit. But faith and belief together with love deserve the reward, and so it is received by grace. For our life is founded on faith with hope and love. This is revealed to whom God wills, and he plainly teaches and expounds and declares it, with many secret details which are a part of our faith and belief, which are to be known to God's glory. And when the revelation, given only for a time, has passed and is hidden, then faith preserves it by the grace of the Holy Spirit to the end of our lives. And so in the revelation there is nothing different from the faith, neither less nor more, as will be seen by our Lord's intention in this same matter, when the whole revelation is completed.

The Thirty-Second Chapter

On one occasion our good Lord said: Every kind of thing will be well; and on another occasion he said: You will see yourself that every kind of thing will be well.

And from these two the soul gained different kinds of understanding. One was this: that he wants us to know that he takes heed not only of things which are noble and great, but also of those which are little and small, of humble men and simple, of this man and that man. And this is what he means when he says: Every kind of thing will be well. For he wants us to know that the smallest thing will not be forgotten. Another understanding is this: that there are many deeds which in our eyes are so evilly done and lead to such great harms that it seems to us impossible that any good result could ever come of them. And we contemplate this and sorrow and mourn for it so that we cannot rest in the blessed contemplation of God as we ought to do. And the cause is this: that the reason which we use is now so blind, so abject and so stupid that we cannot recognize God's exalted, wonderful wisdom, or the power and the goodness of the blessed Trinity. And this is his intention when he says: You will see yourself that every kind of thing will be well, as if he said: Accept it now in faith and trust, and in the very end you will see truly, in fullness of joy.

And so in the same five words said before: I may make all things well, I understand a powerful comfort from all the works of our Lord God which are still to come.

There is a deed which the blessed Trinity will perform on the last day, as I see it, and what the deed will be and how it will be performed is unknown to every creature who is inferior to Christ, and it will be until the deed is done. The goodness and the love of our Lord God want us to know that this will be, and his power and his wisdom, through the same love, want to conceal it and hide it from us, what it will be and how it will be done. And the cause why he wants us to know it like this is because he wants us to be at ease in our souls and at peace in love, disregarding every disturbance which could hinder our true rejoicing in him.

This is the great deed ordained by our Lord God from without beginning, treasured and hidden in his blessed breast, known only to himself, through which deed he will make all things well. For just as the blessed Trinity created all things from nothing, just so will the same blessed Trinity make everything well which is not well. And I marveled greatly at this sight, and contemplated our faith, with this in my mind: Our faith is founded on God's word, and it belongs to our faith that we believe that God's word will be preserved in all things. And one article of our faith is that many creatures will be damned, such as the angels who fell out of heaven because of pride, who now are devils, and many men upon earth who die out of the faith of Holy Church, that is to say those who are pagans and many who have received baptism and who live unchristian lives and so die out of God's love. All these will be eternally condemned to hell, as Holy Church teaches me to believe.

And all this being so, it seemed to me that it was impossible that every kind of thing should be well, as our Lord revealed at this time. And to this I had no other answer as a revelation from our Lord except this: What is impossible to you is not impossible to me. I shall preserve my word in everything, and I shall make everything well. And in this I was taught by the grace of God that I ought to keep myself steadfastly in the faith, as I had understood before, and that at the same time I should stand firm and believe firmly that every kind of thing will be well, as our Lord revealed at that same time. For this is the great deed which our Lord will do, and in this deed he will preserve his word in everything. And he will make well all which is not well. But what the deed will be and how it will be done, there is no creature who is inferior to Christ who knows it, or will know it until it has been done, according to the understanding which I received of our Lord's meaning at this time.

The Fifty-Ninth Chapter

And we have all this bliss by mercy and grace, and this kind of bliss we never could have had and known, unless that property of goodness which is in God had been opposed, through which we have this bliss. For wickedness has been suffered to rise in opposition to that goodness; and the goodness of mercy and grace opposed that wickedness, and turned everything to goodness and honour for all who will be saved. For this is that property in God which opposes good to evil. So Jesus Christ, who opposes good to evil, is our true Mother. We have our being from him, where the foundation of motherhood begins, with all the sweet protection of love which endlessly follows.

As truly as God is our Father, so truly is God our Mother, and he revealed that in everything, and especially in these sweet words where he says: I am he; that is to say: I am he, the power and goodness of fatherhood; I am he, the wisdom and the lovingness of motherhood; I am he, the light and the grace which is all blessed love; I am he, the Trinity; I am he, the unity; I am he, the great supreme goodness of every kind of thing; I am he who makes you to love; I am he who makes you to long; I am he, the endless fulfilling of all true desires. For where the soul is highest, noblest, most honourable, still it is lowest, meekest and mildest.

And from this foundation in substance we have all the powers of our sensuality by the gift of nature, and by the help and the furthering of mercy and grace, without which we cannot profit. Our great Father, almighty God, who is being, knows us and loved us before time began. Out of this knowledge, in his most wonderful deep love, by the prescient eternal counsel of all the blessed Trinity, he wanted the second person to become our Mother, our brother and our saviour. From this it follows that as truly as God is our Father, so truly is God our Mother. Our Father wills, our Mother works, our good Lord the Holy Spirit confirms. And therefore it is our part to love our God in whom we have our being, reverently thanking and praising him for our creation, mightily praying to our Mother for mercy and pity, and to our Lord the Holy Spirit for help and grace. For in these three is all our life: nature, mercy and grace, of which we have mildness, patience and pity, and hatred of sin and wickedness; for the virtues must of themselves hate sin and wickedness.

And so Jesus is our true Mother in nature by our first creation, and he is our true Mother in grace by his taking our created nature. All the lovely works and all the sweet loving offices of beloved motherhood are appropriated to the second person, for in him we have this godly will, whole and safe forever, both in nature and in grace, from his own goodness proper to him.

I understand three ways of contemplating motherhood in God. The first is the foundation of our nature's creation; the second is his taking of our nature, where the motherhood of grace begins; the third is the motherhood at work. And in that, by the same grace, everything is penetrated, in length and in breadth, in height and in depth without end; and it is all one love.

Walter Hilton

Walter Hilton (ca. 1340–1396) was an Augustinian canon who wrote what is credited as the first systematic treatment of mysticism and belief written in the English language, the *Scala Perfectionis*, the Ladder of Perfection, which describes the movement of the human soul from sin to redemption and became a medieval best seller of sorts, favored by royalty.

Hilton was trained in law, including in Church canon law, but at some point in the 1370s he retired to live the life of a hermit after developing a devotion to the ways of the Carthusians, an order of men and, separately, women, devoted to silence and contemplation. By the 1380s he abandoned solitary life and entered the Augustinian Thurgarton Priory, Nottinghamshire.

Educated in civil and canon law, and with educated friends, in 1386 he wrote a counsel of spiritual perfection, *De Utilitate et Prerogativis Religionis*, for his friend, a lawyer who was entering the Carthusians. He wrote many letters of spiritual counsel and other longer works, including commentaries on scripture and a letter now entitled The Mixed Life, which advises a layman not to give up his household and posessions to become a contemplative.

The first book of The Ladder is addressed to a recently enclosed anchoress, and gives direct instructions in its ninety-three chapters on extinguishing the "foul image of sin" in her soul. Hilton writes that the image of the Trinity in the human soul (drawing on the work of St. Augustine) is perverted in its three powers (intellect, reason, will, reflecting the Father, Son, and the Holy Spirit respectively) through meditations on the seven deadly sins (wrath, greed, sloth, pride, lust, envy, and gluttony).

The second book of The Ladder opens addressed to apparently the same reader for the purpose of—he says—answering her further questions, but the work seems larger in scope and is perhaps written for the wider audience "listening in," as it were, to his advice. The major themes are reformation of the soul in faith, and also in faith a feeling. The latter task is described metaphorically as a journey to Jerusalem.

The first book of The Ladder apparently circulated independently of the later second book, and both were fairly influential in the fifteenth century.

The selection that follows opens with the direct, almost commonsensical advice that the soul that wishes to advance in spiritual matters must first know itself, beginning with the fact that the soul cannot be known through the body. It is in withdrawal from bodily things and from all the five senses that the individual can begin to learn about the spirit. Once able to attest to some knowledge of the spirit, the soul can (and must) seek higher knowledge—the nature of God. Here Hilton invokes a nearly common spiritual metaphor of the mirror—that the soul is the mirror held up to God so as to understand God's nature, but that only insofar as the mirror is kept clean can it perform this necessary function.

The selection that follows also makes comment about "feeling" in spiritual matters—that both beginners and proficients express deep feeling, even weeping, yet the understanding of God is wholly within the imagination and not within the understanding. Hilton teaches that the true understanding of God is of three kinds: faith alone, faith and the imagination of Jesus Christ, and the "spiritual sight of the divine nature in the manhood," that is, a deep understanding of the coexistence of the human and the divine within the person of Jesus Christ. The first two understandings are good, but incomplete, and allow the soul to worship God, but incompletely. The third, the actual understanding of the nature of Jesus Christ, allows the understanding to love that reality—not the Christ talked about through faith alone, nor the bodily Christ formed in the imagination, but the spiritual reality of Jesus that can then be transformed into love for all of God's nature.

Even so, he writes, it is good to maintain the practice of imagination in prayer and reverence of Jesus, and to accept the spiritual feelings thereby stirred up even though they are only outward signs of the effects of grace upon the soul. Hilton's point: there are some souls that will be fired by God's grace and some that will be fired by an act of the imagination, and the higher action of the soul is to give up the feelings evidenced (and sometimes caused by) interior activity of the individual, preferring to wait for the true interior graces of contemplation. So only will Jerusalem or true "contemplation in perfect love of God" be attained.

Hilton's work describes the mystical dark night, but not so thoroughly as John of the Cross, the Carmelite mystic in the following section.

Hilton is celebrated in the Church of England (March 24) and in the Episcopal Church (USA) (September 28).

Phyllis Zagano

THE LADDER OF PERFECTION, BOOK TWO

30. How a man is to have knowledge of his own soul, and how he should set his love in Jesus, God and Man: one Person.

A soul that wants to have knowledge of spiritual things needs first to have knowledge of itself. For it cannot have knowledge of a nature above itself unless it has knowledge of itself; and that is when the soul is so gathered into itself, separated from the consideration of all earthly things and from the use of the bodily senses, that it feels itself as it is in its own nature, without a body. Then if you desire to know and see what your soul is, you shall not turn your thought into your body in order to search for it and feel it, as if it were hidden inside your heart as your heart is hidden and held inside your body. If you search like this, you shall never find it in itself. The more you seek to find and feel it in the way you would feel a bodily thing, the further you are from it. For your soul is not a body, but a life invisible; it is not hidden and held inside your body as a smaller thing is hidden and held within a greater, but holding your body and giving it life, much greater in power and virtue than your body is.

Then if you want to find it, withdraw your thought from every outward bodily thing, and so from the awareness of your own body and from all your five senses, as much as you can; and think spiritually of the nature of a rational soul, as you would think in order to know any virtue, such as truth, humility or any other. Just so think that a soul is a life—deathless and invisible—having power in itself to see and know the supreme truth and to love the supreme goodness that is God. When you see this, then you feel something of yourself. Do not seek yourself in any other place, but the more fully and clearly that you can think about the nature and dignity of a rational soul—what it is, and what is the natural working of it— the better you see yourself. It is very hard for a soul that is rough and much in the flesh to have sight and knowledge of itself, or of

320

an angel or of God: it falls at once into the imagination of a bodily shape, and it supposes by that to have the sight of itself, and so of God, and so of spiritual things; and that cannot be. For all spiritual things are seen and known by the understanding of the soul, not by imagination. Just as a soul sees by understanding that the virtue of justice is to yield to each thing what it ought to have, so likewise the soul can see itself by understanding.

Nevertheless, I do not say that your soul is to rest still in this knowledge, but by this it shall seek higher knowledge above itself, and that is the nature of God. For your soul is only a mirror in which you shall see God spiritually. Therefore, you shall first find your mirror and keep it bright and clean from fleshly filth and worldly vanity, and hold it well up from the earth so that you can see it, and in it likewise our Lord. For this is the end for which all chosen souls labor in this life, in their purpose and their intention, even though they have no special feeling of this. Therefore, it is as I have said before: that many souls—beginning and proficient—have many great fervors and much sweetness in devotion, and are all burning in love, as it seems; and yet they do not have perfect love or spiritual knowledge of God. For you must know that however great the fervor that a soul feels—so much that it seems to him that the body cannot bear it—or even though he melts altogether into weeping: as long as his thinking and his consideration of God is mainly or entirely in imagination and not in understanding, he has not yet come to perfect love or to contemplation.

For you are to understand that the love of God is of three kinds. All are good, but each one is better than another. The first comes through faith alone, without the grace of imagination or spiritual knowledge of God: this love is in the least soul that is reformed in faith, in the lowest degree of charity, and it is good, since it is enough for salvation. The second love is what a soul feels through faith and the imagination of Jesus in his humanity. This love is better than the first, when the imagination is stirred by grace, for the eye of the spirit is opened to behold our Lord's manhood. The third love is what the soul feels through spiritual sight of the divine nature in the manhood, as it may be seen here: that is the best and most valuable, and that is perfect love. A soul does not feel this love until he is reformed in feeling. Beginners and proficient souls do not have this love, for they do not know how to meditate upon Jesus or love him spiritually, but (as it were) all humanly and carnally, according to the conditions and likeness of man; and with that point of view they shape all their work, by their thoughts and their affections. They fear him as a man, and worship him principally in human imagery, and go no further. For instance, if they have done wrong and trespassed against God, they then think that God is angry with them, as a man would be if they had trespassed against him. Therefore they fall down as if at our Lord's feet with sorrow of heart, and cry for mercy, and when they do so they have a good trust that our Lord will of his mercy forgive them their trespass. This kind of practice is very good, but it is not as spiritual as it might be. In the same way, when they want to worship God they present themselves in their thought as it were before our Lord's face in a bodily likeness, and imagine a wonderful light where our Lord Jesus is; and then they bow before him, honor him and fear him, and put themselves fully at his mercy, for him to do with them whatever he will. Similarly, when they want to love God they behold him, honor him and fear him as a man, not yet as God in man—either in his passion or in some other thing to do with his manhood—and in that beholding they feel their hearts greatly stirred to the love of God.

This kind of practice is good and comes of grace, but it is much less and lower than the practice of understanding: that is when the soul by grace beholds God in man. For in our Lord Jesus there are two natures: the manhood and the divinity. Then just as the divine nature is more excellent and honorable than the manhood, so the spiritual consideration of the divinity in Jesus the man is more honorable, more spiritual and more deserving of reward than the consideration of the manhood alone, whether one beholds the manhood as mortal or as glorified. And just so, for the same reason, the love that a soul feels in considering and thinking of the divinity in man, when it is shown by grace, is more honorable, spiritual and deserving of reward than the fervor of devotion that the soul feels by imagining only the manhood, however much it shows outwardly. For in comparison with that, this is only human, since in the imagination our Lord does not show himself as he is, or that he is; for the soul could not at that time bear such a thing, because of the frailty of the fleshly nature.

Nevertheless, to such souls that do not know how to think spiritually of the divine nature our Lord Jesus tempers the invisible light of his divinity, so that they should not err in their devotion but be comforted and strengthened through some kind of inward beholding of Jesus, to forsake sin and the love of the world. He clothes that invisible light in the bodily likeness of his manhood and shows it to the inner eye of a soul, which he feeds spiritually with the love of his precious body: a love of such great power that it slays all wicked love in the soul and strengthens it to suffer bodily penance for love of Jesus, as well as other bodily distress in time of need. And this is the shadowing of our Lord Jesus over a chosen soul, in which shadowing a soul is kept from the burning of worldly love; for just as a shadow is made by a light and a body, so this spiritual shadow is made by the blessed invisible light of the divinity and the manhood united to it, shown to a devout soul. Of this shadow the prophet speaks thus. *Spiritus ante faciem nostram Christus Dominus: sub umbra eius vivemus inter gentes.* Our Lord Jesus Christ is a spirit before our face: under his shadow we shall live among the nations. That is, our Lord Jesus in his divinity is a spirit that cannot be seen as he is in his blessed light by us living in the flesh: therefore as long as we are here we shall live under the shadow of his humanity. But although it is true that this love in imagination is good, nevertheless a soul should desire to have spiritual love in the understanding of the divine nature, for that is the end and the full blessedness of the soul, and all other considerations in the body are but means leading the soul to it. I do not say that we should separate God from

323

man, but we are to love Jesus, both God and man: God in man, and man in God; spiritual, not carnal.

This was our Lord's teaching to Mary Magdalene (who was to be contemplative), when he spoke thus, *Noli me tangere; nondum enim ascendi ad Patrem meum.* Do not touch me; I have not yet ascended to my Father. That is to say, Mary Magdalene ardently loved our Lord Jesus before the time of his passion, but her love was much in the body, little in the spirit; she well believed that he was God, but she loved him little as God, for at that time she did not know how; and therefore she allowed all her affection and all her thought to go to him as he was, in the form of man; and our Lord did not blame her then, but greatly praised it. But afterward, when he had risen from death and appeared to her, she would have honored him with the same kind of love as she did before, and then our Lord forbade her, saying thus: "Do not touch me"—that is, Do not set the rest or the love of your heart upon that human form you see with your bodily eye alone, to rest in it, because in that form I have not ascended to my Father, that is, I am not equal to the Father. For in human form I am less than he. Do not touch me thus: but set your thought and your love upon that form in which I am equal to the Father—that is, the form of the divinity—and love me, know me, and honor me as God and man divinely, not as a man humanly. That is how you shall touch me, because I am both God and man, and the whole reason why I shall be loved and honored is that I am God and took the nature of man; therefore make me a God in your heart and in your love, and worship me in your understanding as Jesus, God in man-supreme truth, supreme goodness and blessed life—for that is what I am. This is how our Lord taught her, as I understand, and also all other souls who are disposed to contemplation and fit for it, that they should do the same.

Nevertheless, for other souls that are neither subtle by nature nor made spiritual through grace, it is good to keep on with their own practice—in imagination with human affection—until more grace comes to them freely. It is not safe for anyone to abandon one good thing before he sees and feels a better. The same may be said of other kinds of feeling that are like bodily ones, such as hearing delightful song, feeling a comfortable heat in the body, or perceiving light or the sweetness of bodily savor. These are not spiritual feelings, for spiritual feelings are felt in the powers of the soul; principally in understanding and love, and little in imagination; but these feelings are in the imagination, and therefore they are not spiritual feelings. Even when they are best and most true, they are still only outward signs of the inward grace that is felt in the powers of the soul.

This can be clearly proved by holy scripture, which says this: *Apparuerunt apostolis dispertitae linguae tan quam ignis, seditque supra singulos eorum Spiritus Sanctus.* The Holy Spirit appeared to the apostles on the day of Pentecost in the likeness of burning tongues, and inflamed their hearts and sat upon each of them. Now, it is true that the Holy Spirit, who is God invisible in himself, was neither that fire nor those tongues that were seen, nor that burning which was felt in the body, but he was felt invisibly in the powers of their souls, for he enlightened their reason and kindled their affection through his blessed presence so clearly and so ardently that they suddenly had the spiritual knowledge of truth and the perfection of love, as our Lord promised them, saying thus: *Spiritus Sanctus a'ocebit vos omnem veritatem.* That is: The Holy Spirit shall teach you all truth. Then that fire and that burning was nothing else but a bodily sign, shown outwardly as witness to that grace which was felt within; and as it was in them, so it is in other souls that are visited and illuminated inwardly by the Holy Spirit and have with it such outward feeling, in comfort and as witness to the inward grace. But that grace is not, as I suppose, in all souls that are perfect, but where our Lord wills. For other souls that are imperfect and have such feelings outwardly, not having yet received the inward grace, it is not good to rest too much in such feelings, except inasmuch as they help the soul to more stability of thought in God, and to more love. For some maybe true and some may be pretended, as I have said before.

John of the Cross

Juan de Yepes Álvarez (1542–1591) grew to manhood during the famous reforming ecumenical Council of Trent (1645–1661) of the Catholic Church, which condemned various heresies and defined dogma, particularly regarding Scripture and Tradition, original sin, justification, sacraments, the Eucharist, and the veneration of saints.

Jesuit-educated, John entered the Carmelite order at the age of twenty-one, and was ordained priest in 1567. Seeking deeper silence, he intended to enter the Carthusian order, but was dissuaded by the Carmelite nun Teresa of Avila (1515–1582), whom he joined in reforming the entire Carmelite order. Known as "discalced" ("shoeless") Carmelites, he and Teresa founded monasteries throughout Spain. However, the branch of the order he was criticizing—the "calced" Carmelites—imprisoned him on the night of December 2, 1577, on a charge of his refusing to return to his original monastery. Following nine months of imprisonment—including public lashing before the entire community of friars—John escaped his tiny cell on August 15, 1578.

John wrote his most famous poem, the "Spiritual Canticle," during his imprisonment, and that experience is reflected in his other works—"The Sayings of Light and Love," "The Ascent of Mount Carmel," "The Dark Night," "The Spiritual Canticle," and "The Living Flame of Love." Of these, he is perhaps best generally known for "The Dark Night" (often called "The Dark Night of the Soul"—a phrase he never uses), which comprises a complete spiritual and psychological treatise on the stages through which an individual progresses on the way to and in attaining contemplative prayer and union with God.

The selections that follow come from the beginning of the book, where John explains his intent and presents his poem, and from early in the book where he begins to explain the concept of "dark night." His intent is to teach beginners about prayer, and to explain to those whom he calls "proficients"—those more practiced in the discipline of prayer—about the attainment of divine union in contemplative prayer. The stages he outlines in the longer explanations of the poem, those of the purgative, illuminative, and unitive, are common to other explanations of the progression of stages of prayer in that they in order first clear the soul of attachment to sin and earthly things, then demonstrate to the soul understandings of the truths of faith and of the self, and finally, the movement to absolute union as a work of God passively allowed by the individual, having passed through the dark night.

The dark night itself comprises two stages, that of the senses and that of the spirit. The dark night is initially marked by an inability to practice what is called discursive mediation (the use of the faculties of intellect and reasoning in prayer), and is combined with an absence of emotional satisfaction from spiritual things, even as the soul maintains deep commitment to Christ as the way toward union with God. This leads to aridity in prayer and even emotional disturbance and the loss of "feeling" in prayer, but John contends the onset and ensuing stages of dark night are theological, not psychological in nature, even as they may have psychological components.

John's explanations of dark night, of dark night of the sense and dark night of the spirit, are found in two of his works: "The Ascent of Mount Carmel" and "The Dark Night."

The first sign, the dark night of the senses, actually has a double set of signs. In "The Dark Night," John describes them as God's initiative (I:9, 2-8), while the more subtle points of the individual's response are presented in "The Ascent of Mount Carmel" (II:13, 2-4). In the dark night of the sense the key signal is the individual's inability to engage in discursive meditation, powerlessness to direct one's own prayer or receive satisfaction from it. This alone is not sufficient without the soul's concern that it is not serving God—despite its inability to pray as it once did, it is not inclined to move away from earlier practice. The darkness that spreads is fearful, although the soul begins to like the aloneness with God. Still enormous faith—and often a competent spiritual director—is required to convince the soul that the condition is not one of sloth or laziness.

The second sign, or the dark night of the spirit, is briefly described in "The Dark Night" (I:8, 1–3; I:121, 1–2) and in more detail later in the second book of "The Dark Night." He also mentions dark night of the spirit in the second and third books of "The Ascent of Mount Carmel." The three distinct marks of dark night of the spirit are: (1) recognition of the soul's poverty in receiving God's light and interior insight; (2) interior powerlessness—a helplessness or weakness that is overpowering; and (3) another, deeper powerlessness, which compounds the dark night of the spirit's effect on the memory, intellect, and will. The demonstration of the soul's powerlessness and interior darkness is secretly assuaged by the dark contemplation it experiences and moves it to a deepening of the Christian theological virtues of faith, hope, and charity or love.

The following selections comprise the poem "The Dark Night," which is explained throughout the entire book. Portions of the poem are reminiscent of the Song of Songs of the Old Testament or Hebrew Bible. The poem itself secured John's status as one of the finest poets writing in Spanish. John's explanation of the dark night of the senses follows.

Overall, John is known as the finest explicator of the movement from discursive prayer to contemplative prayer in the Christian tradition, and his work is widely read in other traditions as well because of his careful and insightful descriptions of the interior movements of prayer.

Phyllis Zagano

THE ASCENT OF MOUNT CARMEL

This treatise explains how to reach divine union quickly. It presents instruction and doctrine valuable for beginners and proficients alike that they may learn how to unburden themselves of all earthly things, avoid spiritual obstacles, and live in that complete nakedness and freedom of spirit necessary for divine union.

Theme

The following stanzas include all the doctrine I intend to discuss in this book, The Ascent of Mount Carmel. They describe the way that leads to the summit of the mount—that high state of perfection we here call union of a soul with God. Since these stanzas will serve as a basis for all I shall say, I want to cite them here in full that the reader may see in them a summary of the doctrine to be expounded. Yet I will quote each stanza again before its explanation and give the verses separately if the subject so requires.

Stanzas

A song of the soul's happiness in having passed through the dark night of faith, in nakedness and purgation, to union with its Beloved.

1. One dark night,
Fired with love's urgent longings
—Ah, the sheer grace!—
I went out unseen,
My house being now all stilled;

2. In darkness and secure,
By the secret ladder, disguised,

—Ah, the sheer grace!—
In darkness and concealment,
My house being now all stilled;

3. On that glad night,
In secret, for no one saw me,
Nor did I look at anything,
With no other light or guide
Than the one that burned in my heart;

4. This guided me
More surely than the light of noon
To where he waited for me
—him I knew so well—
In a place where no one appeared.

5. O guiding night!
O night more lovely than the dawn!
O night that has united
The lover with his beloved,
Transforming the beloved in her lover.

6. Upon my flowering breast
Which I kept wholly for him alone,
There he lay sleeping,
And I caressing him
There in a breeze from the fanning cedars.

7. When the breeze blew from the turret
Parting his hair,
He wounded my neck
With his gentle hand,
Suspending all my senses.

8. I abandoned and forgot myself
Laying my face on my beloved;

All things ceased; I went out from myself,
Leaving my cares
Forgotten among the lilies.

2. The first night or purgation, to which this stanza refers and which will be under discussion in the first section of this book, concerns the sensory part of the soul. The second night, to which the second stanza refers, concerns the spiritual part. We will deal with this second night, insofar as it is active, in the second and third sections of the book. In the fourth section we will discuss the night insofar as it is passive.

3. This first night is the lot of beginners, at the time God commences to introduce them into the state of contemplation. It is a night in which their spirit also participates, as we will explain in due time. The second night or purification takes place in those who are already proficients, at the time God desires to lead them into the state of divine union. This purgation, of course, is more obscure, dark, and dreadful, as we will subsequently point out.

Commentary on the Stanza

4. In this stanza the soul desires to declare in summary fashion that it departed on a dark night, attracted by God and enkindled with love for Him alone. This dark night is a privation and purgation of all sensible appetites for the external things of the world, the delights of the flesh, and the gratifications of the will. All this deprivation is wrought in the purgation of sense. That is why the poem proclaims that the soul departed when its house was stilled, for the appetites of the sensory part were stilled and asleep in the soul, and the soul was stilled in them. One is not freed from the sufferings and anguish of the appetites until they are tempered and put to sleep. So it was a sheer grace, the soul declares, to have gone out unseen without encumbrance from the appetites of the flesh, or from anything else. It was also fortunate the departure took place at night; that is, that God took from the soul all these things through a privation that was a night to it.

5. It was a sheer grace to be placed by God in this night that occasioned so much good. The soul would not have succeeded in entering it, because souls are unable alone to empty themselves of all their appetites in order to reach God.

6. Summarily, then, we have an explanation of the first stanza. Now we will expound on it verse by verse and explain whatever pertains to our subject. We will follow the method mentioned in the prologue: first cite each stanza and then the individual verses.

Chapter Two

The nature of the dark night through which a soul journeys to divine union.

One Dark Night

1. We can offer three reasons for calling this journey toward union with God a night.

The first has to do with the point of departure because individuals must deprive themselves of their appetites for worldly possessions. This denial and privation is like a night for all their senses.

The second reason refers to the means or the road along which a person travels to this union. Now this road is faith, and for the intellect faith is also like a dark night.

The third reason pertains to the point of arrival, namely God. And God is also a dark night to the soul in this life. These three nights pass through a soul, or better, the soul passes through them in order to reach union with God....

Chapter Three

The first cause of this night—the privation of the appetite in all things. The reason for the use of the expression "night."...

Chapter Thirteen

The manner and method of entering this night of sense.

1. Some counsels are in order now that the individual may both know the way of entering this night and be able to do so. It should be understood, consequently, that a person ordinarily enters this night of sense in two ways: active and passive.

The active way, which will be the subject of the following counsels, comprises what one can do and does by oneself to enter this night. The passive way is that in which one does nothing, but God accomplishes the work in the soul, while the soul acts as the recipient. This will be the subject of the fourth book where we will discuss beginners. Since, with God's help, I will there give counsels pertinent to the numerous imperfections beginners ordinarily possess on this road, I will not take the time to offer many here. Nor is this the proper place to give them, since presently we are dealing only with the reasons for calling this journey a night, and with the nature and divisions of this night.

Nevertheless, if we do not offer some immediate remedy or counsel, this part would seem very short and less helpful. Therefore I want to set down the following abridged method. And I will do the same at the end of my discussion of each of the next two parts (or reasons for the use of the term "night") which, with God's help, will follow.

2. Though these counsels for the conquering of the appetites are brief and few in number, I believe they are as profitable and efficacious as they are concise. A person who sincerely wants to practice them will need no others since all the others are included in these.

3. First, have a habitual desire to imitate Christ in all your deeds by bringing your life into conformity with His. You must then study His life in order to know how to imitate Him and behave in all events as He would.

4. Second, in order to be successful in this imitation, renounce and remain empty of any sensory satisfaction that is not

purely for the honor and glory of God. Do this out of love for Jesus Christ. In His life He had no other gratification, nor desired any other, than the fulfillment of His Father's will, which He called His meat and food [Jn 4:34]....

5. Many blessings flow from the harmony and tranquility of the four natural passions: joy, hope, fear, and sorrow. The following maxims contain a complete remedy for mortifying and pacifying the passions. If put into practice these maxims will give rise to abundant merit and great virtues.

6. Endeavor to be inclined always:

not to the easiest, but to the most difficult;
not to the most delightful, but to the harshest;
not to the most gratifying, but to the less pleasant;
not to what means rest for you, but to hard work;
not to the consoling, but to the unconsoling;
not to the most, but to the least;
not to the highest and most precious, but to the lowest and
        most despised;
not to wanting something, but to wanting nothing;
do not go about looking for the best of temporal things, but
for the worst, and desire to enter for Christ into complete
nudity, emptiness, and poverty in everything in the world.

7. You should embrace these practices earnestly and try to overcome the repugnance of your will toward them. If you sincerely put them into practice with order and discretion, you will discover in them great delight and consolation....

10. As a conclusion to these counsels and rules it would be appropriate to repeat the verses in "The Ascent of Mount Carmel" (the drawing at the beginning of the book), which are instructions for climbing to the summit, the high state of union. Although in the drawing we admittedly refer to the spiritual and interior aspect, we also deal with the spirit of imperfection existent in the sensory and exterior part of the soul, as is evident by the two roads, one on each side of that path that leads to perfec-

tion. Consequently, these verses will here bear reference to the
sensory part. Afterward, in the second division of this night, they
may be interpreted in relationship to the spiritual part.

11. The verses are as follows:

> To reach satisfaction in all
>> desire its possession in nothing.
> To come to possess all
>> desire the possession of nothing.
> To arrive at being all
>> desire to be nothing.
> To come to the knowledge of all
>> desire the knowledge of nothing.
> To come to the pleasure you have not
>> you must go by a way in which you enjoy not.
> To come to the knowledge you have not
>> you must go by a way in which you know not.
> To come to the possession you have not
>> you must go by a way in which you possess not.
> To come to be what you are not
>> you must go by a way in which you are not.
> When you turn toward something
>> you cease to cast yourself upon the all.
> For to go from all to the all
>> you must deny yourself of all in all.
> And when you come to the possession of the all
>> you must possess it without wanting anything.
> Because if you desire to have something in all
>> your treasure in God is not purely your all.

12. In this nakedness the spirit finds its quietude and rest.
For in coveting nothing, nothing raises it up and nothing weighs
it down, because it is in the center of its humility. When it covets
something, in this very desire it is wearied.

SIX

ISLAM

The Qur'an

INTRODUCTION

Muslims believe the Qur'an is the revealed word of God. Prophet Muhammad (570–633) started receiving the revelation at the age of forty, and he continued to receive revelation for the last twenty-three years of his life.

Composed of 114 chapters (*surah*) and approximately 6,200 verses (*āyah*), the Qur'an literally means "reading" or "recitation." The Qur'an is meant to be a performed text, spoken aloud by believers. It is an important part of liturgical prayers, where select chapters and verses are recited every day. The opening chapter, *Al-Fatihah*, is recited as part of every prayer, mandatory and supplicatory. To read the Qur'an over the course of the month of fasting for Muslims, Ramadan, is considering auspicious, because the Qur'an was revealed during this month.

Because it is considered to be the word of God, to recite it beautifully, and correctly, is an imperative, and many Muslim-majority countries will have recitation competitions. That the word is also to be written beautifully has given rise to the art of Islamic calligraphy. This calligraphy adorns spaces of worship, houses, clothes, household items, and, in the modern period, such things as web pages. By virtue of being the words of God, these artworks possess a certain power and blessing (*barakah*), that are transmitted to the consumer of the words.

The Qur'an is not structured in a linear narrative, like the Hebrew Bible or the Christian Gospels. Rather, because of the oral/aural nature of the text, it is arranged by theme, rhyme, meter, and time of revelation. Although the words are believed to have come from God, the arrangement is understood to be

339

human. Aside from the story of Joseph, the longest narrative in the Qur'an, there is very little that would demand that the Qur'an be ordered in a story-like format. It is full of aphorisms, descriptions of God, stories of the apocalypse, and allusions to stories of biblical figures. Only about 6 percent of the text is what we would consider legalistic. Because of the wide variety of material in the Qur'an, its fragmented nature, and the Qur'an's importance to Muslim ritual life, it has proven to be a rich source that Muslims have mined for spiritual understandings.

God is described in incredibly visceral language, having a throne that covers the heavens and the earth (2:255). God is also described in intimate language, being closer to us than our own jugular veins (50:16), and having conversations with humanity before creation (7:172). The transcendent nature of God is also present, for example when God is described as the light in a lamp (24:35). This tension between the near and far nature of God (57:3) reminds Muslims to have *taqwa*, God-consciousness in their daily lives.

That *taqwa* is manifest through a variety of ways. Chapter 55 of the Qur'an has a repeating verse that is a rhetorical question: "How many favors of your Lord will you deny?" This chapter, called "The Compassionate," is a call for Muslims to be ever grateful. One of the best-known of the legalistic verses (2:177) commands the sharing of wealth with those less fortunate. This act is arguably a sign of gratefulness to God for the bounty that believers receive.

That same verse (2:177) also speaks of these acts as being righteous, and it is the righteous who possess *taqwa*. Therefore, acts are a defining aspect of faith, but in this instance it is acts of generosity that are emphasized over acts of worship. This verse helps to highlight the distinction between religion (*dīn*) and faith (*imān*). A Muslim may practice all the religious rituals but not have faith. Many communities attempt to infuse ritual observance with a deep sense of faith; perhaps the best known of these communities are the Sufis.

The term *Sufism* is often used to mean Islamic mysticism. While Sufis are perhaps the largest group of Muslims who formally engage in mystical readings of Islamic texts, they are not the only group. For example, many Shi'ah groups also have esoteric interpretations of the Qur'an, engaging in *ta'wil*, or exegesis by divinely appointed representatives (3:7). However, as Sufis remain the largest grouping of individuals engaged in esoteric *tafsir* or Qur'an commentary, the selections in this section represent the diversity of the Sufi tradition.

The Qur'an, however, is not just a book that defines spirituality for those with mystical inclinations. It is an oral/aural text whose language, rhythm, meter, and rhyme demand to be recited by the believer. It has resonance with the heart, the mind, and the soul. It forms the basis for religious legal thought, and inspires some of the finest art, from architecture, to painting, to calligraphy. Much of the traditional poetry found in Muslim contexts refers to the contents of the Qur'an, keeping the text close to people's hearts.

Hussein Rashid

1. Sūrat al-Fātiḥah

In the name of Allah,
the All-beneficent, the All-merciful (1)

All praise belongs to Allah,
Lord of all the worlds, (2)
the All-beneficent, the All-merciful, (3)
Master of the Day of Retribution. (4)
You [alone] do we worship,
and to You [alone] do we turn for help. (5)
Guide us on the straight path, (6)
the path of those whom You have blessed
—such as have not incurred Your wrath
nor are astray. (7)

2. Sūrat al-Baqarah

Piety is not to turn your faces
to the east or the west;
rather, piety is [personified by] those who have faith
in Allah and the Last Day,
the angels, the Book,
and the prophets,
and who give their wealth, for love of Him,
to relatives, orphans,
the needy, the traveler
and the beggar, and for [the freeing of] the slaves,
and maintain the prayer and give the *zakāt*,
and those who fulfill their covenants,
when they pledge themselves,
and those who are patient in stress and distress,
and in the heat of battle.
They are the ones who are true [to their covenant],
and it is they who are the Godwary. (177)

....

Allah!—there is no god except Him—
Is the Living One, the All-sustainer.
Neither drowsiness befalls Him nor sleep.
To Him belongs whatever is in the heavens
and whatever is on the earth.
Who is it that may intercede with Him
except with His permission?
He knows that which is before them
and that which is behind them,
and they do not comprehend
anything of His knowledge
except what He wishes.
His seat embraces the heavens and the earth,
and He is not wearied by their preservation,
and He is the All-exalted, the All-supreme. (255)

3. Sūrat Āl-i-'Imrān

It is He who has sent down to *you* the Book.
Parts of it are definitive verses,
which are the mother of the Book,
while others are metaphorical.
As for those in whose hearts is deviance,
they pursue what is metaphorical in it,
courting temptation and courting its interpretation.
But no one knows its interpretation except Allah
And those firmly grounded in knowledge;
they say, 'We believe in it;
all of it is from our Lord.'
And none takes admonition
except those who possess intellect. (7)

7. Sūrat al-A'rāf

When *your* Lord took from the Children of Adam,
from their loins, their descendants
and made them bear witness over themselves,
[He said to them,] 'Am I not your Lord?'
They said, 'Yes indeed! We bear witness.'
[This,] lest you should say on the Day of Resurrection,
'Indeed we were unaware of this.' (172)

19. Sūrat Maryam

And *mention* in the Book Mary,
when she withdrew from her family
to an easterly place. (16)
Thus did she seclude herself from them,
whereupon We sent to her Our Spirit
and he became incarnate for her
as a well-proportioned human. (17)
She said, 'I seek the protection of the All-beneficent from
    you,
Should you be Godwary!' (18)
He said, 'I am only a messenger of your Lord
that I may give you a pure son.' (19)
She said, 'How shall I have a child
seeing that no human being has ever touched me,
nor have I been unchaste? (20)
He said, 'So shall it be.
Your Lord says, "It is simple for Me."
And so that We may make him a sign for mankind
and a mercy from Us,
and it is a matter [already] decided.' (21)
Thus she conceived him,
then withdrew with him to a distant place. (22)
The birth pangs brought her
to the trunk of a date palm.

She said, 'I wish I had died before this
and become a forgotten thing, beyond recall.' (23)
Thereupon he called her from below her [saying,]
'Do not grieve!
Your Lord has made a spring to flow at your feet. (24)
Shake the trunk of the palm tree,
freshly picked dates will drop upon you. (25)
Eat, drink, and be comforted.
Then if you see any human,
say,
"Indeed I have vowed a fast to the All-beneficent,
so I will not speak to any human today.' " (26)
Then carrying him she brought him to her people.
They said, 'O Mary,
you have certainly come up with an odd thing!' (27)

24. Sūrat Al-Nūr

Allah is the Light of the heavens and the earth.
The parable of His Light is a niche wherein is a lamp
—the lamp is in a glass,
the glass is as it were a glittering star—
lit from a blessed olive tree,
neither eastern nor western,
whose oil almost lights up,
though fire should not touch it.
Light upon light.
Allah guides to His Light whomever He wishes.
Allah draws parables for mankind,
and Allah has knowledge of all things. (35)

38. Sūrat Ṣād

When *your* Lord said to the angels,
'Indeed I am about to create a human being
out of clay. (71)

So when I have proportioned him
and breathed into him My Spirit,
then fall down in prostration before him.' (72)
Thereat the angels prostrated,
All of them together, (73)
but not Iblis;
he acted arrogantly
and he was one of the faithless. (74)
He said, 'O Iblis!
What keeps you from prostrating
before that which I have created
with My [own] two hands?
Are you arrogant,
or are you [one] of the exalted ones?' (75)

50. Sūrat Qāf

Certainly We have created man
and We know to what his soul tempts him,
and We are nearer to him
than his jugular vein. (16)

55. Sūrat Al-Raḥmān

In the name of Allah,
the All-beneficent, the All-merciful

The All-beneficent (1)
has taught the Qur'an. (2)
He created man, (3)
[and] taught him articulate speech. (4)
The sun and the moon are [disposed] calculatedly, (5)
and the herb and the tree prostrate [to Allah]. (6)
He raised the sky and set up the balance, (7)
declaring, 'Do not infringe the balance! (8)
Maintain the weights with justice,

and do not shorten the balance!' (9)
And the earth, He laid it out for mankind. (10)
In it are fruits and date-palms with sheaths, (11)
grain with husk, and fragrant herbs. (12)
So which of your Lord's bounties
Will you both deny? (13)
He created man
out of dry clay, like the potter's, (14)
and created the jinn out of a flame of fire. (15)
So which of your Lord's bounties
Will you both deny? (16)
Lord of the two easts,
and Lord of the two wests! (17)
So which of your Lord's bounties
will you both deny?(18)
He merged the two seas, meeting each other. (19)
There is a barrier between them
which they do not overstep. (20)
So which of your Lord's bounties
will you deny? (21)
From them emerge the pearl and the coral. (22)
So which of your Lord's bounties
will you both deny? (23)
His are the sailing ships on the sea
[appearing] like landmarks. (24)
So which of your Lord's bounties
will you both deny? (25)

Everyone on it is ephemeral, (26)
yet lasting is the Face of *your* Lord,
majestic and munificent. (27)
So which of your Lord's bounties
will you both deny? (28)
Everyone in the heavens and the earth asks Him.
Every day He is engaged in some work. (29)

So which of your Lord's bounties
will you both deny? (30)

We shall soon make Ourselves unoccupied for you,
O you, notable two! (31)
So which of your Lord's bounties
will you both deny? (32)
O company of jinn and humans!
If you can pass through
the confines of the heavens and the earth,
then do pass through.
But you will not pass through
except by an authority [from Allah]. (33)
So which of your Lord's bounties
will you both deny? (34)

57. Sūrat al-Ḥadīd

He is the First and the Last,
the Manifest and the Hidden,
and He has knowledge of all things. (3)

96. Sūrat al-'Alaq

In the name of Allah,
the All-beneficent, the All-merciful

Read in the name of your Lord who created;
created man from a clinging mass. (2)
Read, and *your* Lord is the most generous, (3)
who taught by the pen, (4)
taught man what he did not know. (5)
Indeed man becomes rebellious (6)
when he considers himself without need. (7)
Indeed to *your* Lord is the return. (8)
Tell me, he who forbids (9)
a servant when he prays, (10)

tell me, should he be on [true] guidance, (11)
or bid [others] to Godwariness, (12)
tell me, should he call him a liar and turn away (13)
—does he not know that Allah sees? (14)
No indeed! If he does not stop,
We shall seize him by the forelock, (15)
a lying, sinful forelock ! (16)
Then let him call out his gang! (17)
We [too] shall call the keepers of hell. (18)
No indeed! Do not obey him,
but prostrate and draw near [to Allah]! (19)

97. Sūrat al-Qadr

In the name of Allah,
the All-beneficent, the All-merciful

Indeed We sent it down
on the Night of Ordainment. (1)
What will show you
what is the Night of Ordainment? (2)
The Night of Ordainment
is better than a thousand months. (3)
In it the angels and the Spirit descend,
by the leave of their Lord,
with every command. (4)
It is peaceful until the rising of the dawn. (5)

99. Sūrat al-Zalzalah

In the name of Allah,
the All-beneficent, the All-merciful.

When the earth is rocked with a terrible quake (1)
and the earth discharges her burdens, (2)
and man says, ' What is the matter with her?' (3)
On that day she will relate her chronicles (4)

for her Lord will have inspired her. (5)
On that day, mankind will issue forth in various groups
to be shown their deeds. (6)
So whoever does an atom's weight of good
will see it, (7)
and whoever does an atom's weight of evil
will see it. (8)

103. Sūrat al-'Aṣr

In the name of Allah,
the All-beneficent, the All-merciful.

By Time! (1)
Indeed man is in loss, (2)
except those who have faith
and do righteous deeds,
and enjoin one another to [follow] the truth,
and enjoin one another to patience. (3)

107. Sūrat al-Mā'ūn

In the name of Allah,
the All-beneficent, the All-merciful.

Did you see him who denies the Retribution? (1)
That is the one who drives away the orphan, (2)
and does not urge the feeding of the needy. (3)
Woe to them who pray, (4)
—those who are heedless of their prayers, (5)
those who show off (6)
but deny aid. (7)

109. Sūrat al-Kāfirūn

In the name of Allah,
the All-beneficent, the All-merciful.

Say, 'O faithless ones! (1)
I do not worship what you worship, (2)
nor do you worship what I worship; (3)
nor will I worship what you have worshiped (4)
nor will you worship what I worship. (5)
To you your religion, and to me my religion.' (6)

114. Sūrat al-Nās

In the name of Allah,
the All-beneficent, the All-merciful

Say, 'I seek the protection of the Lord of humans, (1)
Sovereign of humans, (2)
God of humans, (3)
from the evil of the sneaky tempter, (4)
who puts temptations into the breasts of humans, (5)
from among the jinn and the humans.' (6)

Translated by 'Ali Quli Qara'i

Rabia al-Adawiyya

Rabia al-Adawiyya (d. 801 CE) was born and died in Basra in modern-day Iraq; hence she is also known as Rabia al-Basri. As one of
the earliest Sufis, a type of Muslim mystic, she is considered the
archetype of the Muslim consumed by love of God. Very little is
known about her life, although there is a consistent hagiography
that is told by later mystics. Although she is credited with a great
number of verses and aphorisms, there is very little that can definitively be attributed to her. All of the works attributed to her show
a woman consumed by *taqwa*, or God-consciousness.

Legend holds that Rabia was born to a poor family. It was
during this time of deprivation that she learned from her parents
about faith in God. Her father refused to beg and was visited in a
dream by Prophet Muhammad, who told him how to earn
money. As this dream became reality, the father and Rabia became
further convinced that God was the provider of everything.

Rabia was eventually taken captive during a raid and sold
into slavery. She remained so committed to prayer that she would
toil during the day and spend the night in worship. One night,
the master saw her in prayer, surrounded by light. He believed
himself to be in the presence of a holy person and immediately
freed her.

She returned to Basra and started an ascetic, celibate life. As
word of her commitment to devotional life spread, she began to
attract students. She also entered into debates with other early
Sufis, most notably Hasan al-Basri, who is more representative of
an intellectual approach to God.

There are two stories of Rabia that exemplify the type of
approach to God to which she adhered. The first is when a student asked her if she hated Satan. Her reply was that she was so

consumed by love of God that she had no energy to hate Satan. The second story is about her running through the streets of Basra with a pail of water in one hand and a torch of fire in the other. People asked her what she was doing, and she replied that she wanted to put out the fires of hell and to burn down heaven. People accused her of being mad, and she responded that she did not want to worship God from fear of hell or from the promise of heaven. Rather, she wanted to worship God for the love of God alone.

The selection of poetry from Rabia speaks to both her purported biography and her approach to worshipping God. She cherishes God as a companion who is always with her and is her "Friend" and "Sustainer." She also speaks of having two loves for God: one that is selfish and that allows her to ignore the demands of this world, and a love that is worthy of God.

While we cannot speak with any certainty of Rabia's biography, there is a very clear image of what she represents to Muslims on a spiritual quest. She is the seeker who is lost in God. Her love and passion subsume all other interests and her sense of being. It is this proximity to God that so many Muslims strive for in their own approaches to the Divine.

Hussein Rashid

My peace, O my brothers, is in solitude,
And my Beloved is with me alway[s],
For His love I can find no substitute,
And His love is the test for me among mortal beings,
When-e'er His Beauty I contemplate,
He is my "mihrāb,"[1]
towards Him is my "qibla"[2]
If I die of love, before completing satisfaction,
Alas, for my anxiety in the world, alas for my distress,

O Healer (of souls) the heart feeds upon its desire;
The striving after union with Thee has healed my soul,
O my Joy and my Life abidingly,
Thou vast the source of my life and from Thee also
    came my ecstasy.
I have separated myself from all created beings,
My hope is for union with Thee, for that is the goal
    of my desire.

O my Joy and my Desire and my Refuge,
My Friend and my Sustainer and my Goal,
Thou art my Intimate, and longing for Thee sustains me,
Were it not for Thee, O my Life and my Friend,
How I should have been distraught over the spaces
    of the earth,
How many favors have been bestowed, and how
    much hast Thou given me.
Of gifts and grace and assistance,
Thy love is now my desire and my bliss,
And has been revealed to the eye of my heart that
    was athirst,

1 [a niche in the front of every mosque]
2 [toward Mecca, the direction in which Muslims pray.]

Islam

I have none beside Thee, Who dost make the
 desert blossom,
Thou art my joy, firmly established within me,
If Thou art satisfied with me, then
O Desire of my heart, my happiness has appeared.

I have made Thee the Companion of my heart,
But my body is available for those who desire its company,
And my body is friendly towards its guests,
But the Beloved of my heart is the guest of my soul.

I have loved Thee with two loves, a selfish love and a love
 that is worthy (of Thee),
As for the love which is selfish, I occupy myself therein
 with remembrance of Thee to the exclusion of all others,
As for that which is worthy of Thee, therein Thou raisest
 the veil that I may see Thee.
Yet is there no praise to me in this or that,
But the praise is to Thee, whether in that or this.

Junayd Baghdadi

Junayd Baghdadi (d. 910 CE) was, as his name suggests, centered in Baghdad, in modern-day Iraq. Like Rabia, Junayd was a Sufi, a type of Muslim mystic. Rather than extolling the path of all-consuming love, however, he advocated a more rational approach to God. His thought would become the foundation for what became known as "sober" Sufi orders, as opposed to "ecstatic" Sufi orders.

While the ecstatic Sufis, exemplified by figures like al-Hallaj and Rumi, lost themselves in God's love, the sober Sufis were more systematic and rationalist in their thinking. Junayd and al-Ghazāli are exemplars of the latter type of Sufism, and are often in conversation with their ecstatic counterparts. Many of these Sufis, both sober and ecstatic, spoke of annihilation (*fanā*) of oneself in the Divine. Where they disagreed was in the process of achieving that state and what that state meant.

For Junayd, who wrote a work dedicated to *fanā* (annihilation), to achieve union with God was a multistep journey. He argues for withdrawal from the world and dedication to acts of worship. Ultimately, the mystic will lose herself in God's essence. However, Junayd argues that the goal of the mystic is not to remain in a state of annihilation, but to return and remain (*baqa*). Later commentators argue that Junayd's sequence of events are nearly impossible to achieve, and should therefore be read as aspirational.

Part of the challenge in reading Junayd's work is that his words are very precise and technical, and he assumes knowledge on the part of the audience. This complexity may be intentional on his part. Like many Sufi thinkers, he argues that knowledge of Sufism is not for the average person; it is meant for an initiated

357

elite. While many of his intellectual heirs would maintain that only a select few should have access to the knowledge they spoke about, and they continued to speak in a highly technical language, their works were not as cryptic, a trend we will see in the figure of al-Ghazāli.

Junayd, referred to as the Sultan of Sufis for his contributions to mystical thought, is one of the earliest proponents of a systematic sober school. While his work is not as accessible as some of his ecstatic counterparts, or later sober thinkers, it still remains an important part of the tradition.

Hussein Rashid

THE BOOK OF FANĀ

Praise be to God and God's blessing to Muhammad and his family,
peace upon them all.
The words of the Imām Abū al-Qāsim al-Junayd ibn Mulammad,
may Allah sanctify his spirit.

Praise be to God, who cut off attachments from those who
cut themselves off for him, who granted the realities to those who
cling to him and rely upon him by founding them (aujadahum)
and granting them his love. He confirmed the knowers in his
party, placed them in ranks of endowment, and showed them a
power which he made appear from out of himself and through
which he granted them of his favor, so that passing thoughts
would not dominate and obstruct them.

No attribute leads to deficiency in relation, because of their
relationship with the realities of *tawhīd*, through the implementa-
tion of *tajrīd* (stripping, peeling), in accordance with the call, and
the finding in him of favor, through apparitions of the unseen, in
nearness to the loved one.

Then I heard him say: He endowed me with himself and
became hidden in me from myself. I am the most harmful of
things to myself: Woe to me from myself! Did he not deceive me
and through me cheat me of himself? My presence was the cause
of my loss. The gratification I took in witnessing turned to
absolute struggle.

In the distress of my heart-secret, my powers fail. I find no
taste in existence, no sweetness in mastery of witness, no bliss in
bliss, no torment in torment. Tastes desert me, languages fail; no
attribute lights, no motive incites. In manifestation his command
was as it was in origination.

I said: How then does this pronouncement appear from you
when no attribute comes to light and with no motive to incite?

359

He said: I pronounced while hidden from my own condition. Then there appeared to me an overpowering, manifest, explicit sign. He annihilated my construction just as he constructed me originally in the condition of my annihilation.

I did not influence him who is pure of all influence. I did not tell of him who masters all telling. Did he not efface my trace in his attribute? In my effacement, my knowledge vanished in his nearness. He is the creator and the reviver.

I said: What do you mean by saying he annihilated my construction just as he constructed me originally in the condition of my annihilation?

He said: Do you not know that the Almighty said (7:17˙1): When your lord took out from the sons of Adam, from their loins, their progeny, and had them witness over themselves: 'Am I not your lord?' They replied: 'You are! We so witness.'

The Almighty informed us that he addressed them and that they are nonexistent but for in his existencing-of-them. He existed their created nature in a sense other than their existence-in-themselves—a sense that no one can know but he and no one can find but he. He was founding them, encompassing them, witnessing them in the beginning in their condition of annihilation from their own abiding, which was their condition from all eternity. That is the lordly existence and the divine understanding which belongs to no other than the Almighty. For this reason we say that, insofar as he is existing the godservant, his will is carried out upon the servant, however he wills, through his exalted attribute which none can share. That existence was the most perfect existence and the most realized, without doubt; it is the first, the overwhelming, the most truly overpowering, most properly subjugating everything to which it appears, effacing every trace of every thing and extinguishing the existence of every thing. There is no human attribute or existence to maintain such an existence for the reasons we have mentioned in exalting the truth and its triumph. This is an eternal guise upon the spirits.

Bliss is not any recognized kind of bliss, generosity in the real is not any known kind of generosity, because the Almighty does not perceive and is not perceived and does not change. No one knows the modality (*kayfiyya*) of his subtle graces (*latā'if*) for his creatures. The meaning of that is lordly, known by no other than he. No one is capable of that. So we said that the real annihilates anything to which it appears, and when it subjugates, it is first in subjugating and most real in overcoming and overpowering.

I said: What do those with such an attribute find when the attribute has effaced the name of their existence and their knowledge?

He said: Their existence-through-the-real-through-them; and what appears to them in an overpowering word and sovereignty; not what they sought, then recalled, and imagined after being overtaken; the real effaces them, annihilates them; it does not adhere to them and is not related to them.

How then can they describe or find what they have not undertaken, what they have not borne upon themselves, what they have not approached, that of which they have no knowledge? The proof is in the extant tradition. Is it not related from the Prophet, peace and blessings of God upon him, that he said: Allah Almighty said: My servant continues to come nearer to me through free acts of devotion until I love him. When I love him, I am the hearing with which he hears and the seeing with which he sees?

There is more discussion in the hadith, but I am concerned with the evidence of this particular passage. Now if he is the hearing with which he hears and the seeing with which he sees, then how can that be given a how? How can it be delimited in such a way as to be accessible to a category of knowledge? Were anyone to claim such a thing, his claim would be false, because we cannot have knowledge of that as a being with a certain aspect that can be a category of knowledge (*'ilm*) or knowing (*ma'rifa*).

This means that he helps him and supports him and guides him and allows him to witness whatever he wills, however he wills, in reaching the aim and in agreement with the real. That is

the action of Allah Almighty in him and his endowments for him
which are related back to him, not to the one who finds them (al-
wājid lahā). They are not from him or of him or through him, but
they come down upon him from another. In their being other
they are prior to him in their otherness. For this reason these
endowments can occur with this hidden attribute, without being
attributed to him [the human party], as we have explained.

I said: How can presence be the cause of loss? How can the
enjoyment of witnessing become absolute struggle? People here
know that they enjoy and exist [or find ecstasy (yajid'ūn)] through
presence, without struggle and loss.

He said: That is accepted opinion among the masses and the
familiar known path of their existence. But as for the select and
the select of the select, who become alien through the strangeness
of their conditions—presence for them is loss, and enjoyment of
the witnessing is struggle, because they have been effaced from
every trace and every signification that they find in themselves or
that they witness on their own. [The real] has subjugated them,
effaced them, annihilated them from their own attributes, so that
it is the real that works through them, on them, and for them in
everything they experience; it is the real which confirms such exigencies in-and-upon them through the form of its completion
and perfection.

They find bliss hidden in it, through enjoyment of existence
in the mode of nonexistence, insofar as the real has taken exclu-
sive possession and complete subjugation. Thus, when the spirits
lost the hidden bliss which ego-selves cannot perceive nor senses
approach, they became accustomed to their annihilation, finding
that their abiding is prevented by their passing away. But when he
makes present for them their thatness (anniyatahā) and makes
them find their species, they are veiled by that from what they had
been in and what had been in them. They choke on their own
selves and become accustomed to their delimited form, because
he had caused them to lose their first perfection and their most
complete nobility and they come back to the categories of discur-

362

sive reason. Grief settles in upon them. The choking of loss is attached to their condition of being-present and to being of their existence. They crave the satisfaction of appetite and return to their want. How could their reemergence from hiddenness and their return to craving after fullness not oppress them?

From here the selves of the knowers rise up ('*araja*) to verdant spaces, pleasing sights, and lush gardens. Anything else is torment for them, including that for which they are yearning from their previous state, which was encompassed by hiddenness and taken over by the beloved. Alas! Allusion to him through the attribute is allusion to that in which nothing can share. His intention in them and from them is what leaves a trace upon them. Whoever is veiled, whoever remembers them or is selected for them, must, through the intention in them, experience the presence of apparition, not the inducements from him to him. So his attribute is secure from annihilation in his realization, slipping away from the presence that he had experienced, in the position of being overwhelmed, worked through, made subject. Then, when he is brought into presence and witnessing, veiling enfolds his presence, and all traces are obliterated in his act of bearing witness.

He can find no cure for the purity of existence that overwhelmed him from the real, Most High. In this way he sees into his highest attribute and his most beautiful names. Now the path of trial opens before the people of trial. They strive, stand firm, are not deceived. A pure power, highness of rank, and dignity of position took possession of them and crushed them.

I said: Amazing! You are telling me that the people of this exalted relation must go through the experience of trial! How is that? How can I understand that?

He said: Understand! When they sought him in his intention and then kept him back from themselves, they sought the veiling of their attributes beneath a shroud of trial with which he would overwhelm them. They sought trial because the pleasure they took in things veiled them from him, so that they acted according to their thatness and occupied themselves with their senses and found pleasure in the vision of themselves in the realms of pride, in the results of their contemplation, and even in being overpowered.

How are you to understand this? No one knows it but its adepts, no one finds it but they, no one else is capable of it. Do you see that they sought him, then refused him, then beseeched him through what appeared to him from himself, and they sought help through the realities in beseeching him against himself?—because he existed them his existence-for-them, and affirmed in-and-upon them the hiddenness of the secrets leading to union with him. Then the traces were effaced and the strands were severed. Relationships continually replaced one another. The ranks were raised higher, with loss of sense and annihilation of self.

Then he made annihilation present to them in their annihilation and he had them witness existence in their existence. What he made present to them and had them witness of themselves was a hidden veil and a subtle curtain. Through it they perceived that the choke of loss and the yoke of struggle were due to the veiling of that which does not accept reasons, by making present that which accepts reasons and takes on the traces of his attribute. They sought what they sought, without knowing it from themselves. They had alighted in the way-station of power and attained the realities of precedence. So he worked in them, preoccupying them. In them was constructed a perfection from him that was and was not according to the attributed, even as the choke of their trial increased.

I said: Describe for me the transformations of trial upon them in their wondrous homeland and nearest abode.

He said: They feel autonomous in what has appeared. They have emerged from their lack, leaving their ladder behind. They clothe themselves in the victory through the struggle of position and the onslaught of pride. They regarded things as their own, without ascent (ta'rīj) to what was his. They employed distinction and difference, in what they saw and found with their own two eyes, while he subjugated them with his own two commands.

When apparitions of the real appeared to them, he gave them refuge in him from themselves by stripping away mastery and position. They left it all behind, without complaint, excited by what they had been singled out to enjoy, taking liberty with him and certain of forgiveness. They saw no necessity of return, no claim against them. At that point, they were encompassed by the guile that took them unawares.

I said: You have dazed my mind and compounded my confusion. Come nearer to what I can understand!

He said: When the people of trial cling to the event of the real in them and the exercise of his decision over them, their heart-secrets are dazed and their spirits are lost for the life of eternity. They find no refuge in their homeland, no protection hiding in their positions. They yearn for the one who puts them to the trial. They sigh at the annihilation caused by a longlost beloved. Loss grieves them. The passion they find makes them abject in thirst for him, ache for him, yearning to find him.

Thirst follows them, wrapping itself more strongly around their insides. They are troubled in knowing, lavish in loss. He works his thirst in them, as if at a funeral. Of every drapery he raises for them a banner. He gives them a taste of loss. He renews in them the vision of more struggle from their inclination toward the traces of hardship, their longing toward exemplars of grief, their imploring a cure, their attachment to the traces of the beloved in whatever appears, their seeing every separation through the eye of nearness. They are hidden in a hidden hiddenness, hidden in the loss of the veil that hid them. He tries them. They do not flinch. How could they be veiled when they are imprisoned before him, called to account before him in his presence, then pardoned before him through perishing in all that he makes appear to them out of their trial, no longer bent on their own self-concern, freed in his love, clinging to him at the waystation of nearness?

They see the measures of gazes from him in the immediacy of their waking. Their perishing drowns as his abiding flows out of them in the harshness of their trial, until the trial delights them and their abiding becomes their intimate companion in him—when they seem near to denying them, when he produces the sting. Exhaustion does not divert them from bearing it. Fullness does not sate them. These are the champions—in what came over them when he gave them the secret. They abide in his over-whelming power, awaiting his command—the command of Allah be done.

The people of trial are of two kinds. There is the one who finds refuge in trial, whose intention subsides, as well as what his desire for things abides and the excitement of the pleasure in the self, and the endowment of sense existence—all that dies down until it hurts him and he is beguiled by it, and then the beguiling ceases as if it were a momentary condition, and he reaffirms his stance in trial as a mark of nobility, seeing that to leave it is a cause of failure and weakness.

The End of the Book of Fanā

Mansur al-Hallaj

Mansur al-Hallaj (d. 922) is regarded as one of the great early mystics for reaching the state of *fanā* (annihilation) in the Divine. His role in Sufi lore is complicated in both theological and political understandings of his achievements. As part of the emerging ecstatic movement of Sufis, he separated from his early teacher, Junayd. He was eventually executed for his beliefs.

Hallaj is perhaps best-known for uttering the phrase *"ana'l-Haqq,"* or "I am the Truth." In this instance, "Truth" is used to mean God and demonstrates Hallaj's total loss of self in his love God. This ecstatic utterance (*shath*) was considered blasphemous by the religious authorities of his time, and he was sentenced to death. One legend of his execution speaks to the proximity of Hallaj to God. As he is hung, the last word to escape from his lips is "Allah." The authorities, fearing that his declaration of God's name would allow people to argue that he was a martyr, decide to quarter him. His blood pools to spell the word "Allah," so his judges decide to burn his body. As the fire quiets and his ashes are revealed, and wind comes and forces the ashes into the pattern of "Allah."

Later ecstatic Sufi commentators, while agreeing to the extreme devotion Hallaj had for God, would develop two separate but related meanings to this story. The first argument is that the average person cannot deal with the realities a Sufi master is aware of. When faced with the idea that God is more immanent than they imagine, the average crowd will react in fear and kill the messenger. The other argument is that Hallaj broke an important rule by revealing secrets of God's proximity to the uninitiated. As a result, he did have to be executed. Other tales of ecstatic utterances happen in private, whereas Hallaj's declaration was public, potentially revealing the power of mystical learnings and leading the laity astray.

As powerful as this story is, the reality of Hallaj's execution seems to be more related to state craft than violation of theological sensibilities. Although it would be easy to see the mystic quest as solely inward looking, for many mystic groups, including the Sufis, spiritual development also meant serving as moral and ethical beacons. Hallaj seems to have run afoul of the ruling dynasty of the time, the Abbasids, by speaking out against corruption and speaking for the disenfranchised. Eventually, as his following grew, he came to the attention of the political authorities, who saw him as a threat. They created charges against him, alleging blasphemy, that ultimately lead to his execution.

It is in the work attributed to Hallaj that we see a keen interest in speaking for the voiceless. The selections of text in this volume are Hallaj attempting to rehabilitate Iblis, without redeeming him. Iblis is the name of Satan before his fall from heaven. For Hallaj, Iblis loved God and that love included never bowing to another being. Therefore, when God commands Iblis to bow to the figure of Adam, Iblis is torn. He loves God and will not bow to another figure, but he must also obey his Beloved. Ultimately, Iblis decides that his love for God means that he must disobey God. Hallaj thus casts Iblis's actions as devotional, rather than treasonous. However, one can also argue that Hallaj also criticizes Iblis for having such a narrow view of God that he could not see the Divine in God's creations.

By approaching the debate in dialogue format, Hallaj allows us to "hear" Iblis. In the first selection, Iblis is compared to the Prophet Muhammad (Ahmad). Whereas Iblis is said to be disobedient, compared to Muhammad's obedience, Iblis says that he was simply affirming God's unity (*tawhid*), and worshipping no one else but God. In the second exchange, with Moses, Iblis argues that his love for God was being tested, not his ability to obey orders. He then expounds about various Sufi states and how they should not be revealed to others not as advanced as he is. In the discourse on Azazil (the Angel of Death), Hallaj argues that we need Iblis to understand God, because we learn through opposition. Finally, Hallaj directly inserts himself into conversation with Iblis and Pharaoh. Each argues that they are fulfilling an oath to serve God, but each one's service is determined by God's needs and understandings.

The counterintuitive readings that Hallaj offers give us an insight as to the debates happening amongst ecstatic Sufis as to what should be publicly revealed. To argue that Iblis is a lover of God and is serving God's purpose can weaken others' certitude as to what is right and what is wrong. There is also in Hallaj's hagiography a sense of the division between sober and ecstatic Sufis. Hallaj is said to have been a student of Junayd, and that they split over their differing interpretations of approaching God. When Hallaj was sentenced to death, Junayd was asked for his opinion. His response was that we can only judge by the external appearance, and God knows the truth of Hallaj's inward state. This statement can be seen as a subtle criticism of Junayd and the sober schools. They are so fascinated with the outward manifestation, like Iblis, that they forgot God's presence in creation.

Hussein Rashid

MUHAMMAD AND IBLIS

1. That strange and learned master, Abū al-Mughīth Husayn ibn Mansūr al-Hallaj—may Allah adorn his place of rest—said:

Making claims is appropriate for no one but Iblis and Ahmad, except that Iblis fell from the 'ayn while Ahmad—God bless him—had revealed to him the 'ayn of 'ayn.

2. Iblis was told: "Bow down!" Ahmad was told: "Look!" The former did not bow and Ahmad turned neither to the right nor left.

(53:17) "The eye did not swerve nor did it exceed its bounds."

3. Iblis made claims but he returned to his power.

4. Ahmad made claims and returned from his power,

5. With the sayings, "O changer of hearts!" and "I cannot measure out your praise."

6. Among the inhabitants of heaven, there was no affirmer of unity (mu-wahhid) like Iblis,

7. When Iblis was veiled by (ulbisa) the 'ayn, and he fled the glances and gazed into the secret, and worshiped his deity stripped of all else,

8. Only to be cursed when he attained individuation and given demands when he demanded more.

9. He was told: "Bow down!" He said, "[to] no other!" He was asked, "Even if you receive my curse?" He said, "It does not matter. I have no way to an other-than-you. I am an abject lover."

370

10. My disavowal in you is *taqdīs* (affirmation of transcendence)
    My reason in you, befuddlement.
    Who is Adam other than you?
    To distinguish them, who is Iblis?
    [And the one in between is Iblis].

11. He said: He disdained and grew proud, turned away and backed around, and what he insisted upon, set down.

He said, "You've grown proud." He replied, "A moment with you would be enough to justify my pride and lording-it-over *(tajabbur)*. So how much more am I justified when I have passed the ages with you. (7:11) 'I am better than him' because of my priority in service. There is not in the two creations anyone more knowing of you than I. I have a will in you and you have a will in me. Your will in me is prior and my will in you is prior. If I bow before an other-than-you or do not bow, I must return to my origin, for (7:11) 'you have created me from fire.' Fire returns to fire. To you belongs the determination and the choice."

12. There can be no distance for me
        distancing you from me
    When I have achieved certainty
        nearness and distance are one.
    Even if I am abandoned,
        abandonment will be my companion.
    How can it be abandonment
        while love is one?
    To you, praise in success,
        in the pure absolute
    For a servant of true heart
        who will bow to no other than you.

371

MOSES AND IBLIS

13. Musa met Iblis on Mount Sinai and said, "O Iblis, what kept you from bowing down?" He answered, "The proclamation of only one object of worship prevented me. If I had bowed down in prayer before Adam, I would have been like you. You were called one time to 'look at the mountain!' and you looked. I was called a thousand times to 'bow down! bow down!' but I did not bow, held back by the meaning of my proclamation."

14. He said, "You abandoned the command!"
He replied, "That was a test, not a command."
He said, "Of course he deformed you."
He answered, "Musa, that and that is masquerade. The condition is unreliable; it will change. Knowing remains as sound as it was before, unchanged; only the figure has been transformed."

15. Musa said, "Do you remember him now?"
"O Musa," he replied, "remembrance does not remember. I am the remembered and he is the remembered. His remembrance is my remembrance, my remembrance, his. Can the two rememberers be anything but together? My service is now purer, my moment freer, my remembrance greater. Formerly I served him out of concern for my own lot; now I serve out of concern for his."

16. We took cupidity from prohibition and defense, harm and advantage. He set me apart, "extased me" *(awjadani)* when he expelled me, so that I would not be mixed with the pure-hearted. He held me back from others because of my zeal, othered me because of my bewilderment, bewildered me because of my exile, exiled me because of my service, proscribed me because of my friendship, disfigured me because of my praise, consecrated me because of my *hijra*, abandoned me because of my unveiling, unveiled me because of my union, made me one with him because of my separation, cut me off because of the preclusion of my fate.

17. By his reality! I have not erred concerning the designing *(tabfīr)* nor rejected the destining *(taqdīr)* nor concerned myself with the change in imaging *(taṣwīr)*, nor am I in such measures the one to be judging! Even if he torments me with his fire forever and beyond, I will not bow before any other than him, abase myself before a figure and body, or recognize a rival or offspring. My proclamation is the proclamation of those who are sincere, and in love I am triumphant. How not?

....

'AZĀZĪL (1)

18. Al-Husayn ibn Mansur al-Hallaj, God's compassion upon him, said:

Concerning the states of 'Azdzil there are different opinions. One is that he was the proclaimer in heaven and on earth. In heaven he was the proclaimer of the angels, showing them the virtues, and on earth he was the proclaimer of humankind, showing them the vices.

19. Things are known through opposites. A fine garment is woven on a course, black backing. Similarly, the angel displays the virtues and says to the virtuous: "Perform them and you will be requited," while Iblis shows the vices and says: "Perform them and you will be requited"—symbolically. Whoever does not know vice will not know virtue.

....

IBLIS, PHAROAH, AND HALLAJ

20. Abu 'Umāra al-Hallaj, the strange master, said:

I competed with Iblis and Pharoah in the domain of valor.

Iblis said, "If I had bowed down, the name of valor would have fallen from me."

Pharoah said, "If I had affirmed belief in the Prophet, I would have been thrown from the station of valor."

21. I said, "If I had gone back on my proclamation, I would have been thrown from the carpet of valor."

22. Iblis said (7:12), "I am better than he" when he saw no other other than he.

Pharoah said [28:37], "I know of no other lord for you than me." He knew no one among his people who could distinguish between the real and the creation.

23. And as for me, I said, "If you do not recognize him, recognize his trace. I am his trace. I am the real!" because I never ceased to be real in the real.

24. My friends and teachers are Iblis and Pharoah. Iblis was threatened with fire but did not go back on his proclamation. Pharoah was drowned in the sea, but did not go back on his proclamation and did not affirm any mediation at all. But I said (10:90), "I believe that there is no God but he in whom the people of Israel believed." Don't you see that Allah (may he be praised) opposed Jibril at his gate and said, "Why have you filled his mouth with sand?"

25. I was killed and my hands and feet were cut off. Still I did not go back on my proclamation.

'AZĀZĪL (2)

26. The name "Iblis" is derived from his name 'Azāzīl: the letter *'ayn'* corresponds to the height of his inner resolve, the zā' [z] to the compounding of dilation in his dilation; the *alif [ā]* to his views on his "thatness"; the second zā [z] to his renunciation in rank *(rutba)*; the *yā'* [i] to his seeking refuge in the knowledge of his priority; and the *lām* [l] to his disputation over his reddening (lamiyya).

27. He said to him: "Why did you not bow in prayer, abject one?"
He replied: "I am a lover; lover abject. You say abject *[mahin]* // but I read in the book *mubīn* [that makes clear] // what would happen to me, O you of the power *matīn* [unbreakable] // How was I to abase myself before him when [8:2] 'you created me from fire and created him from *tīn* [mud, clay]? // 'two contraries that cannot meet, and I am in service senior, more majestic in his favor, in knowledge more learned, in living more complete!'

28. The real, be praised, said to him: The choice is mine not yours.
He said, "All choices, including my own, are yours. You have chosen for me, O Originator! If you forbid me from bowing, you are the Forbidder. If I err in speaking, don't abandon me, All-Hearer! If you will me to bow before him, I am the Obeyer. I know no one more knowing of you than me."

29. Don't blame me, blame from me is *ba'īd* [far away]
Reward me! master, for I am *wahīd* [unique]
In your true threat, I am made true
Desert in desert, my plight is *shadīd* [severe]
Whoever wills a speech, here is my book and testament,
Read it and know I am a *shahīd* [witness, martyr].

30. My brother Iblis was called 'Azāzīl because he was set apart, set apart as intimate friend, not proceeding from beginning to end, but brought forth emergent from his end.

31. His coming forth inverted his rootness-on-site, ignited by his blazing fire of night, from his precedence, blinding light.

32. His watering pond
       dried, cracked ground
    Abundance want,
       lightning fading
    His rain-swords only apparitions
       Blind he wanders off the path

    Alas

33. My brother, if you understand this you
       have piled up stones,
    spectres of imagination,
       then returned in consternation,
    and passed away in cares.

34. The most eloquent of the tribe were dumbstruck at his gate.
       The sages failed to appreciate;
    He was more perfected than they in the position of prayer
       Nearer than they to the one existing
    Spending himself in struggle, more giving
       More faithful than they in the oaths they would swear
    More loyal to the master than they, more near.

35. They fell before Adam in prayer as a favor
       While Iblis, because of his ancient age of witnessing,
          refused.
    His character against the horizon huge,
       his excess a refuge,
    thornweeds fruitful,
       his being cut away an unfolding flower,
    his return, most giving, noble.

Abu Hamid Muhāmmad al-Ghazāli

Abu Hamid Muhāmmad al-Ghazāli (d. 1111) was a polymath who wrote extensively about philosophy, logic, astronomy, and theology. By the twelfth century, the fissure between Sufis and legal scholars had become a chasm, and al-Ghazāli is often credited with bringing them closer together within the Sunni tradition of Islam. His work reflects his own commitment to a mystical understanding of Sunni doctrine, as well as a strict adherence to traditional legal thought.

Al-Ghazāli's father was a member of a Sufi order who died while al-Ghazāli was a young boy. This exposure to Sufism impacted both al-Ghazāli and his younger brother Ahmad. While al-Ghazāli went on to train to become a legal scholar, Ahmad became a Sufi master. Al-Ghazāli found success as a scholar in the Abbasid court in Baghdad. However, in 1095, al-Ghazāli experienced a spiritual crisis, after which he left his family and adopted the mannerisms of a mendicant Sufi.

Although al-Ghazāli is known for engaging in debates with philosophers about the necessity for philosophy in a religious system, it is during his period of self-discovery that he writes what many consider to be his magnum opus, *Ihya' 'Ulum ad-Din* (*The Revival of Religious Sciences*). This text is part Sufi manual, part legal rule book, and part theological treatise. This work is al-Ghazāli's attempt to bring legalistic and mystical thinking into harmony for the Sunni tradition. His long periods of debates with the philosophers and Shi'ah Isma'ili thinkers is evident. At the same time he is deriding these groups, he is incorporating their methodologies into his own work. There are strong resonances between his *rapprochement* and the work of Ibn Sina, or Fatimid thinkers like Qadi Nu'man. However, the work is innovative for his followers, and remains an important work to the present day.

The selection from the work included here is about preparing one's heart for the Sufi way. Al-Ghazāli begins with the idea of a person looking at a mirror. In this scenario, there are three items we must be aware of: the mirror, the image, and the person. The heart is compared to the mirror, and it must be polished and oriented to the person to get an image. Polishing the heart includes keeping away from sin. The heart must be oriented toward the Divine, and the heart must be disciplined, through engagement with religious learning, to appreciate the Divine. He then argues, based on sayings of Prophet Muhammad (*hadith*), that God resides in the hearts of believers, but that they must be trained to appreciate that presence. He ends his discourse on the need for spiritual engagement and experiential learning. It is only through experience that one can have a meaningful faith free from error. His counter-example is that of speculative theologians, who do not have the proof of experience and are therefore capable of leading people into error.

Al-Ghazāli is perhaps the most important thinker of sober Sufism within the Sunni worldview. His ability to adapt and incorporate a wide variety of thought into his work were clearly transformative in the way mystical and legal traditions interacted with one another. The continuing influence of his manual attests to both the depth of his work and the role of mystical thought in contemporary Muslim life.

Hussein Rashid

THE ELABORATION OF THE MARVELS OF THE HEART (KITĀB SHARH 'AJĀ'IB AL-QAIB):

BOOK 21 OF THE REVITALIZATION OF THE RELIGIOUS DISCIPLINES (I IHYĀ' 'ULŪM AD-DĪN)

[14] Clarification 6: The likeness of the heart, particularly in relation to the religious disciplines:

Know that the dwelling place of *'ilm* is the heart. I am referring to the subtle faculty that governs all the limbs, and which all of the members obey and serve. Its relationship to the true natures of things known is like that of a mirror to evanescent images. Just as the evanescent image and the likeness of this image are imprinted upon the mirror and appear there, so everything known has a true nature whose image is imprinted upon the mirror of the heart and becomes visible there. And just as the mirror is a distinct item, and the images of persons are a separate item, and the occurrence of their likeness upon the mirror still another, so that it is a question of three distinct items, so the three in this instance are, specifically, the heart, the true natures of things, and the occurrence of those true natures in the heart and their presence there. The term knower is a reference to the heart in which the likeness of the true natures of things dwell, while that which is known refers to the true natures of things, and knowledge refers to the occurrence of the likenesses in the mirror.

Just as in the act of grasping, that which does the grasping is like the hand, and that which is grasped is like the sword, and the "reception" that characterizes the relationship between sword and hand resulting from the hand's taking the sword is known as grasping—so the heart's reception of the likeness of the thing known is called knowledge. Now the true nature of a thing exists, as does the heart, even when knowledge is not in progress, for knowledge refers

379

to the occurrence of the truth in the heart. Similarly, both the sword and the hand exist independently even when one does not speak of the occurrence of grasping and seizing when there is no sword in the hand. One must note that "grasping" refers to the presence of the sword itself in the hand, whereas that which is known does not itself enter into the heart. So, for example, fire itself does not enter into the heart of one who knows fire; instead, what enters there is its definition and the true nature of it that is congruent with its image. The creation of its likeness in a mirror, therefore, is fundamental, for the individual person as such does not enter into the mirror—only the likeness that is congruent with the person does so. That is how the presence in the heart of a likeness congruent with the true nature of the thing known is called 'ilm.

There are five conditions under which an image is not revealed in a mirror:

[15] First, deficiency in its reflective capability when it is raw iron, before it is rounded, trimmed, and burnished.

Second, the presence of a blemish, rust, or tarnish, even if it is perfectly shaped.

Third, its being deflected away from facing the image and toward something else, as when the image is behind the mirror.

Fourth, the interposition of a veil between the mirror and the image.

And fifth, ignorance with respect to where the desired image is, so that one becomes unable to orient the mirror directly toward the image.

The heart, too, functions as a mirror subject to all of these limitations, in that the essential nature of the Truth is revealed in it, even though hearts may at times be devoid of knowledge, for the following five reasons:

First, an inherent deficiency, as in the instance of the heart of a child to which things known are not revealed because of its undeveloped state.

Second, the tarnish of sins and the imperfections that have accumulated on the face of the heart as a result of a multitude of cravings, robbing the heart of its purity and clarity, so that the efflorescence of the truth in it is foreclosed by its darkness and its accretion of blemishes. The Prophet alludes to that when he says, "When a person yields to sin, understanding withdraws from him never to return." In other words, tarnish settles on the individual's heart and its traces do not disappear. Suppose that it is the individual's intention to pursue (understanding) with some positive action by which to rub off (the tarnish). If, at that point, he brings a good act to bear upon it that is not offset by an evil act, then there will surely be an increase of illumination in the heart. But when an evil act takes precedence, the benefit of a good deed is canceled out but the heart reverts thereby to the condition in which it was prior to the evil act. As a result, light does not increase in the heart. This is an obvious deterioration and diminishment for which there is no remedy. But cannot the mirror that has been sullied then be polished by burnishing, the way one is polished by burnishing to increase its clarity beyond its former sullied condition? It is, then, the concern for obedience to God and turning away from the importunities of the passions that clarifies and purifies the heart. On that point God has said, "Those who struggle on Our behalf We will surely guide to Our ways" (29:69), and the Prophet said, "To anyone who acts upon what he knows, God bequeaths as an inheritance knowledge of what he had not known."

Third, the heart might be deflected from the direction of the spiritual reality that one seeks, so even if the heart of an obedient and upright person is pure, the effulgence of the Truth might not shine forth in it since it is not seeking the Truth and its mirror is not oriented in the requisite direction. Indeed, anxiety over fulfilling specific necessary bodily deeds or securing means of livelihood often intrudes. The individual does not turn his thoughts toward full attentiveness to the Lordly presence and the hidden divine truths. Only the minutiae of the deleterious actions and secret faults of the ego-self upon which the individual reflects are

381

revealed to the individual as he is reflecting upon them, or the exigencies of making a livelihood when he is reflecting on them. Now if preoccupation with actions and the details of ordinary compliance with life's demands can restrict disclosure of the Truth's effulgence, how do you think a person who turns his concern toward worldly cravings and pleasures and attachments could but miss out on disclosure of the truth?

Fourth, there is the veil. It may be that an obedient heart that is victorious over its cravings and has dedicated its thoughts exclusively to one aspect of the ultimate reality still experiences no revelation because it is veiled from it by adherence to immature views arising from unquestioning acceptance of authority and concern for good repute. That condition may intervene between the individual and the reality of the Truth, so that the incongruity of what he has latched onto from the outward meanings afforded by uncritical assent prevents disclosure in his heart. This is, in addition, a great veil that veils countless speculative theologians and partisans of the various schools of legal methodology. Indeed, many upright individuals who reflect on the realms of heaven and earth are veiled by varieties of adherence to uncritical assent that congeal in their souls and take deep root in their hearts, so that a veil comes between them and the perception of realities.

Fifth comes ignorance with respect to the source of discovery of that which one seeks. The person who seeks 'ilm cannot attain knowledge [161] of the unknown except through mindfulness of the disciplines that together bear upon that which he seeks, to such an extent that he reflects on them and coordinates them internally with a specific ordering that religious scholars recognize from their perspective. When that occurs, the individual hits upon the direction of the object of the quest, so that its spiritual reality is manifest to his heart. But one cannot avail oneself of the desired forms of knowledge, which are not innate, except through the matrix of the sum total of the sciences. In fact, one cannot attain any knowledge except by linking together as a pair two previously known specific bits of knowledge. On the basis of their pairing, one attains a third bit of knowledge, much the way a brood of young animals comes about as a result of the conjoining of the male and female of the species. Then, just as when one wishes to produce a mare and cannot do so from a jackass or a camel or a human being, but only from the specific stock of the male and female horse, and that only with the specific conjoining of the two, so every cognition has two specific sources that are meant to be paired and from whose conjunction the desired beneficial knowledge comes about.

Ignorance as to the nature of the conjunction of these sources is an obstacle to knowledge. I have already alluded to an analogy to this in relation to ignorance of the direction in which the image lies. The analogy is this: Suppose the individual wants to see a reflection of the back of his head in the mirror. If he raises the mirror opposite his face, it is not oriented toward the back of his head, and as a result he does not see the back of his head in it. If he then raises it behind and opposite the back of his head, he has turned the mirror away from his eye so that he does not see the mirror or the image of the back of his head in it. The individual must therefore have someone else hold a mirror up behind the back of his head, while the first mirror is in front where the individual can see it. By maintaining a juxtaposition of the two mirrors, then, the image of the back of his head is imprinted upon the mirror oriented toward the back of his head. Then the image in this rear mirror is transferred to the other mirror that is before the eye, and the eye perceives the image of the back of the head. Similarly, therefore, in the course of availing oneself of the sciences there are wondrous paths along which there are deviations and detours even stranger than what I have mentioned occur on the mirror. People capable of discerning a way beyond these deviations are scarcely to be found anywhere on earth. These then are the causes that prevent hearts from the intimate knowledge of the true natures of things.

On the other hand, every heart is naturally disposed to experiential knowledge of spiritual realities, for it is a divine exalted charge that distinguishes (humankind) from the other elements of the universe through this uniqueness and nobility. The word of

God alludes to this, "We did offer the trust to the heavens and the earth and the mountains, but they declined to bear it, for they feared it, but the human being undertook it" (33:72). This indicates that human beings possess a unique characteristic that distinguishes them from the heavens and the earth and the mountains, that renders them capable of undertaking the trust of God. This trust is experiential knowledge and the acknowledgment of the divine transcendent unity, and the heart of every human being is prepared for undertaking the trust and inherently capable of it. However, the conditions I have been discussing impede it from assuming its burdens and attaining the full realization of it. It was on this account that Muhammad said, "Everyone begotten is born with a natural inclination, though his parents make him a Jew or a Christian or Magian." And the words of God's Messenger, "If the devils did not swarm about the hearts of the children of Adam, they would look toward the kingdom of the heavens," are alluding to one of these conditions that stand as a veil between human hearts and the kingdom of heaven.

Another allusion to this is a tradition we have received from Ibn Umar: Someone asked God's Messenger, "O Messenger of God, where is God-on earth or in heaven?" He replied, "In the hearts of his faithful servants." And in a sacred Hadith, God said, "Neither the earth nor the heavens are wide enough for Me, but there is room for Me in the gentle, meek heart of my faithful servant." And according to a report, someone asked, "O Messenger of God, who is the best person?" He answered, "Every believer whose heart is swept clean." Someone asked, "And what is it that sweeps the heart clean?" He answered, "It is the piety and purity in which there is neither deceit nor injustice nor betrayal nor envy." It was in this connection that Umar said, "My heart sees my Lord," for he had lifted the veil through piety. And when [17] the veil has been lifted between an individual and God, the image of the King and the Dominion is manifest in that person's heart, so that he sees a Garden so expansive that it contains Heaven and earth. The whole of it is wider than the heavens and the earth because "Heaven and earth" is an expression for the realm of earthly sovereignty and witnessing through the senses. Even if the breadth of its limits were to exceed all bounds, it would still come to an end after all. But the realm of Lordly Dominion comprises mysteries, hidden from the sight of eyes, that are reserved for the perception of the inward vision and to which there is no end. How fortunate the heart that receives even a fleeting glimpse of that realm, though it is, in itself and in relation to the knowledge of God, limitless!

If you took it in all at one time, you would call the combination of the realm of the earthly sovereignty and the Lordly Dominion the Lordly Presence: The Lordly Presence encompasses all existent things since nothing exists apart from God and His actions. His kingdom and His servants are the results of His actions, and what is manifest to the heart from that, is, according to the Sufis, the Garden, and, according to the people of Truth, a means of realizing the Garden. The breadth of His kingdom in the Garden is commensurate with the breadth of experiential knowledge of Him and is proportionate to what is manifest to the individual concerning God and His attributes and deeds. To be sure, the desired result of deeds of obedience and the actions of all the bodily limbs is the purification, cleansing, and polishing of the heart: "One who purifies it is successful" (91:9). The desired result of its purification is the descent of the lights of faith into it, by which I mean the illumination of the light of experiential knowledge. That is the goal according to the words of the Most High, "When God desires to guide a person, He expands the center of that person's being toward surrender *(islām)*" (6:125) and "Does not a person, the center of whose being God has expanded, have the light of his Lord?" (39:22).

How wonderful is this manifestation and this faith! It has three degrees: The first degree is the faith of the generality of people, the faith of simple uncritical acceptance of authority. The second is the faith of the speculative theologians. It is alloyed with a variety of deductive inference, and it represents a level close to that of the faith of the generality of people. The third is the faith of those endowed with experiential knowledge, and it involves contemplating with the light of certitude. Let me explain these degrees to you by means of a three-part analogy with how one ascertains that Zayd is inside a house.

The first is that someone whose veracity you have checked out—and you neither know him to be guilty of mendacity nor doubt what he says—passes along to you news about Zayd. So your heart is confident about him and trusts his report on the basis of hearing alone. This belief is based purely on uncritical acceptance of authority and is like the faith of the generality of people: When they arrive at the age of discrimination they hear from their fathers and mothers about the existence of God and His knowledge, will, power, and other attributes, and the sending of the messengers, and their veracity, and what God revealed to them. They accept what they hear, depend upon it, and have confidence in it. It never occurs to them to disagree with what they have been told because of their respect for their fathers, mothers, and teachers. This faith is the means of salvation in the next life. Its proponents are among the foremost ranks of the Companions of the Right Hand, but they are not among those who draw near to God because their faith does not encompass the revelation, inward vision, and expansion of the center of one's being through the light of certitude.

Error is possible in connection with what one hears from anyone, even when it is a question of numerous individuals' adherence to creedal statements. So the hearts of the Jews and Christians as well were confident in what they heard from their fathers and mothers, but their belief in that to which they assented was erroneous because their parents had passed along erroneous belief to them. The Muslims hold to the truth, not as a result of their study of it, but because the word of truth was delivered to them.

The second degree is that you hear Zayd's speech and his voice from inside of the house, but from behind a wall. On that basis, then, you infer his existence in the house. Your faith, verification, and certitude as to his existence in the house are in this instance stronger than your verification on the basis of hearsay alone. If, therefore, someone were to tell you he was in the house, and then you heard his voice, your certitude would be increased because voices lead the one who hears the voice to infer the shape and image as if one actually witnessed the image. So your heart makes the judgment that this is the voice of that person. This faith is allied to evidence, but here also one can be led into error. [18] If the voice is similar to another voice, it could be mimicry employed as a ruse, but it has not occurred to the listener that he has any grounds for suspicion, nor does he suspect that this involves a deliberate deception and ruse.

The third degree is that you enter the house and look at Zayd with your own eyes and witness him directly. This is authentic experiential knowledge and certain witnessing, and it is similar to the experiential knowledge of those who draw near to God and those who attest to the truth because they believe on the basis of contemplative vision. On the one hand, their faith is consistent with the faith of the generality of people and of the speculative theologians, but on the other, they are different by virtue of the superiority of the evident proof by which they elude the possibility of error.

In addition, they differ with respect to both the scope of their knowledge and the levels of disclosure. As for the levels of disclosure, an analogy would be that the individual sees Zayd in the house from close proximity and in the courtyard of the house as the sun illumines it, so that his perception of Zayd is complete. Suppose that, by contrast, another individual perceives Zayd in a room or from a distance or later in the evening. The form resembles Zayd in such a way that the viewer is certain that it is Zayd, but the fine details and hidden features of his image are not visible. With regard to disparity as to the scope of knowledge, the first individual sees Zayd and 'Amr and Bakr and others in the house, while the other individual sees only Zayd. Thus the experiential knowledge of the first person most definitely increases in proportion to the number of things known. This, then, is the spiritual state of the heart in relation to the varieties of knowledge, and God knows best what is correct.

Farīd ad-Din 'Attār

Although one of Farīd ad-Din 'Attār's (d. 1221) best-known works, *Tadhkirat al-Awliya* (*Memoirs of the Friends of God*), is a collection of biographical and hagiographical material of Sufi masters, we actually know very little about Attār himself. He was most likely a druggist and deeply influenced by the Sufi and Shia Ismaili thought of his time. Based in Nishapur in modern-day Iran, he was a prolific and masterful mystic poet.

Attār's *Mantiq al-Tayr* (*Conference of the Birds*) is his best-known work in English. The text is loosely modeled on Ahmad al-Ghazāli's *Treatise on Birds*, an allegory for the soul's search for God. Attar's work opens with the mythical hoopoe calling out to all the birds in the world to follow him to search for their king, Simorgh. The birds give him excuses as to why they cannot go, and he parries each of their objections directly and by reference to stories. These allegorical stories are part of Attār's teaching methodology, in order to have the reader reflect on the meaning of the journey in his or her own life.

An example of this dialogue occurs with the peacock. The peacock says that he was the bird of paradise and was in proximity to God before the exile of Adam and Eve. He says that his goal is to return to that perfect place. The hoopoe responds that the peacock has become enraptured with the creation, forgetting the Creator. He further argues that the reason that Adam and Eve had to leave paradise was because they, too, were enamored with it, and they needed to be put in a situation where they would have to remember God.

After getting a cohort of birds to follow him, the hoopoe leads them through eight valleys: Seeking, Love, Knowledge, Detachment, Unicity of God, Bewilderment, Poverty, and Annihi-

389

lation (*fanā*). These valleys represent Attār's vision of the path of attainment for Sufis. One progresses along an axis of conscious knowledge and intellect, until the fifth valley of Unicity of God (*tawhid*). At this point, Attār emphasizes experience and feeling, even commenting that his language must become more obtuse because not everything should be easily accessible.

The hoopoe finally ends at Mount Kaf, the home of the legendary Simorgh, with only thirty birds. Thousands of other birds failed to leave earlier valleys successfully. As they enter the king's chamber, they realize that they are the Simorgh. The realization depends on a pun in Persian. The Simorgh is a mythical bird, but the phrase *sī murgh* means "thirty birds." Attār's message is that God is never separate from the seeker, but is always within, waiting to be discovered. These thirty birds, like the Sufi seeker, must travel on a path to achieve this self-knowledge and understanding.

The fragmented selection of the text is from the moment that the birds realize they are the Simorgh, here described as a "phoenix." The knowledge that descends on them is that they are one with God, whose perfection is being described. They are not separate from, nor can they be separated from the Divine, only from knowledge of the Divine. It is through acts of spiritual discipline that this knowledge is once more made accessible to them.

Hussein Rashid

THE PHOENIX'S SPEECH

The sun of my Perfection is a Glass
Wherein from *Seeing* into *Being* pass
All who, reflecting as reflected see
Themselves in Me, and Me in them, not *Me*,
But all of Me that a contracted Eye
Is comprehensive of Infinity.
Not yet *Themselves*; no Selves, but of the All
Fractions, from which they split and whither fall.
As water lifted from the Deep, again
Falls back in individual Drops of Rain—
Then melts into the Universal Main.
All you have been, and seen, and done, and thought,
Not *You* but *I* have seen and been and wrought;
I was the Sin that from Myself rebelled,
I the Remorse that toward Myself compelled:
I was the Tajidar who led the Track:
I was the little Briar who pulled you back:
Sin and Contrition—Retribution owed
And cancelled—Pilgrim, Pilgrimage, and Road,
Was but Myself toward Myself: and your
Arrival but *Myself* at My own Door:
Who in your fraction of Myself behold
Myself within the mirror Myself hold
To see Myself in, and each part of Me
That sees himself, though drown'd, shall ever see...
Rays that have wandered into Darkness wide
Return, and back into your Sun subside!

Muhyī al-Dīn al-'Arabī

Like many Sufi masters, Muhyī al-Dīn al-'Arabī [Ibn Arabi] (d. 1240) has stories of his life that blend myth with fact. He is known as *Shaykh al-Akbar* (The Great Master), for his monumental output in philosophy, theology, poetry, and Sufi thought. Despite this corpus of literature, popular tradition holds that his only formal education was in Qur'an recitation. His influence is so profound that one commentator has suggested that for the next six hundred years, most Sufi work was simply a footnote to his thought.

Ibn Arabi's two most discussed works are *The Meccan Revelations* (*Al-Futuhat al-Makkiyya*) and *The Gems of Wisdom* (*Fusus al-Hikam*). The first work was started during his pilgrimage to Mecca for the *Hajj*, something that Muslims are obliged to do at least once in their lives if they are able. Although he began it in 1202, he did not finish it until 1233, constantly adding and revising the text. He claims that he was inspired by God to write every word on the pages, creating an omnipedia of Muslim mystical thinking. The text covers a wide variety of disciplines, with topics such as the hidden meanings of each of the twenty-eight letters of the Arabic alphabet, the spiritual meaning of rituals, and reflections on the teachings of the prophets.

Ibn Arabi expands on this theme of prophetic teaching in *Gems of Wisdom*. He argues that each prophet is a particular manifestation of divinity, as each has been sent by God to fulfill a purpose. By understanding each of these prophets and the word each one brings, we can better understand the workings of the universe and the divine plan. The prophetic arc is brought to completion with Muhammad, who is regarded as manifesting the mission of all the previous prophets. A sincere follower of Muhammad can

393

achieve a level of perfection that allows him to become *al-insan al-kamil* (the Perfect Man). This Perfect Man also becomes a manifestation of all realities. Ibn Arabi argues that this stage is achievable and has been achieved by Sufi masters.

Perhaps one of Ibn Arabi's most controversial ideas was what came to be known as "Unity of Being" (*wahdat al-wujud*). Although he never used the term himself, it became a succinct way to describe elements of his thought that were considered pantheistic. The argument is that nothing exists except God and that creation is simply a distraction from understanding this basic truth. In its broadest sense, the concept is not unique to Ibn Arabi. Al-Ghazāli, among others, makes similar formulations. Part of the critique against Ibn Arabi, however, is that his thought is based on ecstatic experience rather than a systematic approach. Consequently, it is considered idiosyncratic and not appropriate for sharing with a general audience.

The first selection comes from Ibn Arabi's collection of love poetry, *Tarjuman al-Ashwaq* (*The Interpreter of Desires*). As with most ecstatic Sufis, poetry became a popular form to convey mystical teachings. The denseness of meaning in poetic language allowed for a multiplicity of meanings to be read into every text. Oftentimes, romantic poetry was used to talk about the believer's longing for God, and poetry allowed the dual meaning to be read out of the text. The poem here talks about love and what appears to be a wedding night, when henna is normally applied to a bride's hands. It ends with the idea that to love God is to erase the differences among people, as we all become absorbed into the all-encompassing Divine Essence.

The next two pieces come from *The Gems of Wisdom*. The piece on Adam references a statement by God to Muhammad that God created the world so that God may be known. This bezel says that Adam was created to be a mirror for God and to be a vehicle for the transmission of God's wisdom on earth. Seth, brother of Cain and Abel, is used as a foil to discuss the nature of Muhammad's prophetic nature. Ibn Arabi draws on a tradition that even though Muhammad was the last prophet, his essence was created first, so that all prophets are reflections of his prophetic light. Finally, Ibn Arabi talks of the deception of earthly love as exemplified by romantic relations. To love a woman in a lustful way is to be taken away from God, but to see union between a man and a woman as a connection between creation and the Creator is to contemplate reality in the most perfect way.

Hussein Rashid

FROM *TARJUMAN AL-ASHWAQ*

O doves that haunt the *arāk* and *bān* trees, have pity!
    Do not double my woes by your lamentation!
Have pity! Do not reveal by wailing and weeping
    my hidden desires and my secret sorrows!
I respond to her, at eve and morn, with the plaintive cry
    of a longing man and the moan of an impassioned lover.
The spirits faced one another in the thicket of *ghadā* trees,
    And bent their branches toward me, and it annihilated me.
And they brought me divers sorts of tormenting desire
    and passion and untried affliction.
Who will give me sure promise of Jam' and al-Muḥaṣṣab
      of Minā?
    Who of Dhāt al-Athl? Who of Na'mān?
They encompass my heart moment after moment, for the
      sake of love and anguish, and kiss my pillars,
Even as the best of mankind [Muhammad] encompassed
      the Ka'ba which the evidence of reason proclaims to
      be imperfect,
And kissed stones therein, although he was a Prophet.
    And what is the rank of the Temple compared with Man?
How often did they vow and swear that they would not
      change,
    but one dyed with henna does not keep oaths.
And one of the most wonderful things is a veiled gazelle,
    who points with red finger-tip and winks with eyelids,
A gazelle whose pasture is between the breast-bone and
    the bowels. O marvel! A garden amidst fires!
My heart has become capable of every form: it is a pasture
    of gazelles and convent for Christian monks,

And a temple for idols and the pilgrim's Ka'ba
  and the tables of the Torah and the book of the Qur'ān.
I follow the religion of Love: whatever way Love's
  camels take, that is my religion and my faith.

. . . .

THE GEM OF DIVINE WISDOM IN
THE WORD OF ADAM

The Reality desired to see the essences of His most beautiful names, whose number is immeasurable—or, if you like, to see His own essence in one universal being who when endowed with existence would reveal all the Divine Command, so that He might behold His mystery in it. For the vision of oneself is not like beholding oneself in a polished metal mirror, for then one is manifest in a form resulting from the place one beholds, which is the mirror.

He created the entire world as a fully formed body without a spirit, so that it was like an unpolished mirror. It is a rule of the divine activity to prepare no locus which does not receive a divine spirit. This is no other than the actualizing of the potentiality of the locus to receive some of the everlasting revelatory outpouring, which ever was and ever shall be. It was Adam who became the polish of that mirror and the spirit of that body.

The angels were faculties of that form of the world which the people of gnosis call "The Great Man" [each man is a microcosm, and the macrocosm is a Man], so that they are to it like the spiritual and physical forms of the human organism. Each of these faculties is veiled from the others by its own nature and can conceive of nothing finer than itself, so that it is its property to hold that it is entitled in itself to the high place that it has with God.

This is a matter which reflective reason cannot grasp; understanding can come here only by the divine unveiling. Only by this unveiling can one know the origin of the cosmic forms which receive their spirits. This being God named Man [insān] and vice-regent [khalīfa]. He is to the Reality as the pupil of the eye [insān al-ʿayn] through him Reality sees its creation and has mercy on it. Thus humanity is both created accident and eternal principle, being created and immortal, the Word which defines and which comprehends. Through him all things came to be; he is the bezel-stone of the signet ring, on which is inscribed the sign with which the King seals His treasures. Thus he is the King's viceroy, who bears his seal and safeguards His treasure, and the world shall not cease to be safeguarded so long as the Perfect Man [insān kāmil] remains in it.

....

WISDOM OF SETH

Some of us are ignorant of knowledge of God, and say, "To know that one cannot know Knowledge is knowledge." Others of us know and do not say such a word, which is the last word; to them knowing gives silence, rather than ignorance. Such a one is the highest knower of God, and such knowledge is given only to the Seal of the Messengers and the Seal of the Friends of God.

Every prophet from Adam to the last Prophet [Muhammad] receives light from the niche of the Seal of the Prophets, even though his clay was formed after theirs, since in reality he was present always, according to his word, God bless him and give him peace: "I was a prophet when Adam was between water and clay." Other prophets only became prophets at the time when they were sent. Similarly, the Seal of the Saints was a Friend of God when Adam was between water and clay, and other saints only became such after they fulfilled the conditions of nearness to God by taking on divine qualities, for He says, "I am the Friend, the Much Praised."

Thus even the messengers of God, as friends of God, receive from the niche of the Seal of the Saints.

Apostlehood and prophecy (and I mean by this the bringing of sacred Law and the mission) cease, but Sainthood never ceases.

The Seal of the Prophets, by virtue of his friendship with God, participates in the Seal of the Saints just as the other prophets do in him. He is at once Messenger, Friend, and Prophet.

The Seal of the Saints is the friend and the heir, who partakes of the Source, and contemplates the hierarchies of being. He is one of the virtues of the Seal of the Prophets, Muhammad, upon whom be peace and God's blessing; foremost of the Collectivity and lord of the sons of Adam by opening the gates of intercession.

....

THE DIVINE REALITY IN WOMEN

Muhammad is the Seal of the Prophets, the first of the three singulars [Ibn al-'Arabī held that the Divine Reality expressed Itself in the triplicity of Essence, Will, and Word], since all other singulars derive from it. Since his reality was given the primal singularity by being given triplicity in its makeup, he said concerning love, "Three things I have been given to love in your world: women, perfume, and prayer." He began with woman because woman in the manifestation of her essence is a part of Man.

Because of this, he loved women because of the perfect contemplation of the Reality in them. [Reality delights in union with Its created image.] Contemplation of the Reality devoid of any base is never possible, since God in His essence does not depend on creation. Since a base is necessary, contemplation of the Reality in women is the greatest and most perfect sort. The greatest union is that of man and woman, since it is like the divine turning to the one He created in His own image, to make him his vice regent and behold Himself in him.

Islam

One who loves women truly loves them with a divine love, while one who loves them in carnal lust approaches his wife or any other woman only for pleasure, without realizing Whose that pleasure is. If he only knew Whom he is enjoying and Who is the enjoyer, then he would be perfect.

Jalāl al-Din Muhammad Rumi

One of the recent best-selling poets in America and arguably the greatest Persian poet is Jalāl al-Din Rumi (d. 1273). His exposure to Sufism exemplifies the tension between legal scholars and mystical seekers. His voluminous and spontaneous poetic output attests to his brilliance and absolute devotion to God. As an ecstatic Sufi master, he inspires the formation of a new Sufi order, the Mevleviyya, known as the Whirling Dervishes.

Rumi was born in modern-day Tajikistan or Afghanistan. Fearing the Mongol invasion, his family moved to Konya in present-day Turkey. His father was a jurist and theologian who was able to successfully resettle the family. Rumi followed in his father's footsteps becoming a legal scholar and joining a Sufi order. However, it was not until he met Shams-i-Tabrīzī that he fully realized what a Sufi commitment to loving God meant.

According to legend, Rumi was walking through the markets of Konya with books in his hands. A poor, mendicant Sufi asked him what was in the books, at which point Rumi said dismissively, "You would not understand." Shams, the poor Sufi, took the books and threw them in a body of water. Rumi took the books out of the water and found them dry. He asked Shams what happened, to which Shams replied, "You would not understand." Shams then became Rumi's mystical guide for several years, after which he disappeared. Rumi was torn apart by grief and wrote one of his massive tomes of poetry, *Diwan-i Shams* (*The Work of Shams*), using Shams as his pen name.

Rumi's poetry is ecstatic and supposedly spontaneous in its creation. The strong rhythmic qualities are, in part, due to the conventions of the poetic genre in which he was writing. Another component relates to the whirling dance credited to Rumi and one of the defining characteristics of his order. The story is that while walking through the metalworkers' section of the bazaar, the rhythmic tapping put Rumi into a trance and he started to whirl. The metalsmiths were apparently chanting the phrase "la illah ila allah," (there is no deity except God), and Rumi recalled the Qur'anic verse that God is closer to a human than the person's jugular (50:16). The recollection of God and of God's immanence inspired and transported Rumi to another state of consciousness.

Rumi's other poetic work is the *Masnavi-i Manavi* (*Poetry of Meaning*). It is a series of stories and poetic instructions for the mystic way. All the selections below are from these six volumes of poetry. The first poem of the *Masnavi* is the "Lament of the Reed," and helps set the tenor of Rumi's vision of humanity's relationship to the Divine. The reed represents the human soul, cut from the reed-bed of the Divine, when the primordial covenant mentioned in the Qur'an was made. In the moment of pre-creation, God asks the souls, "Am I not your Lord?" and all reply, "Yes, we bear witness" (7:172). The struggle of creation is to return to that proximity to God. The separation causes us to wail, like the reed-flute (*ney*), which is made from the cut reed. The flute makes a melancholy and meditative sound, as a symbol of how humanity should be once it realizes what it has lost.

The next selection is about the need for a guide on the Sufi way. After speaking of the animal desires of human beings, and the need to be disciplined by a master, the text mentions Muhammad and Ali. As the prophet of the Muslim community, Muhammad is considered an exemplar for Muslims in general to emulate. Ali is Muhammad's cousin and son-in-law. The question of his political succession after Muhammad's death is a primary cause of the Shia-Sunni division. However, Ali's spiritual nature is undisputed, and he is often described as the first Sufi and transmitter of esoteric knowledge. He is then juxtaposed, through allusion, to Moses, who is honored in the Qur'an as a prophet. Despite Moses' place of privilege in Muslim traditions, he is also described as being too focused on the law and outward forms. He thus provides a useful foil to the spirituality of Ali being described, and echoes Rumi's nature before meeting Shams.

The third selection continues this theme of Moses as being rules-focused, as he chastises a believing shepherd for the way the shepherd prays. Moses is chided by God, both for focusing on ritual over intent and for not realizing the spiritual proximity the shepherd had to God that Moses had weakened. The criticism of ritual observance over inner-meaning continues in "The Pilgrimage of Bayazid." Rumi often returns to the theme of *hajj*, arguing that people go to visit a building, instead of God. To really appreciate what God's house means, one should see that each individual should see the Divine in themselves and each other. In many ways, this last poem is in conversation with Ibn Arabi's ideas of the "Perfect Man," and of God being present in every part of creation.

Hussein Rashid

THE SONG OF THE REED

Now listen to this reed-flute's sad lament
About the heartache being apart has meant:
'Since from the reed-bed they uprooted me
My song's expressed each human's agony,
A breast which separation split in two
Provides the breath to share this pain with you:
Those kept apart from their own origin
All long to go back to rejoin their kin;
Amongst the crowd to mourn alone's my fate,
With good and bad I've learnt to integrate,
That we were friends each one was satisfied,
But none sought out my secrets from inside:
My deepest secret's in this song I wail,
But eyes and ears can't penetrate the veil:
Body and soul are joined to form one whole,
But no one is allowed to see the soul.'
It's fire not air the reed-flute's mournful cry,
If you don't have this fire then you should die!
The fire of love is what makes reed-flutes pine,
Love's fervour thus gives potency to wine;
The reed consoles those forced to be apart,
Its melodies will open up your heart,
Where's antidote or poison like its song
Or confidant, or one who's pined so long?
This reed relates a tortuous path ahead,
Recounts the love with which Majnūn's heart bled:
The few who hear the truths the reed has sung
Have lost their wits so they can speak this tongue;
The day is wasted if it's spent in grief,
Consumed by burning aches without relief,
Good times have long passed, but we couldn't care

If you're with us our friend beyond compare!
While ordinary men on drops can thrive
A fish needs oceans daily to survive:
The way the ripe must feel the raw can't tell,
My speech must be concise, and so farewell!

THE ṢŪFĪ GUIDE

Follow the journey's guide, don't go alone,
The path is filled with trials that chill the bone!
Even on routes which numerous times you've used
Without a guide you're hopelessly confused,
Beware now of this path you've not yet tried!
Don't go alone, keep focused on your guide!
If you're not safe in his protective shade
The ghoul's deep wails will leave you stunned, afraid,
Diverting you straight into further harm,
Much shrewder men than you could not keep calm;
Heed the Qur'ān on those who went astray
And how the wicked Satan made them pay:
He lured them all a thousand miles from here,
Reducing them to nakedness and fear.
Look at their bones and hair, and now take heed,
Don't be an ass, don't let your passions lead!
Grab hold of its thick neck and pull it back
Away from lust towards the guide's own track,
If left alone this donkey's bound to stray
Towards the field with golden mounds of hay,
Don't you forget to hold with force its leash,
Or it will bolt for miles to find hashish!
A donkey stoned—what greater enemy!
That donkey's ruined countless, can't you see?
If you're unsure of what's correct, just do
The opposite of what it wants to do,

405

'Consult them, then do just the opposite!
Or else you'll always be regretting it.'
Don't ever tolerate your carnal lust,
They'll lead you off the path, betray your trust,   (Q 38:26)
While nothing conquers passion better than
The company of fellow travellers can:
The prophet summoned 'Alī to his side,
'Hey, lion of God, brave hero of my pride,
Don't count on courage on its own to cope,
Take refuge also in the tree of hope:
Enter the realm of that pure intellect
Whom no opponent can from truth deflect.
Just like Mount Qāf, he reaches to the sky
His spirit like the Simorgh soars so high,
We could continue with this man's applause
Until the end of time without a pause,
He is the sun, though human to our sight,
Please understand that "God knows best what's right."
'Alī, in preference to all pious deeds
Follow the one whom God's direction leads,
Others persist with acts of piety,
Hoping to flee their egos' tyranny,
Take refuge here instead with this true guide,
Just leave the hidden enemy aside!
Of all the acts of worship it's the best,
It makes you far superior to the rest.'
If he accepts, surrender to the guide
Like Moses, who with Khidr once had tried,
Stay calm, don't question what he should commit,
So he won't say, *Enough, Now we must split!*   (Q 18:8)
If he destroys their boat, don't you go wild,
Don't tear your hair out if he kills a child!
Since God has said this man's hand's like his own,
And, *Up above their hands rests God's alone,*   (Q 48:15)
With God's own hand he slays the helpless boy,

To bring him back with new, eternal joy;
The few who tried this journey on their own
The guide still helped, they didn't walk alone:
His helping hand's for all across the land,
It has to be then naught but God's own hand,
If he can stretch his help out far and wide
There's even more for those stood by his side,
If absent ones receive such gifts for naught
Imagine what those present shall be brought,
You can't compare his faithful followers
With those who choose to be mere onlookers;
Don't be too delicate when he's around,
As weak as water, crumbly like the ground,
If each blow leaves you bitter don't expect
Without pain like a mirror to reflect.

MOSES AND THE SHEPHERD

Once Moses overheard a shepherd pray:
'O you whose every whim we all obey,
Where do you live that I might meet you there
To mend your battered shoes and comb your hair,
To wash your clothes and kill the lice and fleas,
To serve you milk to sip from when you please,
To kiss your little hand, to rub your feet,
To sweep your bedroom clean and keep it neat?
I'd sacrifice my herd of goats for you,
This loud commotion proves my love is true.'
He carried on in this deluded way,
So Moses asked, 'What's that I hear you say?'
'I speak to my creator there on high,
The one who also made the earth and sky.'
Moses replied, 'You've truly lost your way,
You've given up the faith and gone astray,

It's gibberish and babble stupid twit,
You'd better learn to put a cork in it!
Your blasphemy pollutes the atmosphere
And tears to shreds that silk of faith so sheer,
While socks and shoes might be superb for you
How can they fit the sun, have you a clue?
If you don't shut your mouth immediately
A fire will burn up all humanity.
You don't believe? Then please explain this smoke,
And why your soul turned black when you just spoke!
If you're aware that He is God, our Lord,
Why act familiar when that is abhorred?
Friendship like this is worse than enmity,
The Lord's above such acts of piety,
For family friends reserve your generous deeds,
God has no body, nor material needs:
Milk is for babies, who must drink to grow,
And shoes for those with feet, as you must know;
Even when you address his chosen slave
Select your words with care, don't misbehave,
Since God has said, "I'm him and he is Me.
'When I was ill you never came to see':
He wasn't left alone with his disease
That servant who 'through Me both hears and sees'."
Don't talk to saints without the reverence due
It blocks your heart, and blots your record too;
If you address a man by Fātima's name
Though man and woman are inside the same
He'll still seek vengeance for it, if he can,
Even if he's a calm and patient man,
That glorious name which women all revere
Can wound a man more deeply than a spear;
While feet and hands are great for you and me
They'd just contaminate God's purity,
He was not born, nor does the Lord beget,   (Q 112:3)

But reproducing beings are in his debt:
Those with a body once were born—that's sense,
Creation must stay this side of the fence,
That's all because we wither and decay,
Unlike our source we're bound to fade away.'
The shepherd said, 'Your words have struck me dumb,
Regret now burns my soul, and I feel numb.'
He breathed a heavy sigh and rent his cloak,
Then in the desert disappeared like smoke.
A revelation came down instantly:
'Why did you turn a slave away from Me?
Your mission's to unite all far and wide,
Is it instead your preference to divide?
As far as possible don't separate,
"Above all else divorce is what I hate",
I've given each one his own special ways
And his unique expressions when he prays:
One person's virtue is another's sin,
His meat might seem like poison, listening in;
I stand immune to all impurity,
Men's pride and cunning never bother Me,
I don't command for My own benefit,
But so My slaves themselves can gain from it;
For Indians their own dialect seems best,
But folk from Sindh think Sindhi's much more blest,
I'm not made any purer by their praise,
Their own impurities these prayers erase,
And I pay no attention to their speech
But their intention and the heights they reach:
Pure, humble hearts within are what I seek
Regardless of the haughty way they speak.'
The heart's the essence, words are mere effects,
The heart's what counts, the cackle he neglects!
I'm tired of fancy terms and metaphors,
I want a soul which burns so much it roars!

It's time to light one's heart with pure desire,
Burn thought and contemplation with this fire!
How far apart the meek and well-behaved
From ardent lovers who may seem depraved!
Each moment lovers burn themselves away:
A mined village has no tithes to pay,
Don't pick at faults and call him a disgrace,
Don't wash the blood upon love's martyr's face!
His blood exceeds your water's cleanliness:
This martyr's blemish beats all righteousness;
Those at the Ka'ba scrap the *qibla* rule:
What use are boots to divers in the pool?
You don't seek guidance from those drunken men,
So why insist they mend their rags again?
The lovers stand beyond religion's hold,
From God himself truth's creed and laws they're told:
If rubies have no seal stamped there's no harm,
Midst seas of grief love stays serene and calm.
Then in the depths of Moses God concealed
Such secrets that can never be revealed,
Into his heart poured words, pure and refined,
Transparent just like speech and sight combined,
He lost his wits and then found them anew,
From pre- to post-eternity he flew,
I'd just waste time by trying to explain,
It's far beyond the ordinary brain:
This mystery would blow your brain to bits,
While writing it the firmest pencil splits;
Moses, on hearing God's reproach, just ran
Towards the desert searching for that man:
He followed footprints that the shepherd laid,
Scattering dust throughout the track he'd made,
Footprints of drunkards are a special kind
Distinct from those the sober leave behind:
He starts just like a rook, steps straight ahead,

410

Then bishop-like diagonally instead,
Sometimes just like a wave's crest rising high
And then as if a fish has slithered by,
Occasionally he'd write his thoughts in sand
Like fortune-tellers reading what is planned,
At last when Moses found the shepherd there
He gave the message, 'God's decree is fair,
Don't bother with mere custom anymore
But let your heart express what's in its core!
True faith salutes your infidelity,
Through you the world has found security,
Absolved by God *whose will must be fulfilled*   (Q14:27)
Scream out, without the fear that you'll be killed!'
The shepherd said, 'I've gone beyond that stage,
My heart's blood cannot still this thirst assuage,
I've even passed that tree at heaven's end
A thousand spheres beyond—I still ascend:
You cracked the whip and made my stallion vault
Above the heavens with a somersault!
For spurring me towards divinity
God bless that hand which cracked the whip for me!
Right now my state's beyond what tongues can say,
What I've described gives just a glimpse away.'
The image in the mirror that you see
Is yours, and not the mirror's property,
The breath inside the reed its player has blown
Is just a tiny portion of his own,
Whenever you give praise to God, beware
It's worth no more than this poor shepherd's prayer!
You might suppose your own immaculate,
But still for God they're all inadequate,
So when the veil is lifted don't protest:
'What's now revealed we never could have guessed!'

THE PILGRIMAGE OF BĀYAZĪD

For Mecca Bāyazīd one day set out
To make the pilgrimage, to be devout,
At every town he passed along the way
He'd seek what local sages had to say:
He'd wander asking, 'Who here has the light?
Who only leans on truth's supporting might?'
God said, 'When on your travels always seek
The few who take from Me each word they speak!'
Seek treasure, shun the world of gain and loss,
This world is second-best, no more than dross!
In hope of wheat whoever sows his seeds
Soon finds his field has also sprouted weeds,
But if it's weeds you sow no wheat will rise,
Seek masters of the heart, the meek and wise!
Head for the Ka'ba when it's time to go
And you'll see Mecca too, as all must know:
God was, on his *mi'rāj*, the prophet's aim,
He saw the throne and angels all the same.
A new disciple built a house one day,
The master passed and saw it on his way,
He questioned the disciple as a test,
Knowing that his intentions were the best:
'Why did you put a window over here?'
'To let the light come in to make things clear.'
'That's secondary, it's not like breathing air,
Your primary need's to hear the call to prayer!'
While travelling Bāyazīd searched far and wide
To find his epoch's Khidr, the perfect guide,
He found him like a crescent hunched and pale,
Majestic, speaking just like those we hail,
His heart like sunshine though his eyes were blind
Like elephants seeing India in their mind:
Countless delights are seen with eyes shut tight,

412

But when they're opened none are seen in light!
While you're asleep the mysteries are shown
Your heart's a window viewing the unknown,
The mystic even dreams when wide awake,
Prostrate and feel the ground beneath him shake!
So Bāyazīd then asked him, 'How are you?'
The man was poor and had a family too,
'O Bāyazīd, why did you take this road?
Where is it that you're carrying that load?'
'To *hajj*, since day-break I've been travelling.'
'For your expenses how much did you bring?'
'Two hundred silver coins is all I've got,
I've tied them to this garment with a knot.'
'Just walk around me seven times right here,
That's better than the *hajj* for you, fakir!
Then hand your coins to me, you generous man,
Complete your *hajj*, fulfil your mission's plan!
You've run to Ṣafā, entered purity,
You've done the *'umra*, live eternally!
He judges me much loftier, I swear,
Than that mere house of bricks they flock to there:
That Ka'ba is the home of piety,
But I possess his deepest mystery,
Inside the Ka'ba no one's ever stepped
And none but God will my pure heart accept,
When you've seen me, you've seen the lord as well,
Truth's Ka'ba you've just circled, can't you tell?
To serve me is obeying God's decree
So don't suppose he's separate from me:
Open your inner eye, see if you can
Perceive the light of God inside a man!'
This wisdom pierced right into Bāyazīd,
Just like an earring, making him take heed,
For he had heard such wisdom from this friend
Enabling him to reach the journey's end.

Bibliography

GENERAL

Akira, Hirakawa. "Stupa Worship." Translated by Paul Groner. In *The Encyclopedia of Religion*, edited by Mircea Eliade, 92–96. Vol. 14. New York: Macmillan, 1987.

Berger, Peter L. *The Sacred Canopy: Elements of a Sociological Theory of Religion*. Garden City, NY: Doubleday, 1969.

Bhardwaj, Surinder M. "Hindu Pilgrimage." In *The Encyclopedia of Religion*, edited by Mircea Eliade, 353–54. Vol. 11. New York: Macmillan, 1987.

Browne, Lewis, ed. *The World's Great Scriptures: An Anthology of the Sacred Books of the Ten Principal Religions*. New York: Macmillan, 1946.

Burke, T. Patrick. *The Major Religions: An Introduction with Texts*. Cambridge, MA: Blackwell, 1996.

Carmody, Denise L., *Ways to the Center: An Introduction to World Religions*. 4th ed. Belmont, CA: Wadsworth, 1993.

————. *Mysticism: Holiness East and West*. New York: Oxford University Press, 1996.

Carmody, Denise L., and John T. Carmody. *Interpreting the Religious Experience: A Worldview*. Englewood Cliffs, NJ: Prentice-Hall, 1987.

Cunningham, Lawrence S., et al. *The Sacred Quest: An Invitation to the Study of Religion*. 2nd ed. Englewood Cliffs, NJ: Prentice-Hall, 2005.

Davies, J. G. *The New Westminster Dictionary of Liturgy and Worship*. Westminster, PA: Westminster Press, 1986.

Eastman, Roger, ed. *The Ways of Religion: An Introduction to the Major Traditions*. 2nd ed. New York: Oxford University Press, 1993.

Eliade, Mircea, ed. *The Encyclopedia of Religion*. 16 vols. New York: Macmillan, 1987.

Ellwood, Robert S. *Mysticism and Religion*. Englewood Cliffs, NJ: Prentice-Hall, 1980.

————. *Introducing Religion: From Inside and Outside*. 3rd ed. Englewood Cliffs, NJ: Prentice-Hall, 1993.

Fisher, Mary Pat. *Living Religions*. 3rd ed. Upper Saddle River, NJ: Prentice-Hall, 1997.

Hopfe, Lewis M., and Mark R. Woodward. *Religions of the World*. 7th ed. Upper Saddle River, NJ: Prentice-Hall, 1998.

Johnston, William. *The Mirror Mind: Spirituality and Transformation*. San Francisco: Harper and Row, 1981.

Jones, Cheslyn, et al. *The Study of Spirituality*. New York: Oxford University Press, 1986.

Kennedy, Richard. *The International Dictionary of Religion: A Profusely Illustrated Guide to the Beliefs of the World*. New York: Crossroad, 1984.

King, Winston L. "Religion." In *The Encyclopedia of Religion*, edited by Mircea Eliade, 282–93. Vol. 12. New York: Macmillan, 2011.

Levinson, David. *Religion: A Cross-Cultural Dictionary*. New York: Oxford University Press, 1996.

Livingston, James C. *Anatomy of the Sacred: An Introduction to Religion*. 3rd ed. Upper Saddle River, NJ: Prentice-Hall, 1998.

Ludwig, Theodore M. *The Sacred Paths: Understanding the Religions of the World*. 2nd ed. Upper Saddle River, NJ: Prentice-Hall, 1996.

Markham, Ian S., ed. *A World Religions Reader*. Cambridge, MA: Blackwell, 1996.

Matthews, Warren. *World Religions*. St. Paul, MN: West, 1991.

Mitchell, Donald W., and James Wiseman, eds. *The Gethsemani Encounter: A Dialogue on the Spiritual Life by Buddhist and Christian Monastics*. New York: Continuum, 1999.

Monk, Robert C., et al. *Exploring Religious Meaning*. 5th ed. Upper Saddle River, NJ: Prentice-Hall, 1998.

Monroe, Charles R. *World Religions: An Introduction*. Amherst, NY: Prometheus Books, 1995.

Myerhoff, Barbara G., Linda A. Camino, and Edith Turner. "Rites of Passage: An Overview." In *The Encyclopedia of Religion*, edited by Mircea Eliade, 380–86. Vol. 12. New York: Macmillan, 1987.

Nigosian, S. A. *World Faiths*. 2nd ed. New York: St. Martin's Press, 2011.

Noss, David S., and John B. Noss. *A History of the World's Religions*. 9th ed. New York: Macmillan, 1994.

Novak, Philip, ed. *The World's Wisdom: Sacred Texts of the World's Religions*. San Francisco: HarperSanFrancisco, 1994.

O'Grady, John F. "Spirituality Without Religion." *Chicago Studies* 36 (1997): 87–101.

Parrinder, Geoffrey. *The Idea of the Holy*. Translated by John W. Harvey. 2nd ed. London: Oxford University Press, 1950.

——. *Worship in the World's Religions*. Totowa, NJ: Littlefield, Adams, 1976.

Pieper, Josef. *Leisure: The Basis of Culture*. Translated by Alexander Dru. New York: New American Library, 1952.

Porterfield, Amanda. *The Power of Religion: A Comparative Introduction*. New York: Oxford University Press, 1998.

Rice, Edward. *Eastern Definitions*. Garden City, NY: Doubleday, 1980.

Schmidt, Roger. *Exploring Religion*. Belmont, CA: Wadsworth, 1980.

Smart, Ninian. *Worldviews: Crosscultural Explorations of Human Beliefs*. 2nd ed. Englewood Cliffs, NJ: Prentice-Hall, 1995.

———. *The Religious Experience*. 5th ed. Upper Saddle River, NJ: Prentice-Hall, 1996.

Smart, Ninian, and Richard D. Hecht, eds. *Sacred Texts of the World: A Universal Anthology*. New York: Crossroad, 1982.

Smith, Jonathan, and William Scott Green, eds. *The HarperCollins Dictionary of Religion*. San Francisco: HarperSanFrancisco, 1995.

Tremmell, William Calloley. *Religion: What Is It?* 2nd ed. New York: Holt, Rinehart and Winston, 1984.

Turner, Edith. "Pilgrimage: An Overview." In *The Encyclopedia of Religion*, edited by Mircea Eliade, 327–30. Vol. 11. New York: Macmillan, 1987.

Turner, Victor. *The Ritual Process: Structure and Anti-Structure*. Ithaca, NY: Cornell University Press, 1969.

Van Ness, Peter H., ed. *Spirituality and the Secular Quest*. Vol. 22 of *World Spirituality: An Encyclopedic History of the Religious Quest*. New York: Crossroad, 1996.

Van Voorst, Robert E. *Anthology of World Scriptures*. Belmont, CA: Wadsworth, 1994.

Webster's New World Dictionary of the American Language. Second College Edition. Cleveland: William Collins.

Wilson, Andrew, ed. *World Scripture: A Comparative Anthology of Sacred Texts*. New York: Paragon House, 1995.

Wilson, John E. *Religion: A Preface*. Englewood Cliffs, NJ: Prentice-Hall, 1982.

Young, William A. *The World's Religions: Worldviews and Contemporary Issues*. Englewood Cliffs, NJ: Prentice-Hall, 1995.

Zaehner, R. C., ed. *The Concise Encyclopedia of Living Faiths*. Boston: Beacon Press, 1959.

HINDUISM

Chaudhuri, Nirad C. *Hinduism: A Religion to Live By.* New York: Oxford University Press, 1979.

Erndl, Kathleen M. *Victory to the Mother: The Hindu Goddess of Northwest India in Myth, Ritual, and Symbol.* New York: Oxford University Press, 1993.

Haberman, David L. *Journey Through the Twelve Forests: An Encounter with Krishna.* New York: Oxford University Press, 1994.

Hiltebeitel, Alf. "Hinduism." In *The Encyclopedia of Religion,* edited by Mircea Eliade, 336–60. Vol. 6. New York: Macmillan, 1987.

Hopfe, Lewis M., and Mark R. Woodward. *Religions of the World.* 7th ed. Upper Saddle River, NJ: Prentice-Hall, 1998.

Kinsley, David R. *Hinduism: A Cultural Perspective.* Englewood Cliffs, NJ: Prentice-Hall, 1982.

Klostermaier, Klaus K. *A Survey of Hinduism.* 2nd ed. Albany: State University of New York Press, 1994.

Narayan, Kirin. *Storytellers, Saints, and Scoundrels: Folk Narrative in Hindu Religious Teaching.* Philadelphia: University of Pennsylvania Press, 1989.

O'Flaherty, Wendy Doniger, trans. *The Rig Veda, An Anthology: One Hundred and Eight Hymns Selected, Translated, and Annotated.* New York: Penguin, 1981.

Olivelle, Patrick, trans. *The Early Upanishads: Annotated Text and Translation.* New York: Oxford University Press, 1998.

Organ, Troy Wilson. *Hinduism: Its Historical Development.* Woodbury, NY: Barron's, 1974.

Seneviratne, H. L. *Rituals of the Kandyan State.* London: Cambridge University Press, 1978.

Sivaraman, Krishna, ed. *Hindu Spirituality: Vedas through Vedanta.* Vol. 6 of *World Spirituality: An Encyclopedic History of the Religious Quest.* New York: Crossroad, 1989.

Sundarajan, K. R., and Bithika Mukerji, eds. *Hindu Spirituality: Post-classical and Modern.* Vol. 7 of *World Spirituality: An Encyclopedic History of the Religious Quest.* New York: Crossroad, 1991.

Teasdale, Wayne. "The Eternal Religion: Spirituality in Hinduism." *Chicago Studies* 36 (1997): 74–86.

Van Buitenen, J. A. B. *The Bhagavadgita in the Mahabharata: Text and Translation.* Chicago: University of Chicago Press, 1981.

CHINESE

Ames, Roger T. and Henry Rosemont, trans. *The Analects of Confucius: A Philosophical Translation*. New York: Ballantine Books, 1999.

Berk, William. *Chinese Healing Arts: Internal Kung-fu*. Culver City, CA: Peace Press, 1979.

Chan, Wing-Tsit, trans. and comp. *A Source Book in Chinese Philosophy*. Princeton: Princeton University Press, 1963.

―――. trans. *The Way of Lao Tzu (Tao-te ching)*. New York: Macmillan, 1963.

Cleary, Thomas, trans. *The Inner Teachings of Taoism*. Boston: Shambhala Publications, 1986.

―――. *The Taoist I Ching*. Boston: Shambhala Publications, 1986.

―――. *The Buddhist I Ching*. Boston: Shambhala Publications, 1987.

―――. *Understanding Reality*. Honolulu: University of Hawaii Press, 1987.

―――. *Awakening to the Tao*. Boston: Shambhala Publications, 1988.

―――. *I Ching: The Tao of Organization*. Boston: Shambhala Publications, 1988.

―――. *The Book of Balance and Harmony*. San Francisco: North Point Press, 1989.

―――. *I Ching Mandalas*. Boston: Shambhala Publications, 1989.

―――. *Back to Beginnings*. Boston: Shambhala Publications, 1990.

―――. *Further Teachings of Lao Tzu: Understanding the Mysteries*. Boston: Shambhala Publications, 1991.

―――. *The Secret of the Golden Flower*. San Francisco: HarperCollins, 1991.

―――. *Vitality, Energy, Spirit: A Taoist Sourcebook*. Boston: Shambhala Publications, 1991.

DeWoksin, Kenneth. *Doctors, Diviners, and Magicians of Ancient China: Biographies of Fang-shih*. New York: Columbia University Press, 1983.

Dong, Y.P. *Still as a Mountain, Powerful as Thunder*. Boston: Shambhala Publications, 1993.

Eliade, Mircea. *Shamanism*. Princeton: Princeton University Press, 1964.

Fingarette, Herbert. *Confucius: The Secular as Sacred*. Long Grove, IL: Waveland Press, 1998.

Hawkes, David. *The Songs of the South*. New York: Penguin, 1985.

Henricks, Robert G. *Lao-tzu Te-tao-ching*. New York: Ballantine, 1989.

Kohn, Livia, ed. *Taoist Meditation and Longevity Techniques*. Ann Arbor: University of Michigan Press, 1989.

419

————. *Taoist Mystical Philosophy*. Albany: State University of New York Press, 1991.

————. *Early Chinese Mysticism*. Princeton: Princeton University Press, 1992.

————. *The Taoist Experience*. Albany: State University of New York Press, 1993.

Lau, D.C., trans. *Tao Te Ching*. New York: Penguin Books, 1963.

Lo, Benjamin. *The Essence of T'ai-chi Ch'uan: The Literary Tradition*. Richmond, CA: North Atlantic Books, 1979.

Lu, Kuan Yü. *The Secrets of Chinese Meditation*. New York: Samuel Weiser, 1964.

————. *Taoist Yoga*. New York: Samuel Weiser, 1970.

Maspero, Henri. *Taoism and Chinese Religions*. Amherst: University of Massachusetts Press, 1981.

Merton, Thomas, trans. *The Way of Chuang Tzu* (2nd ed.). New York: New Directions, 2010.

Mitchell, Stephen, trans. *Tao Te Ching*. New York: Harper, 1988.

————. *The Second Book of the Tao*. New York: Penguin, 2009.

Robinet, Isabelle. *Taoist Meditation*. Albany: State University of New York Press, 1993.

Saso, Michael. *Taoism and the Rite of Cosmic Renewal*. Pullman: Washington State University Press, 1989.

————. *Blue Dragon, White Tiger: Taoist Rites of Passage*. Washington, DC: Taoist Center, 1990.

————. *The Gold Pavilion: Taoist Ways to Peace, Healing, and Long Life*. Boston: Tuttle, 1995.

Schipper, Kristofer. *The Taoist Body*. Berkeley: University of California Press, 1993.

Simpkins, C. Alexander and Annellen Simpkins. *Simple Taoism: A Guide to Living in Balance*. Boston: Tuttle, 1999.

Waley, Arthur. *The Way and Its Power: A Study of the Tao Te Ching in Chinese Thought*. New York: Grove Press, 1958.

Watson, Burton. *The Complete Works of Chuang-tzu*. New York: Columbia University Press, 1968.

Welch, Holmes. *Taoism: The Parting of the Way*. Boston: Beacon Press, 1957.

Wong, Eva. *Seven Taoist Masters*. Boston: Shambhala Publications, 1990.

————. *Cultivating Stillness*. Boston: Shambhala Publications, 1992.

————. *Lao Tzu's Treatise on the Response of the Tao*. San Francisco: HarperCollins, 1993.

————. *Lieh-tzu: A Taoist Guide to Practical Living.* Boston: Shambhala Publications, 1995.

————. *Feng-shui: The Ancient Wisdom of Harmonious Living for Modern Times.* Boston: Shambhala Publications, 1996.

————. *The Shambhala Guide to Taoism.* Boston: Shambhala Publications, 1997.

Wu, Jing-nuan. *Ling Shu, or The Spiritual Pivot.* Washington, DC: Taoist Center, 1993.

BUDDHISM

Bocking, Brian. *Nāgārjuna in China: A Translation of the Middle Treatise.* Lewiston, NY: Edwin Mellen Press, 1995.

Braverman, Arthur, trans. *Mud and Water, A Collection of Talks by the Zen Master Bassui.* San Francisco: North Point Press, 1989.

Buswell, Robert E. "Doubt." In *The Encyclopedia of Buddhism,* edited by Robert E. Buswell, Jr. Vol. 1. New York: Macmillan Reference USA/Thomson/Gale, 2004.

Carter, John Ross and Mahinda Palihawadana, trans. and ed. *The Dhammapada.* New York: Oxford University Press, 1998.

Conze, Edward, trans. *Buddhist Scriptures.* New York: Penguin, 1959.

Conze, Edward. *The Prajñāpāramitā Literature.* Tokyo: Reiyukai, 1978.

Covill, Linda, trans. *Handsome Nanda.* New York: New York University Press: JJC Foundation, 2004.

Cuevas, Brian J. *The Hidden History of the Tibetan Book of the Dead.* Oxford: Oxford University Press, 2003.

Gethin, Rupert. *The Foundations of Buddhism.* Oxford: Oxford University Press, 1998.

Gyatso, Tenzin. *Essence of the Heart Sutra: The Dalai Lama's Heart of Wisdom Teachings.* Translated and edited by Geshe Thupten Jinpa. Boston: Wisdom Publications, 2002.

Hanh, Thich Nhat. *The Heart of Understanding: Commentaries on the Prajñāpāramitā Heart Sutra.* Edited by Peter Levitt. Berkeley: Parallax Press, 1988.

————. *Living Buddha, Living Christ.* London: Rider, 1995.

————. *The Miracle of Mindfulness: The Classic Guide to Meditation by the World's Most Revered Master.* London: Rider, 2008.

Hinuber, Oskar von. "Dhammapada." In *The Encyclopedia of Buddhism,* edited by Robert E. Buswell, Jr. Vol. 1. New York: Macmillan Reference USA/Thomson/Gale, 2004.

"Hoichi, the Earless." *Kwaidan*. DVD. Directed by Masaki Kobayashi. Criterion Collection, 2000. Originally released in 1964.

Kapleau, Philip. *The Three Pillars of Zen: Teaching, Practice, and Enlightenment*. 35th anniversary edition. New York: Anchor Books, 2000.

Khoroche, Peter. "Aśvaghoṣa." In *The Encyclopedia of Buddhism*, edited by Robert E. Buswell, Jr. Vol. 1. New York: Macmillan Reference USA/Thomson/Gale, 2004.

"Kumarajiva." In *Columbia Electronic Encyclopedia*, 6th Edition. Last updated October 1, 2009. New York: Columbia University Press.

Lopez, Donald S. *Elaborations on Emptiness: Uses of the Heart Sūtra*. Princeton, NJ: Princeton University Press, 1996.

————. *Prisoners of Shangri-La: Tibetan Buddhism and the West*. Chicago: University of Chicago Press, 1998.

McDaniel, Justin. "The Art of Reading and Teaching the *Dhammapada*: Reform, Text, Contexts in Thai Buddhist History." *Journal of the International Association of Buddhist Studies* 28.2 (2005): 299–337.

"Punishment." *Spring, Summer, Fall, Winter...and Spring*. DVD. Directed by Kim Ki-duk. Culver City, CA: Columbia TriStar Home Entertainment, 2004.

Reynolds, Frank E., and Charles Hallisey. "Buddhism: An Overview." In *The Encyclopedia of Religion*, edited by Mircea Eliade, 334–51. Vol. 2. New York: Macmillan, 1987.

Seager, Richard Hughes. *Buddhism in America*. New York: Columbia University Press, 1999.

Stevenson, Daniel B. "Tales of the Lotus Sūtra." In *Buddhism in Practice*, edited by Donald J. Lopez, Jr. Princeton, NJ: Princeton University Press, 1995.

Stone, Jacqueline I. "Lotus Sūtra (Saddharmapuṇḍarīkasūtra)." In *The Encyclopedia Of Buddhism*, edited by Robert E. Buswell, Jr. Vol. 1. New York: Macmillan Reference USA/Thomson/Gale, 2004.

————. "Nichiren." In *The Encyclopedia of Buddhism*, edited by Robert E. Buswell, Jr. Vol. 2. New York: Macmillan Reference USA/Thomson/Gale, 2004.

————. "Original Enlightenment." In *The Encyclopedia of Buddhism*, edited by Robert E. Buswell, Jr. Vol. 2. New York: Macmillan Reference USA/Thomson/Gale, 2004.

Suzuki, Shunryu. *Zen Mind, Beginner's Mind: Informal Talks on Zen Meditation and Practice*, edited by Trudy Dixon. New York: Weatherhill, 1970.

Thurman, Robert A. F. *The Tibetan Book of the Dead: As Popularly Known in the West: Known in Tibet as the Great Book of Natural Liberation*

Through Understanding in the Between. New York: Bantam Books, 1994.

The Tibetan Book of the Dead. DVD. Produced by NHK Japan, Mistral Film of France and the National Film Board of Canada. New York: Wellspring Media, 2004.

Watson, Burton, trans. *The Lotus Sūtra.* New York: Columbia University Press, 1993.

JUDAISM

Blau, Joseph L. *Modern Varieties of Judaism.* New York: Columbia University Press, 1964.

Corrigan, John A., et al. *Readings in Judaism, Christianity, and Islam.* Upper Saddle River, NJ: Prentice-Hall, 1998.

Borowitz, Eugene B. "Judaism: An Overview." In *The Encyclopedia of Religion,* edited by Mircea Eliade, 127–48. Vol. 8. New York: Macmillan, 1987.

Buber, Martin. *Moses: The Revelation and the Covenant.* New York: Harper Torchbooks, 1958.

Cohn-Sherbok, Dan, ed. *The Sayings of Moses.* Hopewell, NJ: Ecco Press, 1991.

Dosick, Wayne D. *Living Judaism: The Complete Guide to Jewish Belief, Tradition, and Practice.* San Francisco: HarperSanFrancisco, 1995.

Epstein, Isidore. *Judaism: A Historical Presentation.* Harmondsworth, Middlesex, UK: Penguin, 1959.

Glazer, Nathan. *American Judaism.* 2nd ed., rev. Chicago: University of Chicago Press, 1957.

Green, Arthur, ed. *Jewish Spirituality: From the Bible Through the Middle Ages.* Vol. 13 of *World Spirituality: An Encyclopedic History of the Religious Quest.* New York: Crossroad, 1986.

———. *Jewish Spirituality: From the Sixteenth Century Revival to the Present.* Vol. 14 of *World Spirituality: An Encyclopedic History of the Religious Quest.* New York: Crossroad, 1987.

Heschel, Abraham Joshua. *The Earth Is the Lord's* and *The Sabbath.* New York: Harper Torchbooks, 1966.

Jones, Alexander, ed. *The Jerusalem Bible.* Garden City, NY: Doubleday, 1966.

Neusner, Jacob. *Between Time and Eternity: The Essentials of Judaism.* Encino, CA: Dickenson, 1975.

———. *The Way of Torah: An Introduction to Judaism.* 5th ed. Belmont, CA: Wadsworth, 1993.

Schallman, Herman E. "Judaic Spirituality." *Chicago Studies* 36 (1997): 39–46.

Trepp, Leo. *Judaism: Development and Life.* 2nd ed. Encino, CA: Dickenson, 1974.

Wiesel, Elie. *Souls on Fire: Portraits and Legends of Hasidic Masters.* Translated by Marion Wiesel. New York: Random House, 1972.

CHRISTIANITY

Borg, Marcus, and Ray Riegert, eds. *Jesus and Buddha: The Parallel Sayings.* Berkeley, CA: Seastone, 1997.

Buber, Martin. *Moses: The Revelation and the Covenant.* New York: Harper Torchbooks, 1958.

Cameli, Louis J. "Spirituality in the Western Catholic Tradition." *Chicago Studies* 36 (1997): 5–15.

Cohn-Sherbok, Dan, ed. *The Sayings of Moses.* Hopewell, NJ: Ecco Press, 1991.

Corrigan, John A., et al. *Readings in Judaism, Christianity, and Islam.* Upper Saddle River, NJ: Prentice-Hall, 1998.

Cross, F. L., ed. *The Oxford Dictionary of the Christian Church.* London: Oxford University Press, 1958.

Cunningham, Lawrence. *The Catholic Faith: An Introduction.* New York: Paulist Press, 1987.

Cunningham, Lawrence S., and Keith J. Egan. *Christian Spirituality: Themes from the Tradition.* New York: Paulist Press, 1996.

Dillenberger, John, and Claude Welch. *Protestant Christianity: Interpreted Through Its Development.* 2nd ed. New York: Macmillan, 1988.

Downey, Michael. *Understanding Christian Spirituality.* New York: Paulist Press, 1997.

Dunne, Carrin. *Buddha and Jesus: Conversations.* Springfield, IL: Templegate, 1975.

Dupre, Louis, and Don E. Saliers, eds. *Christian Spirituality: Post-Reformation and Modern.* Vol. 18 of *World Spirituality: An Encyclopedic History of the Religious Quest.* New York: Crossroad, 1989.

Happel, Stephen, and David Tracy. *A Catholic Vision.* Philadelphia: Fortress Press, 1984.

Holmes, Urban T. *A History of Christian Spirituality: An Analytical Introduction.* New York: Seabury Press, 1981.

Leclercq, Jean. *The Love of Learning and the Desire for God: A Study of*

Monastic Culture. Translated by Catharine Misrahi. New York: Fordham University Press, 1961.

Lefebure, Leo D. "Buddhism and Catholic Spirituality." *Chicago Studies* 36 (1997): 47–61.

Martos, Joseph. *Doors to the Sacred: A Historical Introduction to Sacraments in the Catholic Church.* Liguori, MO: Triumph Books, 1991.

McGinn, Bernard, and John Meyendorff, eds. *Christian Spirituality: Origins to the Twelfth Century.* Vol. 16 of *World Spirituality: An Encyclopedic History of the Religious Quest.* New York: Crossroad, 1985.

McKenzie, Peter. *The Christians: Their Beliefs and Practices.* Nashville: Abingdon Press, 1988.

Meeks, Wayne A., ed. *The HarperCollins Study Bible: New Revised Standard Version with the Apocryphal/Deuterocanonical Books.* London: Harper-Collins, 1989.

Pelikan, Jaroslav. *Jesus Through the Centuries: His Place in the History of Culture.* New Haven: Yale University Press, 1985.

———. "Christianity: An Overview." In *The Encyclopedia of Religion,* edited by Mircea Eliade, 348–62. Vol. 3. New York: Macmillan, 1987.

Raitt, Jill, ed. *Christian Spirituality: High Middle Ages and Reformation.* Vol. 17 of *World Spirituality: An Encyclopedic History of the Religious Quest.* New York: Crossroad, 1989.

Schillebeeckx, Edward. *Christ, The Sacrament of the Encounter with God.* Translated by Paul Barrett. English text revised by Mark Schoof and Laurence Bright. New York: Sheed and Ward, 1963.

———. *Jesus.* New York: Seabury Press, 1979.

Tugwell, Simon. *Ways of Imperfection: An Exploration of Christian Spirituality.* Springfield, IL: Templegate, 1985.

Wainwright, Geoffrey. "Christian Spirituality." In *The Encyclopedia of Religion,* edited by Mircea Eliade, 452–60. Vol. 3. New York: Macmillan, 1987.

Ware, Timothy. *The Orthodox Church.* Baltimore: Penguin, 1972.

Weaver, Mary Jo. *Introduction to Christianity.* Belmont, CA: Wadsworth, 1984.

Weborg, John. "Protestant Spirituality: A Reprise." *Chicago Studies* 36 (1997): 26–38.

Zagano, Phyllis. *Woman to Woman: An Anthology of Women's Spiritualities.* Edited, with an introduction. Collegeville, MN: The Liturgical Press, 1993.

———. *Twentieth-Century Apostles: Christian Spirituality in Action.* Edited, with an introduction. Collegeville, MN: The Liturgical Press, 1999.

Zagano, Phyllis. Series Editor, Liturgical Press Spirituality in History Series: *The Dominican Tradition*, ed. Thomas McGonigle, OP and Phyllis Zagano (2006); *The Benedictine Tradition*, ed. Laura Swan, OSB (2007); *The Ignatian Tradition*, eds. Kevin F. Burke, SJ and Eileen Burke Sullivan (2009); *The Franciscan Tradition*, ed. Regis J. Armstrong, OFM and Ingrid Peterson OSF (2010); *The Carmelite Tradition*, ed. Steven Payne, OCD (2011).

ISLAM

Ali, Ahmed. *Al-Qur'an: A Contemporary Translation.* Princeton: Princeton University Press, 1984.

Corrigan, John A., et al. *Readings in Judaism, Christianity, and Islam.* Upper Saddle River, NJ: Prentice-Hall, 1998.

Cragg, Kenneth. *The House of Islam.* 2nd ed. Encino, CA: Dickenson, 1975.

Cragg, Kenneth, and Marston Speight. *Islam from Within: Anthology of a Religion.* Belmont, CA: Wadsworth, 1980.

Denny, Frederick M. *Islam and the Muslim Community.* San Francisco: HarperSanFrancisco, 1987.

Esposito, John L. *Islam: The Straight Path.* 3rd ed. New York: Oxford University Press, 1998.

Guillaume, Alfred. *Islam.* Harmondsworth, Middlesex, UK: Penguin, 1954.

Jeffery, Arthur, ed. *Islam: Muhammad and His Religion.* Indianapolis: BobbsMerrill, 1958.

Jomier, Jacques. *How to Understand Islam.* New York: Crossroad, 1989.

Martin, Richard C. *Islam: A Cultural Perspective.* Englewood Cliffs, NJ: Prentice-Hall, 1982.

Nasr, Seyyed Hossein. *Islamic Art and Spirituality.* Albany: State University of New York Press, 1987.

————, ed. *Islamic Spirituality: Foundations.* Vol. 19 of *World Spirituality: An Encyclopedic History of the Religious Quest.* New York: Crossroad, 1987.

————, ed. *Islamic Spirituality: Manifestations.* Vol. 20 of *World Spirituality: An Encyclopedic History of the Religious Quest.* New York: Crossroad, 1991.

Rahman, Fazlur. *Islam.* Garden City, NY: Doubleday, 1966.

————. "Islam: An Overview." In *The Encyclopedia of Religion,* edited by Mircea Eliade 304–22 Vol. 7. New York: Macmillan, 1987.